An Advanced Course in Database Systems
Beyond Relational Databases

Suzanne W. Dietrich and Susan D. Urban

Arizona State University

An Alan R. Apt Book

PEARSON
Prentice
Hall

Upper Saddle River, New Jersey 07458

Library of Congress Cataloging-in-Publication Data

Dietrich, Suzanne Wagner.
  An advanced course in database systems : beyond relational databases / Suzanne W.
Dietrich and Susan D. Urban.
    p. cm.
Includes bibliographical references and index.
ISBN 0-13-042898-1
    1. Relational databases.   2. Object-oriented databases.   I. Urban, Susan.   II. Title.

QA76.9.D3D523 2005
005.75′6–dc22   2004054883

Vice President and Editorial Director, ECS: *Marcia J. Horton*
Publisher: *Alan Apt*
Associate Editor: *Toni Holm*
Supplements Editor: *Sarah Parker*
Vice President and Director of Production and Manufacturing, ESM: *David W. Riccardi*
Executive Managing Editor: *Vince O'Brien*
Managing Editor: *Camille Trentacoste*
Production Editor: *Colleen Franciscus*
Manufacturing Manager: *Trudy Pisciotti*
Manufacturing Buyer: *Lynda Castillo*
Director of Creative Services: *Paul Belfanti*
Art Director: *John Christiana*
Executive Marketing Manager: *Pamela Hersperger*
Marketing Assistant: *Barrie Reinhold*
Cover Image: *Mexican Gold Poppies and Saguaro Cacti.* © *George H. H. Huey/CORBIS*
Back Cover Image: *Horse,* © *Karen Falgoust; Hot Air Balloon,* © *Suzanne Dietrich*

© 2005 Pearson Education, Inc.
Pearson Prentice Hall
Pearson Education, Inc.
Upper Saddle River, NJ 07458

Printed in the United States of America

10 9 8 7 6 5 4 3 2 1

ISBN 0-13-042898-1

Pearson Education Ltd., *London*
Pearson Education Australia Pty. Ltd., *Sydney*
Pearson Education Singapore, Pte. Ltd.
Pearson Education North Asia Ltd., *Hong Kong*
Pearson Education Canada, Ltd., *Toronto*
Pearson Educación de Mexico, S.A. de C.V.
Pearson Education—Japan, *Tokyo*
Pearson Education Malaysia, Pte. Ltd.
Pearson Education, Inc., *Upper Saddle River, New Jersey*

Contents

List of Figures

List of Tables

Preface

This book goes beyond the relational database coverage of a typical first course in databases. The topics covered include object-oriented conceptual data modeling, object-oriented databases, object-relational databases, and databases and the Web. Designed for a second database course for undergraduates, the book provides both depth of coverage and a wealth of examples to illustrate the concepts. The book can also be easily adapted for use at the graduate level, assuming an introductory database course on relational databases. Research papers can supplement the text coverage with the latest research topics. The target audience of the book also includes the professional engineer who understands relational database technology. The book can help guide the engineer through the latest technological advances in object databases and Web access to databases.

We assume a familiarity with relational databases, the SQL industry-standard query language, and fundamental object-oriented programming language concepts. These assumptions are consistent with the targeted audience of the book. Where needed, the book is self-contained by providing a review of the relational features of the SQL standard.

Organization

Chapters 1 and 2 provide coverage of object-oriented conceptual data models that graphically describe the data stored in a database. This text bridges the gap between the established Enhanced Entity Relationship (EER) diagrams from the database community and the Unified Modeling Language (UML) conceptual class diagrams used by software engineers in industry. Both of these conceptual data models provide advanced semantic modeling features that address class inheritance, constraints on subclass memberships, and class relationships.

Before offering a detailed approach to mapping the conceptual data models to the relational data model, Chapter 3 covers the relational features of the SQL standard, reviewing the basics of the SQL data definition and manipulation language, as well as introducing advanced relational features such as integrity constraints, triggers, and SQL-invoked routines. Chapter 4 uses side-by-side illustrations to show the mapping of the various EER and UML features to the relational data model, including a detailed discussion of how to maintain the inherent constraints given by the EER or UML diagrams.

The next part of the book focuses on recent developments associated with the interaction between databases and the Web. Specifically, Chapter 5 provides detailed coverage of the JDBC API as a sample call-level interface to relational databases. Chapter 6 covers the Extensible Markup Language (XML), which has become a de facto standard for data exchange. Most relational database products are XML enabled, providing the capability to transfer data between XML documents and the data structures of the database itself. Most database products use either Document Type Definitions or XML Schema for specifying the structure of an XML document. Both specifications are included in the chapter, which also illustrates the exchange of data through the use of XML.

Chapters 7 and 8 examine object data management in the context of object-oriented databases and object extensions to relational databases. Chapter 7 provides in-depth coverage of the ODMG standard for object-oriented databases, including a description of the Object Definition Language (ODL), an approach to mapping the object-oriented conceptual data models to ODL, and the Object Query Language (OQL). Chapter 8 covers the object-relational features of the SQL standard, including abstract data types, object tables, object references, and collections. Techniques are presented for mapping EER and UML schemas to the SQL object-relational data model and for maintaining the constraints of the conceptual design. Chapter 9 discusses sample implementations of a database enterprise on various database products, including implementations in a relational database, an object-oriented database, and an object-relational database.

The organization of the chapters allows the application of conceptual data modeling to the design of an enterprise, followed by its mapping to the relational data model. The JDBC API and XML representation of data can then be explored in the context of a relational implementation. Object data management concepts are introduced, covering first the foundations of object-oriented databases and then object extensions to relational databases. The three implementation case studies summarize the application of the mapping of the conceptual data models to the relational, object-relational, and object-oriented data models, providing a basis for a comparative analysis of these three different database paradigms with respect to data design, constraint enforcement, and data access.

Each chapter includes checkpoint sections at strategic locations in the presentation of the material. Each checkpoint summarizes critical concepts covered, as well as exercises for assessing progress with understanding the material at that point in the chapter. The authors' Web site,

```
http://www.eas.asu.edu/~advdb
```

provides implementation examples that support the relational database mapping material in Chapter 4, the JDBC coverage in Chapter 5, the XML coverage in Chapter 6, the object-oriented database concepts in Chapter 7, and the relational, object-relational, and object-oriented case studies in Chapter 9. The Web site also provides links to useful references and database tools.

Acknowledgments

We would like to acknowledge the many organizations and people that have assisted us in the development, writing, and publication of this book. The development of an advanced database course for undergraduates was funded by the National Science Foundation (DUE-9980417), and the book serves as one of the dissemination mechanisms for that work. We also appreciate the funding received from Microsoft Research and the Arizona State University (ASU) Center for Research on Education in Science, Mathematics, Engineering, and Technology (CRESMET). As part of the NSF educational grant, we held two industry workshops to guide us in the development of the topics and course materials. We appreciate the input that we received from the following industry representatives and their companies: B. N. Rao, Honeywell; Lee Gowen, American Express; Leon Guzenda, Objectivity; Gary James, Homebid; Vishu Krishnamurthy, Oracle; John Nordlinger, Microsoft; Mark Rogers, CoCreate; Jeff Smith, Honeywell; Amy Sundermier, Homebid; Roger Tomas, AG Communication Systems (now Lucent); Stephen Waters, Microsoft Research; Arleen Wiryo, Integrated Information Systems; and Cindy Wu, Honeywell. We also held a faculty development workshop as part of the NSF dissemination process, and we would like to thank the workshop participants: Karen Davis, University of Cincinnati; Don Goelman, Villanova University; Lorena Gómez, Instituto Tecnológico y de Estudios Superiores de Monterrey; Mario Guimaraes, Kennesaw State University; Patricia Hartman, Alverno College; Héctor J. Hernández, Texas Tech University; Myrtle Jonas, The University of the District of Columbia; Juan Lavariega, Instituto Tecnológico y de Estudios Superiores de Monterrey; Liz Leboffe, St. John Fisher College; and Martha Myers, Kennesaw State University. We appreciate the development support that we received from various students at ASU: Shilpi Ahuja, Ingrid Biswas, Chakrapani Cherukuri, Marla Hart, Yonghyuk Kim, Ion Kyriakides, Shama Patel, Lakshmi Priya, Mathangi Ranganathan, Dan Suceava, Pablo Tapia, Ty Truong, Arleen Wiryo, Cindy Wu, Yang Xiao, Nilan Yang, and Mei Zheng. The students in the CSE 494 (Advanced Database Concepts) classes offered at ASU from spring 2000 through spring 2004 also deserve recognition for the valuable input they provided on the content, course notes, and implementation examples that accompany the book. We appreciate the thoughtful guidance provided by the reviewers: Sudarshan Chawathe, University of Maryland; Cindy Chen, University of Massachusetts-Lowell; Jeff Donahoo, Baylor University; Don Goelman, Villanova University; William I. Grosky, Wayne State University; Le Gruenwald, University of Oklahoma; Mario Guimaraes, Kennesaw State University; Patricia Hartman, Alverno College; Héctor J. Hernández, Texas Tech University; Myrtle Jonas, University of the District of Columbia; Jeff Naughton, University of Wisconsin; Joan Peckham, University of Rhode Island; William Perrizo, North Dakota State University; Beth Plale, Indiana University; Hassan Reza, University of North Dakota; Shashi Shekhar, University of Minnesota; and Victor Vianu, University of California at San Diego. We would like to thank our publisher, Alan Apt, for his vision and guidance in the publication of this book. We also thank the editorial staff at Prentice Hall that assisted with the book and its supplements: Toni Dianne Holm, Patrick Lindner, and Sarah Parker. We are thankful to John Christiana at Prentice Hall for his design of a personalized book cover. Many thanks to our Production Editor, Colleen Franciscus, at Progressive Publishing Alternatives and her staff in the editing and production of the book. We also want to acknowledge Jake Warde for coordinating the initial reviews of the book.

Finally, we thank our family and friends for their encouragement and support, with special thanks for the photograph of Royal Rio Miss: Karen Falgoust (photographer), William A. Darling (owner), Bruce Darling, and Diane Darling.

Chapter 1

Enhanced Entity Relationship Modeling

Synopsis

The Entity Relationship (ER) model is often used to capture the conceptual design of a database application. After a review of the ER model, this chapter presents the advanced conceptual modeling features of the Enhanced Entity Relationship (EER) model. Advanced features of the EER model include the use of generalization and specialization for forming entities into class hierarchies, specialization constraints for constraining membership in subclasses, and categorization for defining entities as a union of types. Throughout the chapter, emphasis is placed on the different types of constraints that can be captured in an EER conceptual model.

Assumed Knowledge

- Fundamentals of Entity Relationship Modeling

Conceptual modeling is the process of developing a semantic description of an enterprise that is to be captured in the design and implementation of a database application. The process of conceptual modeling is database independent, involving the analysis of application requirements and the development of a high-level semantic design of the database contents and application constraints. Since application constraints define rules for ensuring the validity of the data stored in the database, the database implementation must ultimately conform to the constraints captured in the conceptual design, as well as to any additional constraints that may be expressed against the conceptual design.

The *Entity Relationship (ER)* model has been one of the most well-known techniques associated with conceptual database design. Introduced in 1976 by Peter Chen, the ER model provides a database-independent approach to describing the entities involved in a database application, together with the relationships and constraints that exist between such entities. Since the introduction of the ER model, many different *semantic data models* were defined as knowledge-modeling enhancements to the ER modeling approach. A common theme among most semantic data models was the need to include modeling features that captured an increased level of semantic constraints within the conceptual design. In response to developments with semantic data models, the ER model has evolved into the *Enhanced Entity Relationship (EER)* model, extending the original ER model with more advanced features for conceptual modeling such as those found in semantic data models.

This chapter begins with a review of ER modeling fundamentals, addressing the basics of forming entities and relationships. The advanced features of the EER model are then presented, including the use of *generalization* and *specialization* for forming entities into taxonomic hierarchies and the use of *categorization* for defining entities as a union of types. Throughout the chapter, the constraints associated with an EER schema are emphasized. These constraints will be used in later chapters to illustrate the implementation considerations that are imposed by an EER design of a database application.

1.1   Entity Relationship Review

Recall that an ER design is constructed primarily from two main components: *entities* and *relationships*. Entities represent the "things," or "objects," to be stored in the database, while relationships define the manner in which entities are associated. An ER diagram is constructed after a thorough analysis of application requirements. As an example, consider the application requirements for the ECLECTIC ONLINE SHOPPING ENTERPRISE:

> The ECLECTIC mail-order company would like to provide a means for its customers to shop and place orders over the Web. ECLECTIC provides a wide range of products, such as thing-a-ma-bobs, deely-bobs, and widgets.
>
> ECLECTIC customers have typical information: name (last name and first name), address (street, city, state, and zip code), phone number, and email. To place an order, a customer must be a registered user having a unique login name and password.
>
> The customer shops the online store by category, where a category has a unique code and description. Each type of item in the online store belongs to exactly one category. For example, books might represent one category, while electronics and sporting goods might represent other categories.
>
> An item type is described by a unique item number, a name, and a price and has an associated graphic for display on the Web page. Since inventory items may come in different colors and sizes, a customer selects a specific inventory item by also specifying its color and size. Inventory items are represented in the database by a code that is unique within the item number. The database also records the current quantity in stock of that inventory item for a given color and size. For example, a thing-a-ma-bob is an item type in the electronics category. A thing-a-ma-bob, however, comes in different sizes and colors. The online store may have 50 small, green thing-a-ma-bobs in stock and may have only 30 large, blue thing-a-ma-bobs in stock.

A customer places inventory items in a shopping cart, specifying the quantity of that item being placed in the cart. There is a unique number associated with the cart, along with the date and total price, which is calculated as the sum of multiplying the price of each inventory item in the shopping cart by the quantity ordered. The contents of the shopping cart can be updated until the customer confirms the cart contents by placing an order. The quantity of each item in the shopping cart can also change before the customer places the order. When an order is placed, the shopping cart is reclassified as an order that is ready for shipment. The price of each shopping cart item at the time of the order is recorded for historical purposes and for calculating the final total price of the order, which is the sum of multiplying the price of each inventory item in the shopping cart by the quantity ordered.

A customer can have at most one shopping cart, but many orders. A shopping cart and an order are associated with exactly one customer. When a shopping cart becomes an order, the shopping cart is emptied to prepare for a future shopping session. Information about customer orders is maintained in the database for a period of three years.

Figure 1.1 presents the ER diagram developed as a result of analyzing the requirements of the ECLECTIC ONLINE SHOPPING ENTERPRISE. Since there are several different notational conventions used for the ER model in the literature, the subsequent subsections

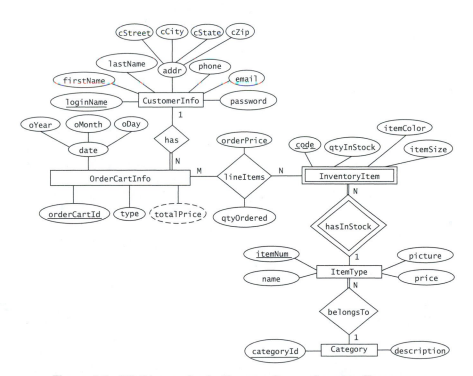

Figure 1.1   ER Diagram for the ECLECTIC ONLINE SHOPPING ENTERPRISE

establish the specific notational conventions that will be used in this book by presenting a review of entities, relationships, and their associated constraints, using the ECLECTIC ONLINE SHOPPING ENTERPRISE as a specific case study. The notational review is supported with a more generic view of the ER model notation, as presented in Figure 1.2, which uses an ABSTRACT ENTERPRISE.

1.1.1   Notational Conventions

In the ER model, entities provide the foundation for the construction of ER diagrams. The description of an entity is referred to as an *entity type*, which is defined by the name of the entity together with its *attributes*. Attributes represent values that characterize an entity. The specific occurrence of an entity type is referred to as an *entity instance*, while the collection of all entity instances of the same type is referred to as the *entity set*.

Relationships define associations between entities. The definition of a relationship between entity types is referred to as a *relationship type*. Like entity types, relationship types can have attributes. The actual occurrence of a relationship between entity instances is referred to as a *relationship instance*, with the collection of relationship instances of the same type referred to as the *relationship set*.

Entities and Relationships

As shown in the generic ER notation of Figure 1.2, each entity is denoted as a rectangle, with the name of the entity, such as A, B, or C, inside of the rectangle. A relationship is denoted as a diamond, with lines connecting the diamond to the entities involved in the relationship. The name of the relationship appears inside of the diamond. In Figure 1.2, entities B and C are related through the bc relationship, while A and B are related through two separate relationships: the ab relationship and the ba relationship.

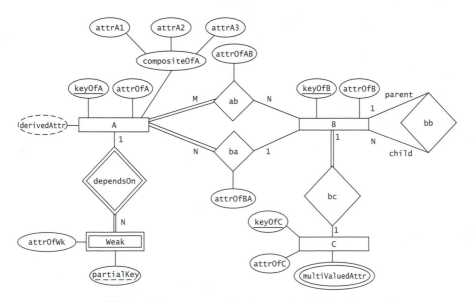

Figure 1.2   ABSTRACT ENTERPRISE in ER Notation

Using a more concrete example, several entities can be extracted from a reading of the requirements description of the ECLECTIC ONLINE SHOPPING ENTERPRISE. As shown in Figure 1.1, one entity type is `CustomerInfo`, representing customers that do online shopping with ECLECTIC. Since a customer can place an order, `OrderCartInfo` is another entity used to represent specific customer orders. The instances of `OrderCart-Info` represent either shopping carts or completed orders. The `has` relationship between `CustomerInfo` and `OrderCartInfo` represents the fact that a customer `has` orders (shopping carts or completed orders). When viewing the relationship in the opposite direction, an order *is placed by* a customer. In the ER model, the relationship name is chosen to describe one specific direction of the relationship.

As stated in the requirements description for the ECLECTIC case study, orders are created when a customer selects different types of items from item categories. Figure 1.1 depicts `Category` and `ItemType` as entities, related by using the `belongsTo` relationship to represent the fact that an item type, such as a thing-a-ma-bob, belongs to a specific category, such as electronics. Since each item type comes in different sizes, colors, and quantities, the `InventoryItem` entity represents the actual items in stock. The `ItemType` entity is related to the `InventoryItem` entity through the `hasInStock` relationship. Notice that the `InventoryItem` entity and the `hasInStock` relationship are enclosed in a double box and a double diamond, respectively. This notation defines a *weak entity*. Weak entities are addressed in more detail later in this section.

The `lineItems` relationship defines an association between `InventoryItem` and `OrderCartInfo`, specifying the inventory items requested on a specific order.

Recursive Relationships

In the ECLECTIC case study, each relationship in Figure 1.1 defines an association between two distinct entity types. A relationship can also be a *recursive* relationship that represents an association between the instances of a single entity type, where one entity instance is connected to another entity instance of the same type.

The generic notation of Figure 1.2 provides an example of a recursive relationship, where B is related to itself through the `bb` recursive relationship. Each instance of B that participates in the recursive relationship plays a specific *role* in the relationship. *Role names*, such as `parent` and `child`, can be added as notations to relationship lines to clarify the semantics of the relationship. A recursive relationship, however, does not always represent a parent–child relationship. As a more specific example, consider a `Person` entity. In addition to defining a parent–child recursive relationship to represent an association between parents and their offspring, recursive relationships can also be defined for `Person` to represent a husband–wife relationship or a sibling–sibling relationship. In all three cases, an instance of `Person` is related to another instance of `Person`, with role names providing the specific meaning of the relationship.

N-ary Relationships

Each relationship in Figure 1.1 is a *binary* relationship, defining a relationship between two entities. As shown in Figure 1.3, a relationship can define an *n*-ary association between several entities. The relationship in Figure 1.3 is specifically referred to as a *ternary relationship*, since three entities—Car, Person, and Bank—are related through

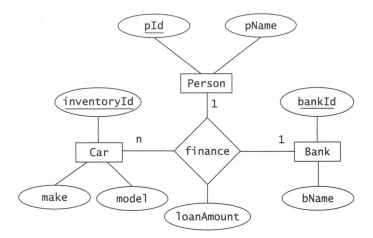

Figure 1.3 N-ary Relationship between `Car`, `Person`, and `Bank`

the `finance` relationship. This relationship might exist in a car dealership application, wherein a person buys a car that is financed by a specific bank. Instead of modeling the application scenario as several binary relationships between the entities involved, the scenario is more accurately represented as a direct relationship between all three entities.

Attributes

The generic notation in Figure 1.2 illustrates that an attribute name is enclosed in an oval and attached by a line to the entity or relationship that it describes. An attribute that is represented by a single oval is known as a *single-valued attribute*, indicating that only one value will be stored for the attribute. As illustrated in the ECLECTIC example of Figure 1.1, the `CustomerInfo` entity has several attributes, including `loginName`, `firstName`, `last-Name`, `phone`, `email`, and `password`. The `OrderCartInfo`, `Category`, `ItemType`, and `InventoryItem` entities also have several single-valued attributes that correspond to the details presented in the ECLECTIC requirements description. For `OrderCartInfo`, the `type` attribute distinguishes between a shopping cart and a completed order, using a value of "S" to indicate a shopping cart and "O" to indicate an order.

An entity can also have a *multivalued attribute*. A multivalued attribute indicates that the entity can have more than one value for the attribute, where each value is of the same type. In entity `C` of Figure 1.2, `multiValuedAttr` provides an example of a multivalued attribute, denoted as a double oval. In the ECLECTIC example, if a customer can have multiple phone numbers and email addresses, then the `phone` and `email` attributes can be changed to double ovals to represent the possibility of multiple values for these attributes.

Another type of attribute is a *composite attribute*, which has two or more single-valued attributes as subcomponents. In Figure 1.2, each subcomponent is denoted by an oval (such as the ovals of `attrA1`, `attrA2`, and `attrA3`) connected by a single line to the oval of the composite attribute (`compositeAttrOfA` of entity `A`).

The ECLECTIC ER diagram in Figure 1.1 provides two different examples of composite attributes. The `CustomerInfo` entity has a composite attribute named `addr` that represents the address of a customer. An address is composed of four subcomponents (cStreet, cCity, cState, and cZip) representing the street, city, state, and zip code of the address. Likewise, in OrderCartInfo, the date of an order is composed of oYear, oMonth, and oDay.

Relationships can also have attributes. Figure 1.2 demonstrates the use of attributes describing the ab and ba relationships. Attributes of relationships can be single valued, multivalued, composite, or derived. In the ECLECTIC application, the qtyOrdered attribute appears as an attribute on the lineItems relationship to record the number of items ordered. Once a shopping cart becomes an order, the price of each inventory item in the cart is recorded in the orderPrice attribute.

An entity can also have a *derived attribute*, which is indicated with a dashed oval, as shown for derivedAttr of entity A in Figure 1.2. A derived attribute represents a value that is not stored in the database. The value of a derived attribute is dynamically calculated with a query or procedure based on other stored or derived attribute values. In the ECLECTIC ER diagram of Figure 1.1, totalPrice is a derived attribute. For a shopping cart, the totalPrice is calculated by using the price attribute of ItemType, since the price of an item can change before the customer finalizes the order. Once a shopping cart becomes an order, the totalPrice is calculated by using the orderPrice attribute on the lineItems relationship.

Keys

Every entity should designate at least one single-valued or composite attribute to serve as a *candidate key*, which uniquely identifies an entity instance in an entity set. A candidate key is minimal in that no subset of its attributes uniquely identifies an entity instance. The name of an attribute that represents a candidate key of an entity is always underlined, as illustrated in Figure 1.2. In Figure 1.1, loginName is a candidate key for CustomerInfo. Likewise, orderCartId, categoryId, and itemNum are, respectively, candidate keys for OrderCartInfo, Category, and ItemType.

An entity can have more than one candidate key. Figure 1.4 illustrates entity Student with two candidate keys, named sID and alternativeKey. The alternativeKey attribute is a composite attribute, composed of firstName, lastName, and dateOfBirth. When multiple candidate keys exist, one of the candidate keys should be designated as the *primary key* when the ER diagram is mapped to a specific database model. A primary key indicates the attribute that will primarily be used to uniquely identify instances of the entity set.

Weak Entities

Recall in our initial discussion of entities in Figure 1.1 that some entities were denoted as single-line rectangles, while InventoryItem was denoted as a double-line rectangle.

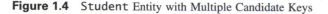

Figure 1.4 Student Entity with Multiple Candidate Keys

Entities with a single-line rectangle are referred to as *strong entities*. A strong entity has at least one candidate key that is formed from attributes that describe the strong entity. An entity with a double-line rectangle is a *weak entity*. The attributes of a weak entity do not uniquely identify an instance of a weak entity in the database. As a result, a weak entity participates in an *identifying relationship* with another entity, referred to as the *identifying owner* of the weak entity. The weak entity depends on its identifying owner for its identification and existence.

A weak entity has a *partial key*, indicated by an attribute with a dashed underline. Semantically, a partial key uniquely identifies the weak entity in the context of its identifying owner. To create a candidate key for the weak entity, the partial key is combined with the primary key of its identifying owner. As shown in Figure 1.2, the entity with the label Weak is denoted with a double rectangle. The Weak entity is linked by a double line to the dependsOn identifying relationship, which is denoted by a double diamond. Entity A is the identifying owner of Weak by its participation in the dependsOn relationship. The candidate key of Weak is the combination of keyOfA and partialKey.

A classic example of a weak entity is illustrated in Figure 1.5, showing dependents as weak entities that are identified by employees. Each dependent cannot exist without being related to an employee. The partial key of Dependent is dName and the key of the identifying owner Employee is eId. Since many employees can have dependents with the same name, the dName of each dependent must be combined with the eId of its identifying owner to create a unique identifier for each instance of Dependent.

Returning to the ECLECTIC example in Figure 1.1, InventoryItem is a weak entity, since the requirements description states that the code for each inventory item is unique only within a specific item type. For example, suppose the code is an abbreviated combination of itemColor and itemSize. A specific instance of InventoryItem for a thing-a-ma-bob ItemType could have a code of "BL" as an abbreviation for blue and large. But a different instance of InventoryItem for a thing-a-ma-jig ItemType could also have a code of "BL". The code is unique only when used in combination with the itemNum of the ItemType to which it is associated in the hasInStock relationship. As a result, InventoryItem is a weak entity that is dependent on the ItemType identifying owner, as denoted by the double rectangle for InventoryItem that is connected by a double line to the hasInStock identifying relationship, which is enclosed by a double diamond.

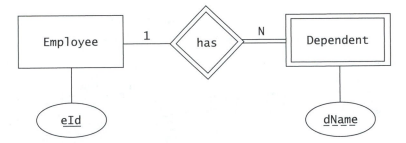

Figure 1.5 Dependent as a Weak Entity with Employee as an Identifying Owner

1.1.2 Relationship Constraints

A review of the ER model would not be complete without a discussion of *structural constraints* on relationships. There are two types of structural constraints: *cardinality constraints* and *participation constraints*. Cardinality constraints define the number of entities that can participate in a relationship. Participation constraints, by contrast, define whether participation in a relationship is required or optional. Together, cardinality and participation constraints define the semantics of relationships between entities.

Cardinality constraints can be one-to-one (1:1), one-to-many (1:N), many-to-one (N:1), or many-to-many (M:N), as illustrated in Figure 1.2. For two entities A and B, a cardinality number is placed across the relationship from A next to the related entity B, indicating the number of instances of B that can be related to an instance of A. In the opposite direction, a number is placed next to A to indicate the number of A instances that can be related to a B instance.

Participation constraints can either be *partial* or *total*. Partial participation, which is denoted as a single line between a rectangle and a diamond, defines optional participation in a relationship. Total participation, which is denoted as a double line between a rectangle and a diamond, indicates required participation in a relationship.

Figure 1.1 provides examples of several 1:N relationships, each of which illustrates total and partial participation. The Category entity has a 1:N belongsTo relationship with ItemType, where ItemType participation in the relationship is total. This relationship indicates that each instance of ItemType must belong to a specific category. In a similar manner, CustomerInfo is related to OrderCartInfo through a 1:N has relationship, where each customer can have many different orders, but each order is associated with only one customer. Furthermore, each instance of OrderCartInfo has total participation in the relationship and is therefore required to be associated with an instance of CustomerInfo.

Total participation defines a special type of relationship referred to as an *existence dependency*. In an existence-dependent relationship, the entity with total participation cannot exist in the database without being connected to an entity on the other side of the relationship. An existence dependency can often lead to implementation policies that propagate the deletion of entities. For example, if instance t of ItemType is related to instance c of Category, the deletion of c could cause the deletion of t. Alternatively, the deletion of c could first require that t be reconnected to a different instance of Category.

Weak entities are *always* existence dependent on the identifying owner entity, thus requiring total participation on the part of the weak entity. In Figure 1.1, inventory items are modeled as the InventoryItem weak entity that depends on ItemType through the 1:N hasInStock relationship. Each instance of ItemType can optionally be connected to many instances of InventoryItem. Each instance of InventoryItem is required to participate in a relationship with only one instance of ItemType as a means of establishing unique identity. In general, a relationship between a weak entity and an owner entity can be 1:1 or 1:N. In a 1:N relationship, the owner entity is always on the 1 side of the relationship.

The inventory items associated with OrderCartInfo are captured through the M:N lineItems relationship. Each entity has partial participation in the relationship. As a result, an inventory item does not have to appear on any order (not a very popular item), and an order does not have to have any items, as in the case of a shopping cart that has just been created. Furthermore, since the relationship is M:N, a given inventory item can appear on more than one order cart (many customers order blue, large thing-a-ma-bobs) and an order can contain many different types of inventory items (thing-a-ma-bobs and thing-a-jigs). The `qtyOrdered` attribute indicates the quantity of each item ordered; the `orderPrice` indicates the price of the item at the time a shopping cart is converted to a completed order.

Cardinalities for N-ary Relationships

Determining cardinalities for a relationship that is not binary is more difficult than for a binary relationship. Consider again the ternary `finance` relationship between `Car`, `Person`, and `Bank` in Figure 1.3. To determine the cardinality on the `Car` end of the relationship, consider how many times a specific (p, b) pair can be related to c, where c is an instance of `Car`, p is an instance of `Person`, and b is an instance of `Bank`. One (p, b) pair can be related to many c entities, since a person can work with a specific bank to finance the purchase of many cars. A (c, b) pair, however, can be related only to one p entity, assuming that a car can only be sold and financed to one person. As a result, a 1 is placed next to the `Person` entity. Likewise, the 1 on the `Bank` end of the relationship states that a (c, p) pair can only be related to one b entity, indicating that the sale of a car to a person can be financed only by one bank. In general, the lines between an entity and a relationship in a nonbinary relationship can be labeled with a 1 to represent participation in one relationship instance or with a letter, such as M, N, or P, to represent participation in many relationship instances, creating many different relationship combinations.

A nonbinary relationship r can always be modeled by introducing an entity e to denote the relationship r. For each entity e_i involved in r, a binary relationship is then created between e_i and e. Figure 1.6 illustrates an alternative representation for the semantics in Figure 1.3. In this representation, `Finance` is modeled as an entity, while `Car`, `Person`,

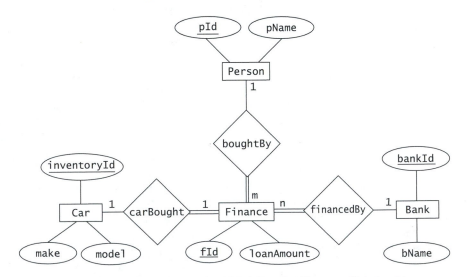

Figure 1.6 Binary Approach to Modeling the `finance` Relationship

and Bank have binary relationships with Finance. Notice that Finance has total participation with Car, Person, and Bank, since an instance of Finance indirectly represents a relationship between the other three entities. In other words, each instance of Finance represents the occurrence of a person buying a car with financing from a specific bank. The cardinalities on the relationships going into the Finance entity in Figure 1.6 are consistent with the cardinalities from the ternary relationship in Figure 1.3, indicating that a car can be financed only once, but that a person and a bank can participate in many Finance relationships. (That is, a person can buy many cars, and a bank can finance many cars.)

(Min, Max) Pairs

Cardinality and participation constraints in the ER model can be refined with the use of *(min, max) pairs*. A (min, max) pair denotes the minimum and maximum number of times that an entity instance can participate in the relationship type. When this alternative notation is used, the 1:1, 1:N, and M:N cardinalities are replaced with (min, max) pairs on the edge linking the entity to the relationship, which is in contrast to the cardinality ratio that is placed across the relationship diamond to the related entity.

Figure 1.7 presents a revised version of Figure 1.2 using (min, max) pairs. In the 1:1 bc relationship between C and B, the (0, 1) pair on the edge between C and bc denotes that instances of C need not participate in the bc relationship, but can participate at most once in the bc relationship. In other words, the bc relationship indicates that an instance of C may not be related to any instances of B or, at most, it may be related to one instance of B. The (1, 1) pair on the edge between B and the bc relationship denotes that instances of B must participate exactly once in the bc relationship. A minimum value or lower bound of at least 1 implies total or required participation in the relationship. A minimum value of 0 implies partial participation.

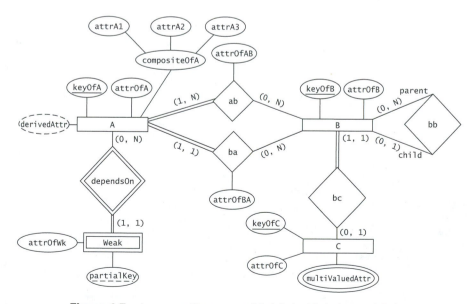

Figure 1.7 ABSTRACT ENTERPRISE Modeled with (min, max) Pairs

Since (min, max) pairs subsume the semantics of the cardinality ratios and participation constraints, the use of double lines to indicate total participation is optional. However, the use of a double line indicating the association of a weak entity to its identifying relationship is always preferred, even in the presence of (min, max) pairs, so that the identifying relationship is easier to locate in the ER diagram. The reader should compare the (min, max) notation in Figure 1.7 with the notation in Figure 1.2 to verify that the two diagrams represent the same relationship semantics. The (min, max) notation is typically used to provide more specific details about lower and upper bounds on cardinality relationships.

1.1.3   Checkpoint: ER Modeling

A summary of the constraints associated with the ER model appears in Table 1.1. The ECLECTIC ONLINE SHOPPING ENTERPRISE provides a case study illustrating the use of entities, relationships, and the ER constraints from Table 1.1 for modeling a specific enterprise. The ER model requires keys on entities to identify instances uniquely.

TABLE 1.1   ER Constraint Summary

ER Constraint		Meaning of the Constraint
Classes		
Key Constraint		A key constraint defines every class to have an attribute or a collection of attributes having a value that is used to uniquely identify instances of the class.
Structural Constraints on Relationships		
Cardinality Constraints: 1:1, 1:N, M:N		Cardinality constraints define the number of relationships that an instance of a class can participate in with an instance of another class.
Participation Constraints: Total vs. Partial		Participation constraints define whether an instance of a class is required to participate in a relationship. *Total* defines required participation. *Partial* defines optional participation.
(Min, Max) Constraints:		(Min, Max) constraints are a combination of cardinality and participation constraints, providing specific lower and upper bounds for participation in relationships.
Min = 0	Partial participation	
Min >= 1	Total participation	
Max = n	An upper bound on relationship participation, where n can be a specific integer value	

Structural constraints on relationships include cardinality constraints and participation constraints, indicating total or partial participation. The use of (min, max) pairs provides a notation that combines the specification of cardinality and participation constraints.

There are several constraints on the ECLECTIC ONLINE SHOPPING ENTERPRISE that cannot be directly represented in the ER diagram. For example, a customer can have only one shopping cart, but many orders. Since shopping carts and orders have been modeled as one OrderCartInfo entity in a 1:N relationship with CustomerInfo, the application will need to enforce the constraint that there can be only one instance of OrderCartInfo with a type of "S" for each customer. Furthermore, since order information must be maintained for three years, inventory items cannot be deleted if they have appeared on any order within the last three years. Subsequent chapters address implementation issues for such constraints in the context of specific database models.

Exercises

1. Revise the ECLECTIC ONLINE SHOPPING ENTERPRISE in Figure 1.1 to use (min, max) pairs instead of the basic cardinality notation. Also, generate a list of all ER constraints associated with the schema.

2. Generate two ER schemas (one version that uses the basic cardinality notation and another version that uses (min, max) pairs) for the GET FIT HEALTH CLUB ENTERPRISE:

   The health club needs a database to manage information about club activities. The health club has members of a family organized into club accounts. Each account has an account number, the date the account was opened, and contact information such as the family address and phone number. Since each account represents a family, an account is associated with several family members. The club maintains information about each member, such as the member identifier, first name, last name, age, and monthly fee. One member of each family is also identified as the primary account contact person.

   The health club offers several classes, such as yoga, step aerobics, and spin classes. The database needs to maintain information about each type of class, such as the class id, class name, and class description. Each class is offered several times a week. For example, yoga might be offered at 6A.M. on Mondays, noon on Wednesdays, and 5P.M. on Fridays. The database needs to maintain the time and day schedule for each class. The schedule should indicate the instructor for each offering of the class.

   To monitor member activity, the health club also needs to maintain attendance for each date on which the class occurs. For example, the club would like to generate an attendance list for the 6A.M. Monday yoga class when it was taught on Monday, January 6, and also on Monday, January 13. Members of the health club can attend any of the classes offered by the club.

   The health club needs to maintain information about instructors of classes. The information includes an instructor identifier, first name, last name, and classes that an instructor is scheduled to teach. Instructors can also work as personal trainers for the members of the club. As a personal trainer, the instructor works one on one with the members, teaching muscle-conditioning techniques. Personal trainers charge a fee to members who contract their services for a specified duration (one month, three months, or six months). The health club has agreed to maintain information about personal-training services between instructors and members, such as the duration, fee, and start date of each contracted service.

3. Generate two ER schemas (one version that uses the basic cardinality notation and another version that uses (min, max) pairs) for the MEDICAL PRACTICE ENTERPRISE:

> Consider a medical practice that wants to maintain information about doctors, patients, patient visits, and diagnoses. A doctor is uniquely identified by a doctor Id. The doctor's name and year of degree are also recorded. A patient is uniquely identified by a patient id and is further described by last name, first name, and date of birth. Each patient is associated with exactly one account, which is uniquely identified by an account id and has an associated balance and responsible party. Each patient visit is recorded and is described by the date, textual description, charge, and the diagnoses for that visit. The name of the doctor who saw the patient on that visit is also recorded. A diagnosis has a unique code and a description.

4. Generate two ER schemas (one version that uses the basic cardinality notation and another version that uses (min, max) pairs) for the MUSIC AGENCY ENTERPRISE:

> A music survey agency wants to keep track of CD titles, the songs in each title, the musical group that recorded the CD, the recording label that produced the CD, the artists who wrote the songs in the CD, and the ratings for each CD title and song title.
>
> A recording label has a unique id, a name, and a location. Each recording label produces several CD titles. Each CD title may be produced by one, and only one, recording label. A CD title has a title and a unique code. The year in which the CD was released and the number sold so far must also be recorded.
>
> Each CD title consists of several songs, with a minimum of one song in each CD. Each song has a title and a unique code. The same song could also be present in multiple CD titles. Each song has a unique track number within a particular CD.
>
> For each year, the end-of-the-year rating (top 40) of each CD title and song title must be maintained.
>
> A CD title is recorded by a single musical group, which has a name and a unique code. A musical group may record several CD titles during its life span. The group consists of one or more artists, each of whom has

a first name, a last name, and a unique id. The year in which the artist was born is also recorded. Since any artist may belong to multiple musical groups over time, the database must record the date an artist joined a particular group and the date he or she left the group. One or more artists write each song title on a CD. A single artist may contribute towards the writing of multiple song titles within a CD, but it isn't necessary for an artist to write a song.

5. What does it mean for an entity to be existence dependent? Using the ECLECTIC ONLINE SHOPPING ENTERPRISE in Figure 1.1, identify all entities that are existence dependent. Identify all entities that are weak entities. Is an existence-dependent entity always a weak entity? Is a weak entity always existence dependent? Explain your answer.

6. A medical doctor has an id and a name as attributes. A doctor can have more than one office location, where each location has a location id, address, and phone number. A patient has a patient id, patient name, and billing address. Use an n-ary association to model the concept of an office visit, where a patient schedules a visit for a specific time and day with a doctor in one of the office locations. Indicate the cardinality constraints of the n-ary association.

1.2 Generalization and Specialization

The EER model builds on the original ER modeling concepts described in the previous section to incorporate advanced modeling concepts from semantic data modeling. One of the most significant enhancements is the ability to model entity types into a hierarchical form known as an *ISA hierarchy* or *class hierarchy*. In the EER model, entity types are referred to as *classes* and can be formed into *superclasses* and *subclasses*, related through an *ISA relationship*. An ISA relationship represents the concept that a subclass *is a more specialized type* of a superclass (thus the term ISA). For example, a student is a more specialized form of a person, while a graduate student is a more specialized form of a student. From the opposite point of view, a superclass *is a more generalized type* of a subclass. A student is therefore a more generalized form of a graduate student, and a person is a more generalized form of a student.

The design process of forming a superclass into more specialized subclasses is referred to as *specialization*. Specialization emphasizes attributes and relationships of the subclasses that do not exist at the superclass level. The opposite of specialization is *generalization*, in which a set of subclasses is formed into a superclass, emphasizing the common attributes and relationships of the subclasses. The sections that follow elaborate on the use of specialization and generalization for forming class hierarchies with the ISA relationship, illustrating notational conventions, constraints on specialization, and special modeling considerations for supporting multiple superclasses of a subclass.

1.2.1 Forming Class Hierarchies

To illustrate class hierarchies in the EER model, consider a HOLLYWOOD ENTERPRISE that requires modeling information about the different types of people involved in the production and review of movie and modeling projects. In particular, this application requires capturing information about movie stars, models, agents, and movie critics. All of these different types of people have common characteristics, such as names and addresses, that need to be stored in the database. At the same time, each person type also has additional information that must be captured to describe the characteristics of his or her specific type of job. With the EER model, these different types of people involved with the Hollywood scene can be organized into a class hierarchy that emphasizes their commonalities and their differences.

Figure 1.8 presents the basic notation of the EER model for forming a class hierarchy. In this example, `Person` is a superclass that forms the *root class* of the hierarchy. A root class is also referred to as a *base class*. `MovieProfessional` and `Celebrity` are subclasses of `Person`, indicating that movie professionals and celebrities are specific types of people. This relationship is often expressed as `MovieProfessional ISA Person` and `Celebrity ISA Person`. A subclass is connected to its superclass by using a line with a subset arc representing the direction of the ISA relationship. `Critic` and `Agent` are specific types of movie professionals, while `MovieStar` and `Model` are specific types of celebrities. The `Celebrity` class is therefore a subclass with respect to its generalization relationship to `Person`, but a superclass with respect to its specialization relationship to `MovieStar` and `Model`. A similar observation can be made for the `MovieProfessional` entity with respect to its ISA relationships with `Person`, `Critic`, and `Agent`.

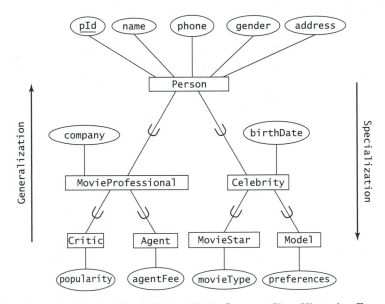

Figure 1.8 Generalization and Specialization in the `Person` Class Hierarchy. From "Database Models," by S. Urban in *Encyclopedia of Electrical and Electronics Engineering*, John G. Webster (editor); copyright © 1999 John G. Webster. This material is used by permission of John Wiley & Sons, Inc.

Classes that are formed into a class hierarchy support the concept of *inheritance*, wherein each subclass inherits all of the attributes that are defined at the superclass level. Since a MovieProfessional ISA Person, an instance of the MovieProfessional class inherits the pId, name, phone, gender, and address attributes that are defined at the Person level. In addition, an instance of MovieProfessional has a company attribute that stores the name of the company for which the movie professional works. This organization of classes allows attributes that are common to a class and all of its subclasses to be expressed at the most common superclass level, instead of repeating such attributes at each level of the class hierarchy.

Each subclass typically introduces new attributes that are not found at the superclass level. An Agent, for example, refines MovieProfessional even further, defining an agentFee that does not exist for instances of the Critic class. The Critic class defines the popularity attribute, capturing whether a critic is viewed as a "friendly" or "hostile" reviewer of movies. Since Critic and Agent are both subclasses of Movie-Professional, instances of both classes inherit the company attribute. Furthermore, the ISA relationship is transitive: If Critic ISA MovieProfessional and MoviePro-fessional ISA Person, then Critic ISA Person. Each instance of the Critic class inherits *all* attributes of MovieProfessional, which includes the attributes that Movie-Professional inherits from the Person class. The same observation can be made for Agent, MovieStar, and Model. Each subclass has its own attributes and inherits the attributes of all of its superclasses.

With respect to class instances, the instances of a superclass include all of the immediate instances of the class and all of the instances of its subclasses. For example, the instances of the Celebrity class include the instances of Celebrity, the instances of MovieStar, and the instances of Model. Likewise, the instances of the Person class include the direct instances of Person, MovieProfessional, Critic, Agent, Celebrity, MoveStar, and Model. Each instance in the database can therefore be viewed at different levels within the hierarchy. Furthermore, since attributes are not inherited upwards in the hierarchy, when a movie professional is viewed as an instance of the Person class, it is incorrect to refer to the company attribute, because, in general, an instance of the Person class is not necessarily an instance of the MovieProfessional class. Subsequent chapters will address the need to distinguish between the immediate instances of a class and the instances of subclasses for query purposes.

The fact that an instance of a subclass is *always* an instance of a superclass is known as the *ISA constraint*. This constraint implies that the deletion of the superclass instance requires the deletion of the instance from all of the subclasses of which it is a member. It would be a violation of the ISA constraint to allow a subclass instance to exist without also being an instance of its superclass. It is possible, however, to create a superclass instance without specializing the instance into one of the subclasses. For example, in Figure 1.8, it is possible to create an instance of Person without specifying that the person is also a MovieProfessional or a Celebrity. The next section addresses specific types of constraints that affect implementation considerations for the insertion, deletion, and modification of class instances.

1.2.2   Constraints on Specialization

The previous section presented a simplistic view of class hierarchies wherein an instance of a subclass is an instance of a superclass. In reality, a designer may need to place more specific constraints on the formation of subclass membership. For example, is it possible for a person to be both a critic and an agent at the same time? Or is it possible to create an instance of the Celebrity class without also indicating whether the celebrity is a movie star, a model, or possibly both?

In the EER model, class hierarchies can be enhanced with constraints that refine the semantics of ISA relationships. In particular, the EER model supports the specification of the *disjoint constraint* and the *completeness constraint*. The disjoint constraint indicates whether an instance of a superclass is restricted to be an instance of only one of its subclasses. If a specialization is not disjoint, then the specialization is overlapping, allowing an instance of the superclass to be an instance of more than one of its subclasses. The completeness constraint specifies whether an instance of a superclass is *required* to be an instance of at least one of its subclasses. If an instance of a superclass is required to be an instance of a subclass, then the specialization is referred to as a *total specialization*. Otherwise, the specialization is a *partial specialization*. A total specialization is also referred to as a *covering constraint*. Disjoint and completeness constraints can be used together to form the semantics of subclass membership with respect to the superclass.

Figure 1.9 illustrates the notational conventions for disjoint and completeness constraints. As shown in Figure 1.9(a), A has a disjoint specialization into its subclasses B and C, which is indicated by the use of a circle enclosing the letter "d" within the ISA specification. As a result, taking the intersection of the instances of B and C should yield the empty set, indicating that an instance of A can be either an instance of B or an instance of C, but not an instance of both B and C. If subclasses are not disjoint, then they are overlapping, meaning that an entity can be an instance of multiple subclasses. The notation for the specification of overlapping subclass membership is indicated in Figure 1.9(b), using a circle to enclose the letter "o". Since D has an overlapping specialization into its

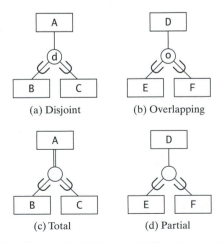

(a) Disjoint   (b) Overlapping

(c) Total   (d) Partial

Figure 1.9   Notation for Disjoint and Completeness Constraints

subclasses E and F, an entity can be an instance of E and F at the same time. The notation used in Figure 1.8 is, by default, assumed to represent overlapping subclass membership.

The notation for indicating the completeness constraint in the EER model is consistent with ER modeling notation for participation constraints. A total specialization indicates total participation of the superclass in the specialization relationship, which is denoted by a double line connecting the superclass to the specialization circle. In Figure 1.9(c), an entity cannot exist as an instance of A without also being an instance of either B or C. This implies that at the time an instance of A is created, the specific subclass or subclasses to which that instance belongs must also be specified. Partial specialization indicates partial participation in the specialization relationship, which is denoted by a single line connecting the superclass to the specialization circle. In Figure 1.9(d), an instance of D is not required to be an instance of E or F. By default, the single lines used in the notational convention of Figure 1.8 also indicate partial specialization. For Figures 1.9(c) and (d), the circle can be filled with either a "d" or an "o" to indicate the disjoint or overlapping constraint, respectively, creating four possibilities for specialization constraints: total disjoint, partial disjoint, total overlapping, or partial overlapping.

Figure 1.10 presents a revised version of Figure 1.8, adding disjoint and completeness constraints. As indicated in Figure 1.10, a Person is not required to be a MovieProfessional or a Celebrity. When an instance of Person does exist at the subclass level,

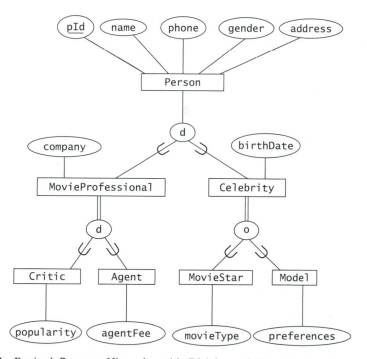

Figure 1.10 Revised Person Hierarchy with Disjoint and Completeness Constraints. From "Database Models," by S. Urban, in *Encyclopedia of Electrical and Electronics Engineering*, John G. Webster (editor); copyright © 1999 John G. Webster. This material is used by permission of John Wiley & Sons, Inc.

the `Person` instance cannot be both a `Celebrity` and a `MovieProfessional` at the same time. Since `Celebrity` has a total participation constraint with its subclasses, creating a `Celebrity` instance also requires the creation of a `MovieStar` or `Model` instance. Furthermore, since `MovieStar` and `Model` are overlapping, a celebrity can be an instance of both subclasses. `MovieProfessional` also has total participation with its subclasses. Membership in the `Critic` and `Agent` classes, however, is disjoint.

1.2.3   Attribute-Defined Specialization

The forms of specialization that have been examined so far are examples of *user-defined specialization*, meaning that the user defines the subclass or subclasses to which a superclass instance can belong. Another form of specialization is *attribute-defined specialization*, where the value of an attribute at the superclass level is used to determine membership in a subclass. Figure 1.11 presents an example of attribute-defined specialization. In this example, the `Project` class is specialized into the `FilmProject` class and the `ModelingProject` class based on the value of the `type` attribute of `Project` being either "F" or "M".

Multiple specializations of a class are illustrated in Figure 1.12. There are three separate specializations in this example, one that organizes `Person` instances according to home country, one that organizes `Person` instances according to gender, and one that organizes `Person` instances by job function. The home country specialization is attribute defined, based on the value of the `homeCountry` attribute of `Person`. For the gender specialization, the `gender` attribute of `Person` is used to determine membership in the `Male` and `Female` subclasses. Each specialization branch can therefore use a different attribute at the superclass level to determine subclass membership. A specialization branch can also be user defined as in the `MovieProfessional` and `Celebrity` specializations.

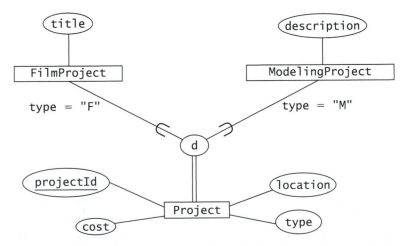

Figure 1.11   The `Project` Attribute-Defined Specialization. From "Database Models," by S. Urban, in *Encyclopedia of Electrical and Electronics Engineering*, John G. Webster (editor); copyright © 1999 John G. Webster. This material is used by permission of John Wiley & Sons, Inc.

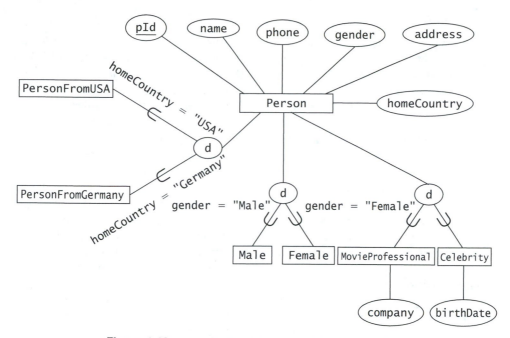

Figure 1.12 Multiple Specializations of the `Person` Class

If the attribute used for specialization is single valued, then membership at the subclass level is always disjoint. If the attribute is multivalued, then overlapping membership is allowed. The specification of disjointness must always be consistent with the attribute type. Furthermore, if the specialization is total, as in Figure 1.11, then the attribute used for specialization is a *required attribute*, meaning that the attribute can never contain a null value. A partial specialization such as the one based on gender in Figure 1.12 implies that a value for the `gender` attribute is optional. However, if the value exists, it should be used to immediately specialize the instance into the appropriate subclass. It is not necessary to have a subclass for every possible value of the specialization attribute. For example, Figure 1.12 includes only the `PersonFromUSA` and `PersonFromGermany` subclasses in the specialization based on homeCountry, even though the homeCountry attribute can store any valid country name.

The modification of a specialization attribute also implies an automatic change in subclass membership. For example, if the type of a project in Figure 1.11 is changed from "F" to "M", then the appropriate instance of `FilmProject` should be deleted, and a new instance should be created in the `ModelingProject` class. The deletion of an instance from a subclass also cannot violate attribute-defined specializations. In general, the deletion of a subclass instance *does not* require the deletion of the corresponding superclass instance. But in the presence of attribute-defined specialization, deletion at the superclass level may be necessary. For example, it is not possible simply to delete a `FilmProject` instance without also deleting the `Project` instance or without changing the `Project` type value. Another option is to disallow deletion at the subclass level.

1.2.4   Multiple Inheritance

Each example presented so far has illustrated the use of a *specialization hierarchy*, in which each subclass has only one superclass. In some modeling situations, it is possible for a subclass to have more than one superclass, thus forming a *specialization lattice*, in which a class with more than one superclass is referred to as a *shared subclass*.

A shared subclass supports *multiple inheritance*, indicating that the subclass inherits attributes from *all* of its superclasses. A shared subclass must satisfy the *multiple-inheritance intersection constraint*, where the entity set of the subclass represents the *intersection* of the superclasses in the lattice. In other words, an entity can be an instance of a shared subclass only if it is an instance of all of its superclasses.

In Figure 1.13, `StarModel` is a shared subclass with `MovieStar` and `Model` as superclasses. The `StarModel` class therefore contains instances that are both movie stars *and* models. Each instance of `StarModel` inherits attributes from `MovieStar`, `Model`, and `Celebrity`. One of the problems with multiple inheritance is that each superclass can have attributes with the same name, thus creating ambiguity in the inheritance process. If the application designer decides to use multiple inheritance, the designer should ensure that the names of all inherited attributes are unique.

The superclasses of a shared subclass must have a common ancestor. Having a common ancestor ensures that instances of the shared subclass are of the same fundamental type of entity. In the `StarModel` shared subclass, the `Person` class is a common ancestor, allowing the system to create only one copy of the common attributes. In contrast, it would not make sense to create a `CatDog` class that inherits from the `Cat` class and from the `Dog` class, since a pet cannot be both a `Dog` and a `Cat` at the same time. A class with multiple superclasses that *do not* have a common ancestor can be modeled by using the category feature of the EER model described in the next section.

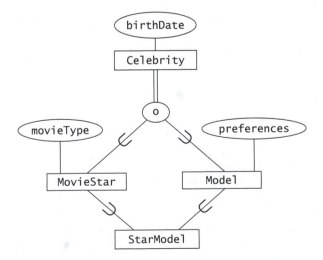

Figure 1.13   The `StarModel` Shared Subclass. From "Database Models," by S. Urban, in *Encyclopedia of Electrical and Electronics Engineering*, John G. Webster (editor); copyright © 1999 John G. Webster. This material is used by permission of John Wiley & Sons, Inc.

1.2.5 Checkpoint: Generalization and Specialization

Table 1.2 provides a summary of constraints for class hierarchies in the EER model. Every subclass must satisfy the ISA constraint. In addition, each specialization can specify the disjoint constraint and the completeness constraint for its subclasses. Optionally, attribute-defined constraints can be used to specify subclass membership based on an attribute at the superclass level. If multiple inheritance is used, then the multiple inheritance intersection constraint must be satisfied.

Exercises

1. Revise the EER of the ECLECTIC ONLINE SHOPPING ENTERPRISE to specialize `OrderCart-Info` into a shopping cart and a past order based on the value of the `type` attribute of `OrderCartInfo`. The shopping cart and past order subclasses should be disjoint. The hierarchy should also be a total specialization. In addition, a past order should have an `orderID`, a `date` (with month, day, and year), and a `totalPrice` as attributes, where `totalPrice` is derived from information in the `lineItems` relationship between `OrderCartInfo` and `InventoryItem`.

TABLE 1.2 EER Constraint Summary

EER Hierarchy Constraint	Meaning of the Constraint
ISA Constraint	The ISA constraint defines an instance of a subclass to also be an instance of its super-class.
Disjoint Constraint: Disjoint vs. Overlapping	The disjoint constraint defines the intersection of the subclasses of a superclass to be the empty set. If subclasses are not disjoint, then they are overlapping.
Completeness Constraint: Total vs. Partial Specialization	The completeness constraint defines whether an instance of a subclass is required to be an instance of one of its subclasses. *Total* defines required participation at the subclass level. *Partial* defines optional participation at the subclass level.
Attribute-Defined Constraint	Membership constraints define the value of an attribute at the superclass level so that it determines automatic membership of the instance at the subclass level.
Multiple-Inheritance Intersection Constraint	The multiple-inheritance intersection constraint defines the instances of a shared subclass to represent the intersection of its superclasses.

2. Develop an EER schema for the FICTITIOUS BANK ENTERPRISE:

> The bank maintains information on its branches. Each branch is identified by a unique code, an address (street, city, state, and zip code), and a phone number. The accounts at each branch are also recorded. Each account has a unique account number, a type (checking or savings), and a balance. An account is associated with exactly one branch, and the date that the account is opened at that branch is also maintained. An account must be classified as either a checking or a savings account. A checking account also maintains whether the account has free checks. A savings account has an associated interest rate.
>
> The bank records data regarding its customers and employees. Both customers and employees have an associated taxpayer identification number, address, and phone number. An employee has a title and salary and works for exactly one branch. The year that the customer joined the bank is also recorded. A customer may have multiple accounts with the bank, and an account may be owned by multiple customers, as in a joint account.

3. Develop an EER schema for the STORE FRANCHISE ENTERPRISE:

> Each franchise has a name, an address for its corporate headquarters, and the name of its chief executive officer. Each store is associated with exactly one franchise and is uniquely identified by its store id and further characterized by its address and phone number.
>
> The stores maintained in the enterprise can be categorized as supermarkets, pharmacies, gas stations, department stores, warehouse clubs, or a combination thereof. Note that not all stores associated with the same franchise are of the same type. For example, some stores that are supermarkets may also have an in-store pharmacy. Other stores may also have gas stations. Some stores are a combination of a supermarket and a department store.

4. Consider the `Person` hierarchy in Figure 1.10. Identify all of the constraints associated with the hierarchy. How will these constraints affect implementation considerations for the following operations on the `Person` hierarchy: (a) inserting an instance into `MovieProfessional`, (b) deleting an instance of `Model`, (c) inserting an instance of `Celebrity`, (d) deleting an instance of `Celebrity`, and (e) deleting an instance of `Critic`?

5. Consider the `Project` hierarchy in Figure 1.11. Identify all of the constraints associated with the hierarchy. How will these constraints affect implementation considerations for the following operations on the `Project` hierarchy: (a) inserting an instance into `Project`, (b) deleting an instance of `FilmProject`, (c) modifying the `type` attribute of `Project` from "F" to "M", and (d) deleting an instance of `Project`?

1.3 Categories and Categorization

Whereas multiple inheritance is used to model the intersection of two subclasses with a common root class, a *category* is used to model the *union* of two or more different types of classes. A category therefore represents a heterogeneous collection of entity instances, unlike other classes, which are homogeneous collections. An instance of a category subclass must be an instance of at least one of its superclasses, but may not necessarily be a member of all of its superclasses.

Figure 1.14 illustrates the notational convention for categories, together with the different types of constraints on categorization. In general, the superclasses of a category are connected by a single line to a union symbol enclosed in a circle. The circle is then connected by a line to the category subclass. A union symbol on the line indicates the direction of the union relationship.

Categories must satisfy either the *total category constraint* or the *partial category constraint*, as summarized in Table 1.3. A total categorization is depicted in Figure 1.14(a) with a double line between the subclass and the circle. If a category is constrained to be total, then every instance of each superclass must participate in the categorization and be an instance of the category subclass. To satisfy the total category constraint, a category must therefore be equal to the union of its superclasses. Partial categorization is shown in Figure 1.14(b) with a single line between the subclass and the circle. If a category is partial, then an instance of a superclass is not required to participate in the categorization and need not be an instance of the category subclass. To satisfy the partial category constraint, the category must be a subset of the union of its superclasses.

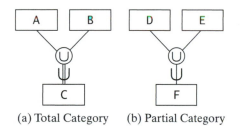

(a) Total Category   (b) Partial Category

Figure 1.14   Notation for Total and Partial Categories

TABLE 1.3   Summary of Category Constraints

Category Constraint	Meaning of the Constraint
Total Category Constraint	The total category constraint defines the instances of a category to be equal to the union of its superclasses.
Partial Category Constraint	The partial category constraint defines the instances of a category to be a subset of the union of its superclasses.

Figure 1.15 illustrates the use of categorization in the HOLLYWOOD ENTERPRISE. In particular, either a person or a company can sponsor a modeling project. Instead of creating two separate sponsor relationships between `Person` and `ModelingProject` and between `Company` and `ModelingProject`, it is useful to define the notion of a sponsor as a category, where a `Sponsor` class is a subset of the union of the `Person` and `Company` classes. A `sponsoredBy` relationship is then defined once between the `Sponsor` class and the `ModelingProject` class. The `Sponsor` class is defined as a partial category to indicate that every `Person` instance and every `Company` instance is not required to be a sponsor. By contrast, an instance of the `Sponsor` class represents an entity that is either a `Person` instance *or* a `Company` instance, but *not* an instance of both the `Person` *and* `Company` classes, as in the case of multiple inheritance and shared subclasses.

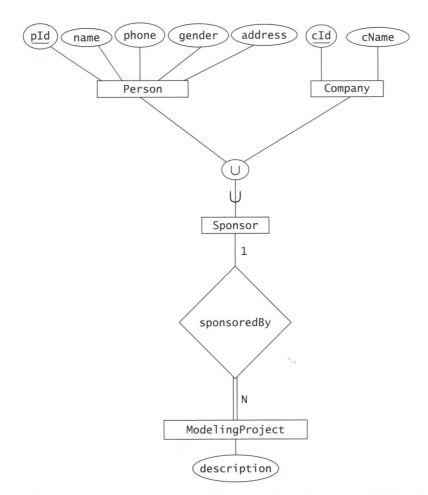

Figure 1.15 The `Sponsor` Partial Category. From "Database Models," by S. Urban, in *Encyclopedia of Electrical and Electronics Engineering*, John G. Webster (editor); copyright © 1999 John G. Webster. This material is used by permission of John Wiley & Sons, Inc.

1.4 Checkpoint

Figure 1.16 shows the complete EER diagram of the HOLLYWOOD ENTERPRISE that has
been presented in this chapter. As a conceptual model of the application, the diagram
in Figure 1.16 defines the entities, attributes, relationships, and constraints that must be
considered in the design of a database that supports the application. The different types
of constraints that can be captured within an EER diagram have been summarized in
Tables 1.2 and 1.3. The constraints of an EER schema subsume the constraints of an ER
schema as summarized in Table 1.1.

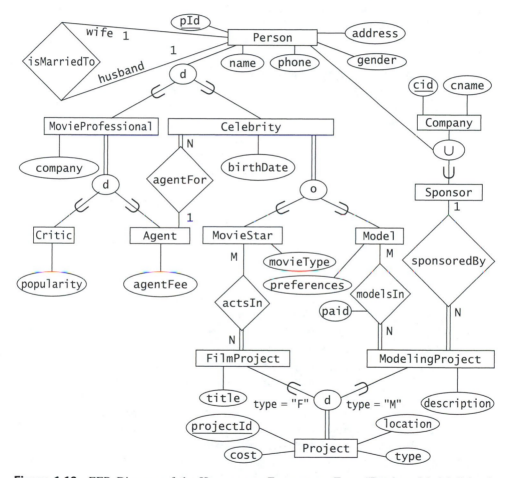

Figure 1.16 EER Diagram of the HOLLYWOOD ENTERPRISE. From "Database Models," by S.
Urban, in *Encyclopedia of Electrical and Electronics Engineering*, John G. Webster (editor); copyright © 1999 John G. Webster. This material is used by permission of John Wiley & Sons, Inc.

Exercises

1. Develop an EER schema for the HORSE RACING ENTERPRISE:

A horse has a registration number, name, type (quarter horse or thoroughbred), gender, and trainer. The heritage of every horse must also be maintained, if the information is available. For example, the mother (dam) and father (sire) should be recorded. It is also necessary to identify the offspring of a given horse.

Information about people involved in the horse-racing business should be maintained. An identifier, a name, an address, and a phone number should be maintained about every person. If a person is a horse trainer, the salary of the trainer should be indicated, along with the names of the horses trained by the trainer. If a person is a jockey, the weight of the jockey must be recorded, along with the date of the last recorded weight. It is sometimes necessary to know whether a person is a trainer and a jockey. Name and contact information can also be maintained about people other than trainers and jockeys.

A stable is a company that breeds, trains, and sells or buys horses. A stable has an identifier, a name, a phone number, and a contact person. A horse trainer works for a specific stable.

A horse can have more than one owner, and an owner can own more than one horse. An owner can be either a stable or a person. Information is always recorded about the most recent date and purchase price of a horse by its current owner(s). Each owner must also record its percentage of ownership of a horse. For example, a horse could be owned by three owners, one with a 50% share and the other two owners with 25% shares.

A racetrack has a track identifier and a track name. Every racetrack has a race schedule indicating the date of each race day and the list of races for each race day. A race day typically has 10 scheduled races, where each race has a race number (from 1 to 10) and a purse. The purse is the amount of money awarded to the winner of the race.

Every race has several entries. Each entry indicates the horse, jockey, and gate position of the horse at the start of the race. After the race, the entry records the finishing position of the horse (first, second, third, etc.). Every horse and every jockey must be able to produce a history of the races in which they have participated.

2. Develop a (min, max) version of the HOLLYWOOD ENTERPRISE.

3. Develop a (min, max) version of the HORSE RACING ENTERPRISE.

4. Explain the fundamental difference between a shared subclass and a category. To support your explanation, can the `StarModel` shared subclass in Figure 1.13 be alternatively represented as a category? Why or why not? Likewise, can the

Sponsor partial category in Figure 1.15 be alternatively represented as a shared subclass? Why or why not?

5. Revise the Sponsor partial category in Figure 1.15 to represent a total category. Then develop an ISA hierarchy representation with Sponsor as a superclass and Person and Company as subclasses of Sponsor. What constraints are required on the hierarchy? Total or partial? Overlapping or disjoint? Is this new representation of the Sponsor hierarchy semantically equivalent to the total category representation of Sponsor? Explain your answer.

1.5 Bibliographic References

Seminal work on the ER model appeared in Chen [1976]. Although there are several different notational variations of the EER model, our presentation is based on the work of Elmasri and Navathe [2003]. Foundational data-modeling issues for Elmasri's version of the EER model were originally addressed in ?], with structural constraints defined in Elmasri and Wiederhold [1980] and categories introduced in Elmasri et al., [1985].

The EER model is based on concepts that originated with research on semantic data modeling. The concepts of generalization and specialization in semantic data models began with the work of Smith and Smith [1977]. Excellent surveys of the semantic-modeling concepts that have influenced the design of the EER model can be found in Hull and King [1987] and in Peckham and Maryanski [1988].

The HOLLYWOOD ENTERPRISE used in this chapter originally appeared in an encyclopedia article on data modeling [Urban 1999].

Chapter 2

The Unified Modeling Language Conceptual Class Diagrams

Synopsis

The previous chapter presented advanced conceptual modeling using the EER model. This chapter continues coverage of advanced conceptual modeling using the Unified Modeling Language (UML) conceptual class diagrams. Unlike the EER model, UML class diagrams provide a more object-oriented approach to database design, supporting the specification of database structure and behavior. The modeling features covered include generalization and specialization of classes, association, and aggregation, as well as the use of discriminators, abstract classes, and interface classes. Emphasis is placed on the constraints that can be captured in a UML conceptual class diagram. Similarities and differences between EER and UML conceptual modeling features are also noted.

Assumed Knowledge

- Enhanced Entity Relationship Modeling (Chapter 1)

The *Unified Modeling Language* (*UML*) is a visual, object-oriented modeling language that captures the structural and dynamic aspects of a software system. Unlike the EER model, the UML is a collection of modeling techniques that apply to many different aspects of the software development process, ranging from database design to the specification of code module interaction. Each modeling technique provides a different static or dynamic view of an application, where the collection of views is referred to as a *model*. The following are some of the UML modeling techniques:

- *Class Diagrams*. A class diagram, also known as a *static structural diagram*, models the entities of an enterprise as classes with attributes and behaviors. A class diagram also establishes the relationships and constraints that exist between classes.

31

- *Object Diagrams.* An object diagram illustrates the specific instances of classes. An object diagram can be used to portray an example of data in a class diagram.

- *Use-Case Diagrams.* A use-case diagram provides a description of a system and how it is used from the user's point of view.

- *State Diagrams.* A state diagram describes the possible states of an object and the changes in state that occur in response to events.

- *Sequence Diagrams.* A sequence diagram illustrates the interaction between objects over time.

- *Activity Diagrams.* An activity diagram is a workflow graph that illustrates tasks that need to be done in a computational process.

- *Collaboration Diagrams.* A collaboration diagram describes how the different elements of a system work together to accomplish a set of global objectives.

The specific focus of this chapter is on the use of class diagrams for object-oriented database design. Since UML class diagrams are based on many of the same database modeling concepts that were originally defined in the EER model, it is useful to have an understanding of both modeling techniques for database design. Although database modeling has traditionally been introduced with EER notation, database developers are increasingly utilizing UML class diagrams in industry, due to the broader scope of the language for use in software design and development. Class diagrams are also prevalent in industry because of the standardization of UML by the Object Management Group. Unlike the EER model, UML provides a more object-oriented approach to database design, supporting the specification of database structure and behavior.

Table 2.1 summarizes the features of class diagrams that are comparable to the EER model, illustrating the differences in terminology between the two modeling techniques. Like the EER model, UML supports the modeling of classes, relationships between classes (known as *association* and *aggregation*), attributes on classes, roles on relationships, structural constraints (known as *multiplicities*), and the generalization and specialization of classes.

TABLE 2.1 Comparison of EER and UML Terminology. From *Succeeding with Object Databases*, by Akmal B. Chaudri and Roberto Zicari. Copyright © 2000 by Akmal B. Chaudri and Roberto Zicari. All rights reserved. Reproduced here by permission of Wiley Publishing, Inc.

UML	EER
Class	Entity/Class
Association and Aggregation	Relationship
Attribute	Attribute
Role	Role
Multiplicity	Structural Constraints
Generalization and Specialization	Generalization and Specialization

UML class diagrams are different from the EER model in that (1) class diagrams offer features for the specification of operations on database objects and (2) class diagrams offer more options for modeling complex relationships. However, class diagrams provide more restrictions on attributes for defining subclass membership than the EER model does. Such attributes are referred to as *discriminators* and have an effect on the use of multiple inheritance. In addition, class diagrams support the concepts of *abstract classes* and *interface classes* that are typically used in object-oriented programming languages. Abstract classes provide a more direct, object-oriented approach to the specification of total specialization as defined in the completeness constraint of the EER model. Interface classes have no counterpart in the EER model, providing a means to specify the inheritance of behavior only.

The category feature of the EER model has no corresponding modeling concept in UML class diagrams. Categories can be simulated in UML, however, through the use of abstract classes and also through the use of a feature known as the *xor constraint* on class associations.

The following subsections present the main features of UML class diagrams from the point of view of database design. Similarities and differences between UML class diagrams and EER diagrams are identified. As in Chapter 1, the constraints associated with UML class diagrams are emphasized. By the end of the current chapter, readers familiar with the EER model will be able to represent an EER diagram in a corresponding and (mostly) equivalent UML class diagram. In the remainder of this book, we will use side-by-side views of equivalent EER and UML diagrams to study the mapping of conceptual database designs to relational, object-oriented, and object-relational database implementations.

2.1   UML Classes

The items of interest in an enterprise are modeled as *classes* in UML, where a class encapsulates the structure and the behavior of *objects* that are instances of the class. The structure includes the attributes that describe the characteristics of each object in the class. The behavior includes the operations that can be executed on a specific object instance.

Figure 2.1 presents the graphical notation for a class as a rectangle with three compartments. The top compartment contains the name of the class. The middle compartment contains a list of attributes for the class. The bottom compartment identifies the method signatures for operations on the class. As illustrated in Figure 2.1, the `Project` class has three attributes and several operations for creating, destroying, and accessing instances of the class. The attributes and operations of a class can be specified at different levels of detail, depending on the current status of the design process. For example, the attribute or operation compartments in a class definition should be omitted if the database design process is in an early stage and such details are not yet available. Attributes and operations can also be listed by name only if attribute types and details about method signatures have not yet been defined.

Stereotypes

The string in guillemets («») above the class name in Figure 2.1 is a *stereotype*. A stereotype provides a way to extend the semantics of a modeling element, such as a class. In

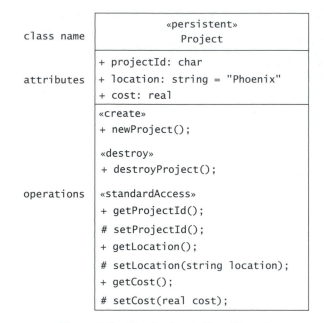

Figure 2.1 The Project Class Example

this case, the «persistent» stereotype identifies the Project class as being a persistent class, meaning that the instances of the class should persist in storage after the process that created the instances has terminated. For database modeling, the «persistent» stereotype indicates that a class should be mapped to an appropriate database representation during implementation. A class without the «persistent» stereotype represents a transient object that does not have persistent storage.

Attributes

The default syntax for attribute specification is

```
[«stereotype»] [visibility] [/] attributeName [multiplicity]:
    [type] [= initialValue]
```

where

«stereotype» is a UML or user-defined stereotype for adding semantics to the meaning of an attribute definition;

visibility uses

+ to denote *public* visibility (any class can access the attribute),

\# to denote *protected* visibility (only the class and its descendants can access the attribute), and

− to denote *private* visibility (only the class can access the attribute);

/ denotes a derived attribute;

attributeName is the name of the attribute;

multiplicity indicates whether an attribute is multivalued;

type is a class name or data type defining the type of value to be stored in the attribute; and

= initialValue indicates a default value to be assigned to an attribute.

The visibility specification is consistent with object-oriented programming language specification of visibility as summarized in Table 2.2. In Figure 2.1, all of the attributes for the Person class are public, indicating that other classes can access the attributes of the class.

Other examples of attribute specification options are pointed out through the use of UML *notes* in Figure 2.2. UML notes are dog-eared rectangles that are used to add comments to a diagram. One note in Figure 2.2 points out the age derived attribute, with an additional note explaining how the derived attribute should be calculated. Notes are also used to point out the emailAddress and phone multivalued attribute multiplicities. The multiplicity specification is placed in square brackets ([]) after the attribute name and indicates either a specific number of values for the attribute or a lower and upper bound on the number of values for the attribute. In general, a multiplicity of [1..1] means exactly one value, [0..1] means a null value or one value, [*] and [0..*] mean zero or more values, and [1..*] means one or more values. If the semantics of an application requires a limit, a star (*) can always be replaced with a specific number. An attribute multiplicity with a single number and no lower bound, such as [5], means that the attribute contains exactly the specified number of values.

Figure 2.2 also points out the pId key attribute and the address composite attribute. UML does not provide any specific notation for the specification of modeling features such as keys and composite attributes. Notes and stereotypes can be used to indicate the

TABLE 2.2 Visibility Rules for Attributes and Operations

	+ **public**	# **protected**	− **private**
attributes	Other classes may examine the attribute value.	Only operations of the class or of a public or protected subclass can examine the attribute value.	Only operations of the class can examine the attribute value.
operations	Other classes may execute the operation.	Operations of the class can only be executed by the class or by public or protected subclasses.	Operations can only be executed by the class.

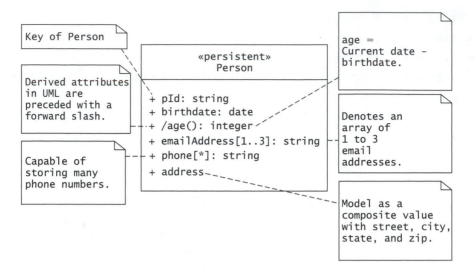

Figure 2.2   Additional UML Class Notation

desired meaning. UML also allows the default attribute specification to be replaced with the syntax of a specific language, such as C++ or Java.

Operations

The default syntax for the specification of a method signature is

```
[«stereotype»] [visibility] methodName ([parameterList]):
    [returnType]
```

where

«stereotype» is a UML or user-defined stereotype for adding semantics to the meaning of an operation;

visibility uses

>   + to denote *public* visibility (any class can execute the method),
>
>   # to denote *protected* visibility (only the class and its subclasses can execute the method), and
>
>   − to denote *private* visibility (only the class can execute the method);

methodName is the name of the method;

parameterList is a comma-delimited list of attribute/type pairs indicating the formal parameters of a method; and

returnType is the class name or data type indicating the type of value that is returned by a function.

Figure 2.1 illustrates the use of stereotypes on method specifications. The «create» stereotype is a UML-defined stereotype that identifies a constructor method for new object instances of the class. The «destroy» UML-defined stereotype indicates the destructor method of a class for deleting object instances. The «standardAccess» stereotype provides an example of a user-defined stereotype that indicates operations for setting and getting the attribute values of an object. Note that operations with the same stereotype can be grouped together under one stereotype specification. As with attribute specifications, operation specifications can use the syntax of a specific programming language.

It is useful to follow naming conventions for the specification of method signatures. The naming conventions followed in this book are as follows:

- Each class has a `newClassName()` method to create an instance of the class. Parameters for the initialization of attributes can be added to the specification if desired.

- Each class has a `destroyClassName()` method to remove instances from the class.

- Each single-valued and multivalued attribute has a `getAttributeName` method to query the attribute value and a `setAttributeName` method to assign a value to an attribute.

- Each multivalued attribute has an `addAttributeName` method to add a single value to the collection of values and a `removeAttributeName` method to remove a single value from the collection of values.

Names for other operations should be used as appropriate according to the semantics of the application.

Figure 2.1 also illustrates the use of the visibility rules from Table 2.2 for operation specifications. The `newProject` and `destroyProject` operations are defined as public operations, indicating that instances of the `Project` class can be created or destroyed from the code of any other class. All of the `get` operations are also public. The `set` operations are specified as protected, indicating that they can be executed only within the `Project` class or any of its subclasses. The next subsection will address the definition of subclasses in more detail.

2.2 Generalization and Specialization

As in the EER model, UML class diagrams support generalization and specialization for forming classes into class hierarchies. Although the notation is different, the meaning of a class hierarchy in UML is the same as in the EER model. In particular, the set of instances for each class must satisfy the ISA constraint, in which an instance of a subclass is always an instance of its superclass. Furthermore, the same constraints on specialization that exist for EER class hierarchies also exist in UML, such as disjoint specialization and total specialization. UML class diagrams also support attribute-defined subclasses, although the use of attributes for specialization is more restrictive in UML. In addition, UML supports the object-oriented programming concept of *abstract classes*, which cannot be directly instantiated. The subsections that follow elaborate on these specific features of generalization and specialization in UML class diagrams.

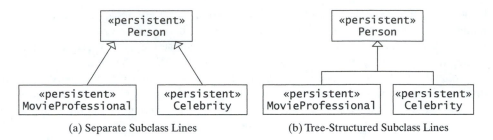

Figure 2.3   Notation for Specialization in UML

2.2.1   Forming Class Hierarchies in UML

The basic notation for the specification of a UML class hierarchy is shown in Figure 2.3. A subclass is always connected to a superclass by a line with an open arrowhead pointing to the superclass. Each superclass–subclass relationship can be drawn as a separate line, as shown in Figure 2.3(a). As a notational convenience, several subclasses can be connected by one arrowhead, forming a tree structure, as illustrated in Figure 2.3(b). There is no semantic difference between the two notations.

Specialization Constraints

The notation in Figure 2.3 is the default notation for disjoint subclass membership. The meaning of a class specialization can also be explicitly defined through the use of *specialization constraints*, which are enclosed in braces ({}) and attached to the specialization link between a subclass and a superclass. The specific constraints are shown in Table 2.3. The `disjoint` constraint specifies that the intersection of a set of subclasses must be the empty set. In other words, an instance of the superclass can be an instance of only one of the subclasses. The `overlapping` constraint indicates that an instance of the superclass can be an instance of multiple subclasses. The `mandatory` constraint specifies that each instance of the superclass is required to be an instance of at least one of its subclasses.

TABLE 2.3   List of Constraints on Specialization

Constraint Type	Description
`disjoint`	Indicates disjoint subclasses.
`overlapping`	Indicates overlapping subclasses.
`mandatory`	Indicates required participation in subclasses.
`complete`	Indicates that all possible subclasses have been specified.
`incomplete`	Indicates that all possible subclasses have not yet been specified.

The complete and incomplete constraints specify whether all of the subclasses have been shown in the class hierarchy; complete indicates that there are no more subclasses to define, and incomplete indicates that not all of the subclasses have been indicated in the diagram yet. Of the constraints listed in Table 2.3, the mandatory constraint is a user-defined constraint, introduced for the purpose of database modeling, while all others are UML-defined constraints.

The UML version of the Person class hierarchy from Figure 1.10 is shown in Figure 2.4. At each level of the hierarchy, specific constraints are attached to each specialization tree. According to the constraints, an instance of Person can be an instance of MovieProfessional or Celebrity, but not both. Since a mandatory constraint was not specified, a Person instance is not required to exist at the subclass level. For the specialization of MovieProfessional, participation at the subclass level is disjoint and mandatory. The insertion of an instance into the MovieProfessional class therefore implies the required insertion of the instance into either Critic or Agent. Because of the overlapping and mandatory constraints on the Celebrity specialization, an instance of Celebrity is required to participate at the subclass level and can be a movie star *and* a model at the same time. Note that the overlapping and disjoint constraints are identical to the corresponding constraints in the EER model. The mandatory constraint corresponds to the completeness constraint of the EER model, indicating total specialization. The absence of the mandatory constraint corresponds to partial specialization.

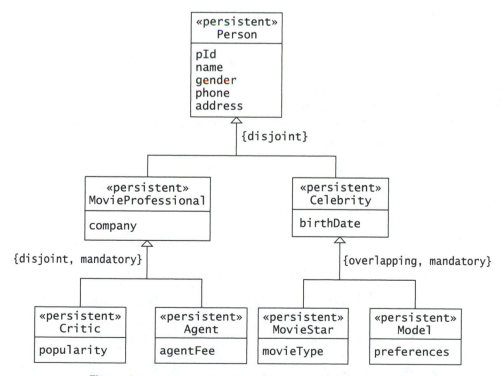

Figure 2.4 Specialization Constraints on the Person Hierarchy

Discriminators

As in the EER model, UML supports membership in subclasses based on the value of
an attribute at the superclass level. The attribute that determines subclass membership is
referred to as a *discriminator*. The use of a discriminator in UML always implies disjoint
and mandatory subclass membership. Furthermore, a subclass must exist for all possible
values of the discriminator.

A discriminator is specified as a label on the specialization link and is considered
to be a *pseudoattribute* of the superclass. A pseudoattribute behaves like a regular class
attribute, except that the domain of the attribute is the set of subclass names. A pseudoattribute does not appear in the attribute compartment of a class definition.

Figure 2.5 illustrates the use of a discriminator to define the subclasses of `Project`.
The discriminator is the `type` pseudoattribute. The possible values for `type` are "Film-
Project" and "ModelingProject."

Because a discriminator implies mandatory subclass membership, the `Project` class in
Figure 2.5 is an *abstract class*, illustrated with the name of the class in italics. An abstract
class is a class that cannot be directly instantiated. In Figure 2.5, a `Project` object can
be created only as an instance of `FilmProject` or as an instance of `ModelingProject`.
Because of the ISA constraint, the object is automatically an instance of `Project`. At the
`Project` level, the object has a `type` attribute that indicates the subclass to which the
object belongs.

If multiple discriminators exist, an instance of the superclass must be specialized
according to each discriminator. The subclasses of each discriminator must be abstract
classes. Different combinations of abstract subclasses for each discriminator must eventually meet using multiple inheritance. As shown in Figure 2.6, the `Person` class has two
discriminators: `teenOrAdult`, indicating whether a `Person` is a `Teenager` or an `Adult`,
and `gender`, indicating whether a `Person` is a `Male` or a `Female`. The four subclasses
of `Person` must be specified as abstract classes, with multiple inheritance classes, such
as `MaleTeenager` and `FemaleAdult`, that inherit from a subclass of each discriminator.

The absence of a discriminator as in Figure 2.3 is the default case, where all subclasses
are assumed to be part of an *empty discriminator*.

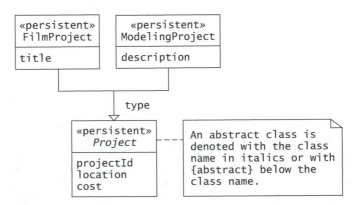

Figure 2.5 Use of a Discriminator for the `Project` Specialization

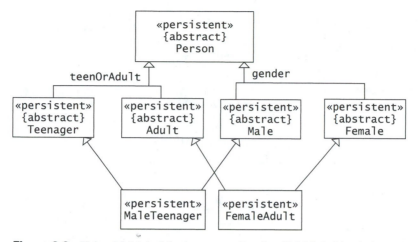

Figure 2.6   Using Multiple Inheritance as a Result of Multiple Discriminators

2.2.2   Abstract and Concrete Classes

The previous subsection introduced the concept of an abstract class, which is a class that cannot be directly instantiated. An abstract class is indicated by putting the name of the class in italics or by placing {abstract} following or below the class name.

An abstract class indirectly acquires instances through the instantiation of its subclasses. As a result, an abstract class always has at least one level of subclasses below it. An abstract class provides a more direct, object-oriented way of specifying total participation as defined in the EER completeness constraint. Every instance of the abstract superclass is always an instance of at least one subclass, since objects can be created only at the subclass level.

A class that can be directly instantiated is referred to as a *concrete class*. All of the classes in Figure 2.4 are concrete classes. In Figure 2.5, FilmProject and ModelingProject are also concrete classes.

In addition to the concepts of abstract and concrete classes, class diagrams make a distinction between *abstract operations* and *concrete operations*. An abstract operation is an operation without an implementation. An abstract operation is always specified in an abstract class, with the name of the operation in italics or with {abstract} appearing after the method signature. The expectation is that the implementation will be provided by a concrete class that inherits the operation. A concrete operation is an operation that does have an implementation. All operations of a concrete class are concrete operations. A class with at least one abstract operation is always an abstract class. An abstract class can also have concrete operations.

To illustrate the use of an abstract class together with abstract operations, consider the Sponsor hierarchy in Figure 2.7. This particular figure also illustrates the manner in which abstract classes can be used to model the concept of total categorization from the EER model.

Recall that the Sponsor class of Figure 1.15 is modeled as a subclass using the partial category notation of the EER model, where a partial category represents a subset of the

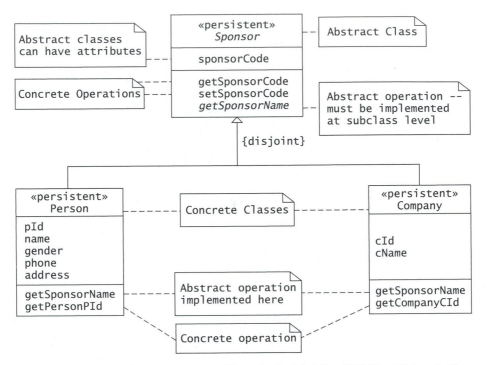

Figure 2.7 The Sponsor UML Class Hierarchy for Modeling EER Total Categorization

union of its superclasses. If the Sponsor class is alternatively modeled as a total category, then Sponsor is exactly equal to the union of its subclasses. In other words, every Person and every Company instance must be a Sponsor. A total category in EER notation can be modeled in UML by inverting the hierarchy, where the superclass is Sponsor, modeled as an abstract class, and the subclasses are Person and Company, modeled as concrete classes. Note that the specialization is also disjoint. Because Sponsor is an abstract class, object instances are never created directly at this level. Objects are created as either instances of Person or instances of Company, but not both. Furthermore, because of the ISA constraint, all instances of Person and Company are instances of Sponsor. The semantics are therefore the same as in the total categorization of the EER model.

Figure 2.7 illustrates the manner in which abstract and concrete operations can be used to enhance the definition of the Sponsor hierarchy. Every Person and Company object will inherit a sponsorCode from the Sponsor class. The Sponsor class also provides the setSponsorCode and getSponsorCode operations for manipulating the sponsorCode attribute. Since these operations are concrete, they are implemented at the Sponsor level, meaning that each subclass inherits the same implementation of the operation.

In contrast, the getSponsorName operation is an abstract operation. Since a Sponsor is either a Person or a Company, and since each corresponding subclass has its own name attribute, a general implementation of the operation cannot be provided at the superclass level. The abstract specification of the operation requires both subclasses to implement the operation as a way to provide a uniform view of each subclass as a sponsor. In the case of a `Person` object, the implementation will return the value of the `name` attribute. In the case of a `Company` object, the implementation will return the value of the `cName` attribute. Users of the database can invoke the `getSponsorName` operation without concern for whether the `Sponsor` is a `Person` or a `Company`. The appropriate operation will be executed, depending on whether the `Sponsor` object is a `Person` or a `Company`. Notice that `Person` and `Company` also have additional concrete operations that are specific to each class.

2.2.3 Checkpoint: Generalization and Specialization

Table 2.4 provides a summary of the specialization constraints supported by UML, compared with the equivalent features in the EER model. As indicated in the table, class hierarchies in UML support all of the same constraints as those found in the EER model. The differences between the use of the constraints in each model are also summarized. UML provides the additional feature of abstract classes as a means of specifying total specialization. Using an abstract class is preferred over using the {mandatory} constraint for total specialization when the subclasses are required to provide implementations for abstract operations at the superclass level. The use of the attribute-defined constraint in

TABLE 2.4   UML vs. EER Comparison of Class Hierarchy Constraints

Class Hierarchy Constraint	UML	EER	Differences
ISA Constraint	√	√	None.

Disjoint Constraint:
  Disjoint vs.
  Overlapping
	√	√	The default EER notation is overlapping. The default UML notation is disjoint.

Completeness Constraint:
  Total vs. Partial
  Specialization
	√	√	Total specialization in UML can be expressed using the {mandatory} constraint or by defining the superclass to be abstract.

Attribute-Defined Constraint	√	√	The attribute is referred to as a discriminator (or pseudoattribute) in UML. A discriminator implies total specialization with an abstract superclass and with disjoint subclass membership. The use of multiple discriminators requires multiple inheritance from the different types of discriminator subclasses.
Multiple-Inheritance *Intersection Constraint*	√	√	None.

UML is also more restrictive, although the semantics of the constraint is the same as in the EER model. Multiple inheritance in UML also has the same semantics as in the EER model.

Exercises

1. Develop a UML class hierarchy to represent horses from the HORSE RACING DATABASE in Exercise 1 in Checkpoint 1.4. Recall that a horse has a registration number, name, type (quarter horse or thoroughbred), and gender. Create subclasses to represent male and female horses using the gender attribute as a discriminator. Is it possible to represent the hierarchy without the use of a discriminator? If so, what specialization constraints should be used? Which representation is preferred?

2. Referring to the solution in Exercise 1, why would you want to have subclasses with no attributes? Discuss the advantages and disadvantages of such a design.

3. Develop a UML class hierarchy to represent the `Person` hierarchy from the HORSE RACING DATABASE in Exercise 1 in Checkpoint 1.4. The following is a modified description of the hierarchy:

   > Information about people involved in the horse racing business should be maintained. An identifier, name, address, and phone number should be maintained about every person. If a person is a horse trainer, the salary of the trainer should be indicated. If a person is a jockey, the weight of the jockey must be recorded, along with the date of the last recorded weight. It is possible for a person to be both a trainer and a jockey. Name and contact information can also be maintained about people other than trainers and jockeys.

   What specialization constraints are appropriate for the `Person` hierarchy?

4. Develop a UML class hierarchy for stores from the STORE FRANCHISE ENTERPRISE from Exercise 3 in Checkpoint 1.2.5. The following is a modified description of the hierarchy:

   > Each store is uniquely identified by its store id and is further characterized by its address and phone number. The stores maintained in the enterprise can be categorized as supermarkets, pharmacies, gas stations, department stores, warehouse clubs, or a combination thereof. Note that not all stores are of one type. For example, some stores that are supermarkets may also have an in-store pharmacy. Other stores may also have gas stations. Some stores are a combination of a supermarket and a department store.

   Can multiple inheritance be used to model the preceding requirements in UML? Why or why not?

5. The use of multiple discriminators in UML is different from the use of attribute-defined subclasses in the EER model. Is it possible to develop a UML version of the `Person` hierarchy from the ER diagram in Figure 1.12, where `homeCountry` and `gender` are discriminators? Why or why not? If it is possible, what assumptions do you have to make about use of the discriminators?

6. Develop the UML class hierarchy equivalent of the EER diagram for the `StarModel` shared subclass in Figure 1.13. Explain how the UML version is different from the EER representation.

7. For the solutions to Exercises 1 and 3, develop meaningful operations for each class. What visibility rules should be added to attribute and operation specifications?

8. The HORSE RACING DATABASE from Exercise 1 in Checkpoint 1.4 describes a horse owner as being either a stable or a person (a modeling feature referred to as a category in the EER model). Assume that every stable must be an owner and that every person must be an owner (a total category in the EER model). Show how this total category can be represented as a class hierarchy in UML, with `Owner` as the root of the hierarchy and `Stable` and `Person` as subclasses. Add a specification for the `printOwnerName` abstract operation to the `Owner` class. How does the abstract operation affect the subclasses? Create examples of concrete operations for the `Owner`, `Stable`, and `Person` classes. How is the `printOwnerName` abstract operation different from the concrete operations?

9. In the original description of the HORSE RACING DATABASE from Exercise 1 in Checkpoint 1.4, a stable *is not* required to be an owner and a person *is not* required to be an owner (a partial category in the EER model). Explain why a partial category cannot be represented as a class hierarchy in UML.

2.3 Associations

As in the EER model, UML class diagrams support the expression of 1:1, 1:N, and M:N relationships between classes. Relationships in UML are referred to as *associations*. The following subsections examine UML notation for modeling the same basic relationships that are supported in the EER model.

2.3.1 Basic Associations

The notation and terminology for associations is illustrated in Figure 2.8, showing a 1:N association between `Sponsor` and `ModelingProject`. A line is always drawn between two classes to indicate an association. Association lines can then be enhanced with *association names*, *role names*, and *multiplicities* to add more semantics to the association.

An association name is similar to a relationship name in the EER model. In Figure 2.8, `sponsors` is the association name. An association name is always expressed with respect to a specific direction of the association. An arrow can be used to indicate how to read the association. For example, the filled right arrow after `sponsors` indicates that the association is read as "A sponsor sponsors modeling projects." If the association were

Association Name	sponsors	An arrow denotes the direction of reading the relationship.
Role Names	sponsoredBy	A ModelingProject is sponsoredBy a Sponsor.
	projectsSponsored	A Sponsor has many projectsSponsored.
Multiplicities	1..1	A ModelingProject must be sponsoredBy one and only one Sponsor.
	0..*	A Sponsor can sponsor no ModelingProjects or many ModelingProjects.

Figure 2.8   Summary of Association Terminology

expressed in the opposite direction, then the name could be changed to isSponsoredBy, with a left arrow in front of the name. In this case, the association would be read as "A modeling project is sponsored by a sponsor."

Role names and multiplicities add more specific meaning to the association. In Figure 2.8, sponsoredBy is the role name of Sponsor in the association, indicating that a modeling project is sponsoredBy a sponsor. On the other side of the association, projectsSponsored is the role name for ModelingProject, indicating that modeling projects are the projectsSponsored by a sponsor. Multiplicities express the cardinality and participation constraints of the relationship. In Figure 2.8, the 1..1 multiplicity indicates that a modeling project is related to exactly one sponsor, while 0..* indicates that a sponsor can sponsor zero or more modeling projects.

The meaning of the multiplicity notation is summarized in Table 2.5. Multiplicities are similar to (min, max) pairs in the EER model, but are denoted as min..max. In

TABLE 2.5   Multiplicity Notation for Associations

min..max notation (related to at least min objects and at most max objects)	0..*	related to zero or more objects
	0..1	related to no object or at most one object
	1..*	related to at least one object
	1..1	related to exactly one object
	3..5	related to at least three objects and at most five objects
shorthand notation	1	same as 1..1
	*	same as 0..*

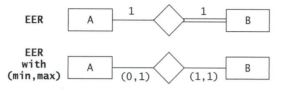

UML

A is associated with 0..1 B objects (partial participation).

B is associated with 1..1 A objects (total participation).

Equivalent EER notation:

Figure 2.9 Equivalent UML and EER Notation for 1:1 Associations

describing how many objects from class B to which an object from class A can be related, the min..max pair is placed on the association line next to class B. This placement is opposite from the placement of (min, max) pairs in the EER model, which labels the line associating the class to the relationship diamond with the minimum and maximum times an object of the class participates in the relationship. The min and max values in UML, however, have the same meaning with respect to cardinality and participation constraints as in the EER model. For example, a min value of zero always indicates partial participation in an association, whereas a min with a value greater than or equal to one indicates total participation. A max value can be expressed as a star (*) to indicate "many" or as a specific number greater than or equal to one. As a shorthand notation, 1 is the same as 1..1, while * is the same as 0..*.

Figure 2.9 provides an example of a 1:1 association in UML, with a comparison of the notation to the equivalent EER form. In the association between A and B, objects from A have partial participation in the association, indicated by the min value of 0 on the min..max pair next to B. As a result, it is possible for an instance of A to be created without establishing an association with an object from B. Objects from B have total participation, indicated by the min value of 1 on the min..max pair next to A. Every object from B is *required* to be associated with exactly one object from A. Figures 2.10 and 2.11 provide similar examples for 1:N and M:N associations, respectively. All three cases of 1:1, 1:N, and M:N associations provide a comparison of the UML notation to the equivalent EER notation.

The use of association names, role names, and multiplicities is optional in a class diagram. In the early stages of the database design process, it is acceptable to only draw a line between two classes to indicate that an association exists, but that the details of the association need to be refined. At a minimum, multiplicities must be specified before a class diagram can be mapped to a specific implementation model.

2.3.2 Association Classes and Reified Associations

Recall that relationships in the EER model can have attributes. For example, in an M:N association between Model and ModelingProject, a model is paid a different salary

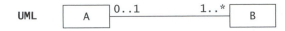

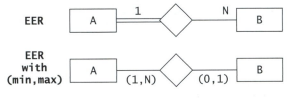

A is associated with 1..* B objects (total participation).

B is associated with 0..1 A objects (partial participation).

Equivalent EER notation:

Figure 2.10   Equivalent UML and EER Notation for 1:N Associations

A is associated with 1..* B objects (total participation).

B is associated with 0..* A objects (partial participation).

Equivalent EER notation:

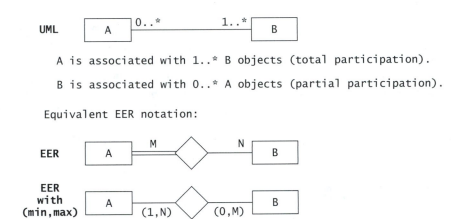

Figure 2.11   Equivalent UML and EER Notation for M:N Associations

for every modeling project to which the model is related. The salary value cannot be an attribute of `Model`, since a model has a different salary for every project. Also, the salary value cannot be an attribute of `ModelingProject`, since a project can have several models that get paid different salaries. The correct way to model this situation is to place an attribute on the relationship between `Model` and `ModelingProject`.

In UML class diagrams, attributes on associations can be modeled with *association classes*. An example of the association class notation is shown in Figure 2.12 for the M:N `modelsIn` relationship between `Model` and `ModelingProject`. The M:N relationship is modeled as described in the previous subsection for M:N relationships. An association class is then attached to the association with a dashed line. As with basic class notation, an association class has a name compartment for the name of the association class. In the figure, the name of the association class is `Paid`. An association class also has an attribute compartment containing a list of attributes that describe the relationship. In the

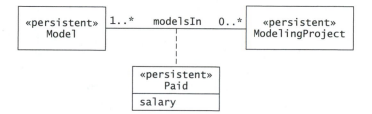

Figure 2.12   Using an Association Class to Model an Attribute on an Association

figure, the only attribute listed is the `salary` attribute, which indicates the salary a model is paid for each project in which the model works. An association class can also have an operation compartment and can participate in associations with other classes.

An alternative notation to the use of association classes is the use of *reified associations*. In a reified association, the association is modeled as a class. The process of transforming an association into a class is called *reification*. When reification is applied, something that is not usually viewed as an object in the application, such as an association between two classes, is modeled as a class.

The association between `Model` and `ModelingProject` is revised in Figure 2.13 as a reified association. In this case, the `Paid` class is no longer an association class and has been elevated to the status of a regular UML class with the name `ModelsIn`. The binary M:N association between `Model` and `ModelingProject` has also been transformed into two separate 1:N binary relationships: one that relates `Model` to `ModelsIn` and one that relates `ModelingProject` to `ModelsIn`. In this representation, each instance of `ModelsIn` is an object that represents a relationship between one model and one modeling project (i.e., the 1 side of each 1:N association). Since a model can optionally model in many modeling projects, the N side of the 1:N association between `Model` and `ModelsIn` is specified as a `0..*` multiplicity. Likewise, since a modeling project is required to have at least one model, the N side of the 1:N association between `ModelingProject` and `Model` is specified as a `1..*` multiplicity. With the use of reification, the M:N association with an association class has been indirectly represented by the two 1:N associations, with an explicit representation of the association as a class.

A reified association is typically used instead of an association class whenever an object on one side of an association can be related more than once to the same object on the other side of the association. In the `ModelsIn` example, a model can model in many projects, but can model in a given project only once. As a result, the association class representation is the most appropriate modeling choice.

Consider a different application that needs to model an M:N association involving employees, the training courses that they take, and the grade that an employee makes

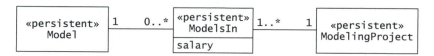

Figure 2.13   Using Reification as an Alternative to an Association Class

in each course. An employee can take many training courses, but if an employee can only take a specific course once, then an association class should be used to represent the grade as an attribute of the association. If, however, an employee can take the same course more than once, then a reified association should be used to distinguish between the different enrollments of an employee in the same course. Another way of looking at the choice between association classes and reified associations is to consider the result of the association. If the result is a set with unique pairs of objects, then an association class should be used. If the result is a bag, with multiple pairs of the same objects, then a reified association should be used.

2.3.3   N-ary Associations

Figure 2.14 presents the UML equivalent of the EER n-ary relationship between Car, Bank, and Person from Figure 1.3. An n-ary association in a UML class diagram is modeled as a diamond, with lines branching out to the classes involved in the association. If the association has attributes, then an association class can be attached to the diamond with a dashed line, as shown in Figure 2.14. Multiplicities are assigned to the n-ary association in the same manner as outlined in Section 1.1.2 for n-ary relationships in the EER model.

   A reified version of the n-ary association is shown in Figure 2.15. The reified class always relates to one of each object type involved in the relationship. In the opposite direction of each relationship (i.e., towards the Finance reified class), each object relates to the reified object as many times as it is allowed to participate in such a relationship.

2.3.4   Checkpoint: Associations

As indicated in Table 2.6, associations in UML support all of the same structural constraints supported in the EER model. The primary difference is found in notational conventions and terminology.

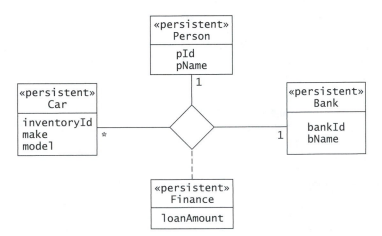

Figure 2.14   Notation for the finance Ternary Relationship

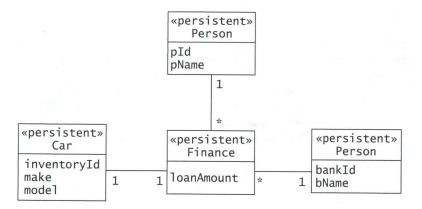

Figure 2.15 Reified Form of the Ternary `finance` Relationship

TABLE 2.6 UML vs. EER Comparison of Structural Constraints

The Structural Constraints	UML	EER	Differences
Cardinality Constraints: 1:1, 1:N, M:N	✓	✓	The use of role names is more common in UML than in EER. A diamond is only used in UML to represent n-ary relationships.
Participation Constraints: Total vs. Partial	✓	✓	Participation constraints in UML are indicated through the use of min..max pairs only, while EER provides the double line notation for total participation.
Min..Max Constraints:	✓	✓	The placement of min..max pairs in UML is opposite from the placement of (min..max) pairs in EER. UML also uses a * to represent many.

Sub-table within *Min..Max Constraints:*

Min = 0	Partial participation
Min >= 1	Total participation
Max = n	An upper bound on relationship participation, where n can be a specific integer value

Exercises

1. Figure 2.16 presents a UML diagram for the following SCHOOL DATABASE ENTERPRISE, which has five main classes, Person, Student, Faculty, Department, and CampusClub:

   > Each instance of Person has a pId, dob (date of birth), firstName, and lastName, where pId is the primary key. Because of the total and disjoint specialization relationship between Person, Student, and Faculty, a Person *must* be either a Student or a Faculty member, but not both. Each Student has a status (freshman, sophomore, junior, or senior) and each Faculty has a rank (assistant professor, associate professor, or professor).
   >
   > A Department has two attributes: a code and a name, with code being the primary key. Each Student and Faculty instance must be associated with a Department through the majorsIn or worksIn relationship, respectively. A Department can have a Faculty instance as the department chair through the chair relationship. Each Faculty member can serve as the chair of at most one Department. A Faculty instance can be the chair only of the Department in which he or she works.

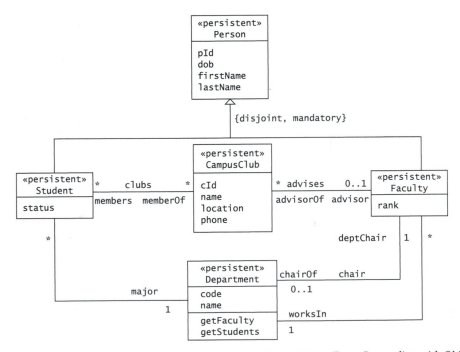

Figure 2.16 UML Diagram of the SCHOOL DATABASE ENTERPRISE. From *Succeeding with Object Databases*, by Akmal B. Chaudri and Roberto Zicari. Copyright © 2000 by Akmal B. Chaudri and Roberto Zicari. All rights reserved. Reproduced here by permission of Wiley Publishing, Inc.

Each `CampusClub` has a `cId`, a `name`, a `location`, and a `phone-Number`, where `cId` is the primary key. A `Student` can optionally be a member of many `CampusClub` organizations. Likewise, a `Campus-Club` can have many `Student` members. A `CampusClub` can have a `Faculty` member as an `advisor`. Each `Faculty` member can advise many `CampusClub` organizations.

Develop an equivalent EER representation of the UML schema in Figure 2.16. Discuss the differences and similarities between UML and EER in the representation of classes, hierarchies, and relationships.

2. Consider the following changes to the requirements for the SCHOOL DATABASE ENTERPRISE from Exercise 1: (a) faculty members can work for more than one department, where the faculty member has a different salary value for each department, and (b) students can major in two departments, where one department is indicated as the primary major and the other department is indicated as the secondary major. Use association classes to model these changes to the SCHOOL DATABASE ENTERPRISE.

3. Modify the solution to Exercise 1 to represent the following change in the relationship between a `campusClub` and a club advisor. Suppose that a club can have a different advisor every semester. In any given semester, the club has only one advisor, but, over time, the club will have a history of many advisors. Maintaining the history of advisors is required. Likewise, a faculty member can serve as an advisor for many clubs. A faculty member can also serve as an advisor for the same club more than once. For example, Joe might be the advisor for the ACM student chapter in the fall, Sue might be the advisor in the spring, and Joe might be the advisor again next fall. First, model these requirements with an association class. Then, develop an alternative version by using reified associations. Is one representation preferred over the other? If yes, why?

4. A medical doctor has an id and name as attributes. A doctor can have more than one office location, where each location has a location id, an address, and a phone number. A patient has a patient id, patient name, and billing address. Use an n-ary association in UML to model the concept of an office visit, where a patient schedules a visit for a specific time and day with a doctor in one of the office locations. Indicate the cardinality constraints of the n-ary association.

5. Exercise 3 in Checkpoint 1.2.5 describes the requirements for the STORE FRANCHISE ENTERPRISE. Show the association that exists between stores and franchises. Use role names and association names in the specification of the association.

2.4 Additional Forms of Association

In addition to the basic associations described in the previous section, class diagrams provide several advanced features for enhancing the semantics of associations between classes. Some of these features, such as *navigability* for representing unidirectional associations, do not have direct modeling counterparts in the EER model. Other features, such as *qualified associations* and *xor (exclusive or) constraints*, can be used to model EER features such as weak entities and partial categories, respectively.

2.4.1 Navigability in Associations

The associations that have been presented so far are referred to as *bidirectional associations*. In a bidirectional association, it is assumed that the corresponding implementation of the schema will allow the user to traverse the association in either direction. For example, in Figure 2.8, an implementation of the Sponsor class will provide a way for an instance of the class to reference the ModelingProject objects involved in the sponsors association. In the opposite direction, an implementation of the ModelingProject class will provide a way for each modeling project to reference the sponsor of the project. The concept of navigability in UML class diagrams allows the designer to restrict the association to be *unidirectional*, meaning that the implementation of the association is stored only in one direction.

The use of navigability is illustrated in Figure 2.17. Navigability is indicated by placing an arrow at one end of the association line, pointing from the referencing object to the referenced object. In other words, the arrow illustrates the direction in which the association can be directly navigated. In the isSponsoredBy association, for example, ModelingProject points to Sponsor to indicate that every ModelingProject object will provide a reference to its corresponding Sponsor object. In the opposite direction, the Sponsor class *will not* explicitly provide a reference to its modeling projects. This does not mean that a sponsor cannot access the projects that it sponsors. In the opposite direction of the navigation, the Sponsor class provides the getProjectsSponsored operation to return the projects sponsored. The operation must be implemented, however, to iterate through instances of the ModelingProject class to return those projects that point to a specific sponsor. The use of such an operation is application dependent and is not a required feature of navigability.

Navigability can be used in either direction in 1:1, 1:N, and M:N associations. Arrows can also be placed on both ends of an association to explicitly indicate a bidirectional relationship, although the default for a bidirectional association is to omit the arrows. In general, the specification of navigability is related to *navigation efficiency* for application requirements. For example, if there is often a need in the HOLLYWOOD ENTERPRISE to traverse from modeling projects to their sponsors, then navigability may be indicated as in Figure 2.17 for efficient access. If there is seldom a need to traverse from sponsors to their projects, then the overhead of maintaining information in the Sponsors class to reference modeling projects can be avoided simply by providing the getProjectsSponsored operation instead.

Navigability is never used with n-ary associations, since it introduces too much complexity into the meaning of navigation with nonbinary associations.

Figure 2.17 Using Navigability for Unidirectional Relationships

2.4.2 Aggregation Associations

An *aggregation association* is a type of association in which one object, known as the *part*, can be modeled as a constituent of another object, known as the *whole*. Another name for this type of association is the *whole–part relationship*.

An example of an aggregation association is shown in Figure 2.18, where Film-Project is the whole and Scene is the part. The open diamond on the FilmProject side of the relationship identifies FilmProject as the whole side of the relationship, being composed of many different scenes. Notice that the association is M:N, indicating that an instance of Scene can be used as a part of several film projects. A film project featuring the life of a famous actress, for example, could include scenes from her original film projects. In aggregation association, a part is also not required to be associated with a whole.

Aggregation does not change the semantics of the association. It is used primarily to provide a different way of looking at the association in the context of the application. One restriction on the use of aggregation is that the open diamond cannot be used on both sides of the relationship. Aggregation can be used in *transitive relationships*, where if *A* is a part of *B*, and *B* is a part of *C*, then *A* is also a part of *C*. The use of aggregation, however, must be *antisymmetric*, meaning that an object cannot be a part of itself. As a result, a class diagram should not contain cycles of aggregation relationships. It is possible, however, for a class to have an aggregation association with itself to represent the concept of recursion (e.g., an inventory item that is composed of other inventory items).

2.4.3 Composition Associations

A stronger form of aggregation is known as *composition association*. In composition association, the part can be associated only with one whole, known as the *composite*. Figure 2.19 illustrates this case for a bicycle inventory application. An instance of Wheel, for example, can be associated with only one instance of Bicycle. The composition is indicated with a solid diamond next to the composite class.

The multiplicity on the diamond side of the relationship must be 1 or 0..1. The composite class is responsible for making sure that each instance of the class is correctly connected to its parts. If a composite object is deleted and the multiplicity from the part

Figure 2.18 Aggregation Association between FilmProject and Scene

Figure 2.19 Composition Association between Bicycle and Wheel

to the composite object is 1, then the associated parts must either be deleted or assigned to another composite object.

2.4.4 Qualified Associations

A *qualified association* in UML provides a way to model the concept of a lookup table or array. Consider a generic array structure, where an array is composed of array values in indexed slots. The qualified association notation for modeling this concept is shown in Figure 2.20. The `Array` class is referred to as the *qualified object*, while the `ArrayValue` class is known as the *target object*. The small box to the right of the `Array` class contains `index`, which is the *qualifier* of the relationship. The qualifier is an association attribute that is unique within the set of target objects that are related to the qualified object. The qualifier can be an attribute of the target object or an attribute of the association that is created when the association between two objects is defined.

A qualified association is typically used in a 1:N association between the qualified object and the target object, where a qualified object can be related to many target objects. The multiplicities in the qualified association, however, describe the cardinality of the relationship between (qualified object, qualifier) pairs and target objects. The multiplicity on the target side of the association defines the number of target objects that can be related to one (qualified object, qualifier) pair. If the multiplicity is $0..1$, then the qualifier selects at most one target object for each qualified object, but does not select a target object for all possible qualifier values. If the multiplicity is $1..1$, then each qualified object is related to one target object for each possible qualifier value. If the maximum value of the multiplicity is greater than one, then the target objects are partitioned according to each (qualified object, qualifier) pair. The multiplicity on the qualified object side of the association can be one or many.

As a more specific example, consider the use of a qualified association to model the concept of weak entities, as illustrated in Figure 2.21. The equivalent EER version was

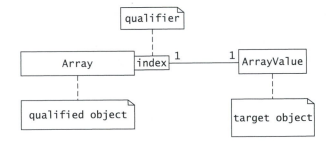

Figure 2.20   Notation and Terminology for a Qualified Association

Figure 2.21   Using a Qualified Association to Model a Weak Entity

previously presented in Figure 1.5. With a qualified association, `Employee` is the qualified object, while `Dependent` is the target object. The dName partial key becomes the qualifier for the association, meaning that each (employee, dName) pair is used to uniquely identify dependents. Notice that in the EER version, the relationship is directly shown as a 1:N relationship. With qualified associations, the 1:N EER relationship is transformed into a 1:1 UML association between (employee, dName) pairs and dependent objects. The multiplicity on the `Dependent` side of the relationship indicates that, for each possible dName value, each employee either has no dependent with that name or has one dependent with that name. An employee can therefore have many dependents, but cannot have more than one dependent with the same name. In the opposite direction, each dependent must be related to one employee.

2.4.5 The Xor Constraint on Associations

When a class can have several associations to other classes, sometimes it is useful to specify that, at any given time, the application must use only one of the associations. The *xor constraint* is used in class diagrams to specify this constraint on the use of associations. The xor constraint can also be used to model partial and total categories from the EER model.

To illustrate this point, Figure 2.22 shows the `Sponsor`, `Person`, and Company classes with two associations, one between `Sponsor` and `Person` and another between `Sponsor` and Company. `Sponsor` is referred to as the *base class*. An xor constraint is specified between the two associations, drawn as a dashed line labeled with {xor}, indicating that a `Sponsor` object can be related to one `Person` object or one Company object, but not both. The multiplicity on the `Person` and Company side of each association is 1, indicating that every instance of `Sponsor` is *required* to be related to either a `Person` or a Company. In the opposite direction, the multiplicity specified can be used to indicate the total or partial participation of `Person` and Company objects with `Sponsor` objects. In Figure 2.22, the multiplicity for each association is 0..1, indicating that each `Person` object and each Company object does not have to be related to a `Sponsor` object, thus capturing the notion of a partial category from the EER model. The multiplicity can be changed to 1..1 on

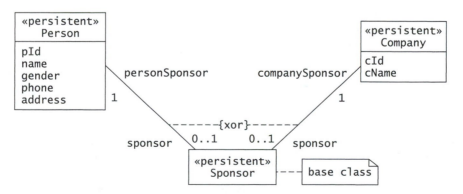

Figure 2.22 Using an Xor Constraint to Model the Partial `Sponsor` Category

each association to represent the concept of a total category, meaning that every `Person` and every `Company` is related to its corresponding `Sponsor` object.

In the EER model, inheritance is used to model a category as shown in Figure 1.15, where `Sponsor` is a subclass and `Person` and `Company` are the superclasses. The inheritance, however, is *exclusive-or* inheritance, where `Sponsor` can inherit from only one of its superclasses. The xor constraint in UML achieves a similar effect through the use of association rather than inheritance. If the designer prefers to model a category in UML by using inheritance, recall that abstract classes can be used as in Figure 2.7. In this approach, however, `Sponsor` (i.e., the category class) is the superclass and `Person` and `Company` are the subclasses. Furthermore, the approach can be used only to model total categories. The xor constraint on associations is a more general approach, since multiplicities can be used to model either total or partial categories.

2.4.6 Checkpoint: Additional Forms of Association

A UML version of the ABSTRACT ENTERPRISE from Figure 1.2 is shown in Figure 2.23. The figure illustrates the similarities between the EER notation and the UML notation for modeling classes, associations, and their structural constraints, using a qualified association to model the weak entity concept. A summary of the additional forms of association in UML is presented in Table 2.7. With the exception of the xor constraint, these additional association features do not define any more new association constraints than those outlined in Table 2.6. Instead, the features enhance the readability of the class

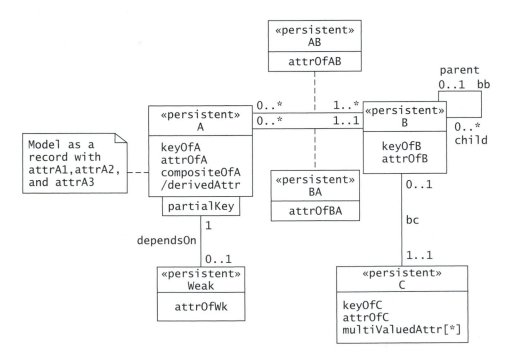

Figure 2.23   UML Class Diagram of the ABSTRACT ENTERPRISE

TABLE 2.7 Summary of Additional Association Features of UML

Additional Association Features of UML	Usage
Navigability	Used as an implementation directive to define the storage of an association in only one direction.
Aggregation Association	Used to define the whole–part relationship between two classes. Aggregation is used to enhance the readability of a class diagram.
Composition Association	Used to define a stronger form of the whole–part relationship in which a part can be connected only to one whole (requires a multiplicity of 1 on the whole side of the association). Can be used to model weak entities from the EER model.
Qualified Associations	Used to model weak entities from the EER model, where the qualifier represents a partial key. The multiplicities on a qualified association define cardinalities between (qualified object, qualifier) pairs (i.e., the identifying owner) and the target object (i.e., the weak entity).
Xor Constraint	Expressed between multiple associations of a class as an implementation directive to indicate an exclusive-or usage of the associations. For each object of the class, only one of the associations should be used, while the other association values are null. The xor constraint can be used to model total and partial categories from the EER model.

diagram. Navigability, for example, provides information about how to implement the association. Aggregation and composition enhance the interpretation of the association as a whole–part relationship, where the association represents whole objects that are composed of part objects. Composition is a more restrictive form of aggregation that permits a part to be related only to one whole. Qualified associations support the EER concept of a partial key for a weak entity in the form of a qualifier attached to a qualified object. The xor constraint is a UML feature that can be used to simulate total and partial categories from the EER model. The constraint requires that, for a set of associations for a class, only one of the associations should be used for each object in the class.

Exercises

1. Develop a UML version of the ER diagram for the ECLECTIC ONLINE SHOPPING ENTERPRISE in Figure 1.1, adding the hierarchy requirements from Exercise 1 in Checkpoint 1.2.5. For each relationship, consider whether the relationship should make use of the UML notation for navigability, aggregation association, composition association, or qualified association.

2. Repeat Exercise 1 for the GET FIT HEALTH CLUB ENTERPRISE, the MEDICAL PRACTICE ENTERPRISE, and the MUSIC AGENCY ENTERPRISE from the exercises in Checkpoint 1.1.3.

3. Figure 2.24 presents an EER diagram of an abstract hierarchy, together with additional classes that model weak entities, a total category, and several other relationships. Develop a UML version of this figure. Can the UML class diagram capture the same semantics as the EER diagram? Discuss any differences between the two modeling notations for the features used in Figure 2.24.

4. The HORSE RACING DATABASE from Exercise 1 in Checkpoint 1.4 describes a horse owner as being either a stable or a person. An owner is required to be either a

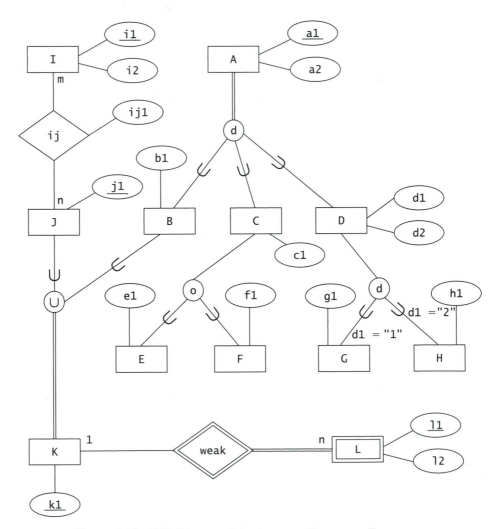

Figure 2.24   EER Diagram of the ABSTRACT HIERARCHY ENTERPRISE

stable or a person, but a stable or person is not required to be a horse owner (a partial category in the EER model). Use an xor constraint to model the associations that exist between a horse owner, a stable, and a person.

2.5   Realization and Interface Classes

The class hierarchies that have been examined so far have addressed the inheritance of structure *and* behavior, where a subclass inherits attributes and operations from its superclass. Sometimes it is desirable for classes in different hierarchies to demonstrate the same type of behavior, even though the classes are of fundamentally different types. Instead of redefining each operation in multiple classes, the operations can be specified once as abstract operations within an *interface*. Classes that need to implement the abstract operations from the interface then participate in a *realization* relationship with the interface.

The notation for the realization of an interface is shown in Figure 2.25. Because an interface is a type of class that provides a name to a collection of abstract operations, an interface is drawn as a rectangle with a compartment for the interface name and a compartment for the list of operations. The word `interface` appears in guillemets above the interface name to indicate that the class is an interface. An interface does not have a compartment for attributes, since an interface supports only the inheritance of behavior. An interface can participate in a unidirectional association, as long as the association specifies navigability pointing into the interface.

A class that realizes the interface is connected to the interface with a dashed line and an arrow pointing towards the interface. In Figure 2.25, `CalculatedValues` is an interface that provides a specification for the `numOfProjects` operation, which is a function that calculates the number of projects in which a person is involved. `MovieStar` realizes the `CalculatedValues` interface; thus, the `MovieStar` class must provide a specific implementation for `numOfProjects`.

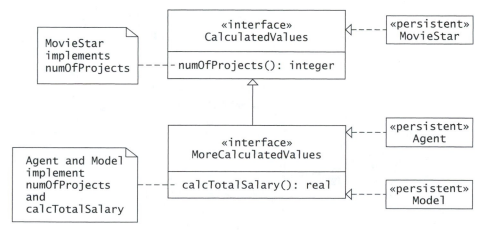

Figure 2.25   Realization of an Interface

As illustrated in Figure 2.25, an interface, such as `MoreCalculatedValues`, can inherit from another interface, such as `CalculatedValues`. As a result, any class that realizes `MoreCalculatedValues` must provide an implementation for each operation specified in `MoreCalculatedValues`, as well as any operation specified in the inherited interface. For example, since `Agent` and `Model` realize `MoreCalculatedValues`, each class must provide an implementation for `calcTotalSalary` and for `numOfProjects`. Note that the implementation of `numOfProjects` will be different in `MovieStar`, `Agent`, and `Model`. The implementation of `calcTotalSalary` will also be different in `Agent` and `Model`. The interface provides a way to specify the behavior once as part of the interface class. Any number of classes can then provide tailored implementations of each operation through a realization of the interface.

An alternative notation for realization is shown in Figure 2.26. In this notation, realization is shown by a line extending from a class and connected to a circle. The circle is labeled with the name of the interface. This particular notation is useful in large diagrams and helps to avoid cluttered diagrams caused by long lines or crossing lines.

Interfaces can be used as an alternative to multiple inheritance and categories, especially when one class needs to inherit from two fundamentally different classes. For example, consider an application that needs to model a company, a person, and a self-employed person. A person and a company are two different types of objects. A self-employed person is a specific type of person who exhibits the characteristics of a company with respect to having a business taxpayer identification number and a need to calculate information about business income. As shown in Figure 2.27, the behavior of a business can be specified within a `Business` interface. A `SelfEmployedPerson` can be defined as a subclass of `Person` to inherit structure and behavior from `Person`. Both `Company` and `SelfEmployedPerson` can then realize the behavior of `Business`. Each class will implement operations for `getTaxPayerID`, `setTaxPayerID`, and `calcTotalIncome` to exhibit the behavior of a business, even though each class represents a fundamentally different type of object.

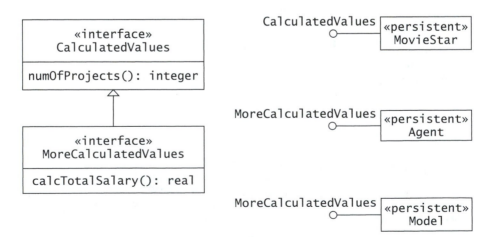

Figure 2.26 Alternative Notation for Realization

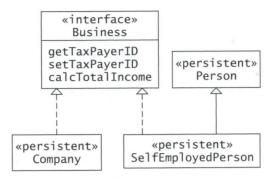

Figure 2.27 Realization of `Business` by `Company` and `SelfEmployedPerson`

2.6 Checkpoint

Figure 2.28 presents the complete UML class diagram of the HOLLYWOOD ENTERPRISE. The UML version of the application represents the same semantics that was captured in the EER version of the application, as shown in Figure 1.16. In addition, the UML version can be further enhanced with operations that define the behavior of the application. (See the exercises that follow.)

Exercises

1. Modify Figure 2.28 to specify operations for the classes of the HOLLYWOOD ENTER- PRISE. Include operations on attributes, as well as other application-oriented oper- ations on relationships between objects (e.g., the assignment of a model to a mod- eling project, cancelling the sponsor of a modeling project, printing the names of actors in a film project).

2. Develop the complete UML class diagram of the HORSE RACING ENTERPRISE from Exercise 1 in Checkpoint 1.4. Include the specification of appropriate operations for each class.

2.7 Bibliographic References

The development of UML was inspired by the introduction of object-oriented program- ming languages and object-oriented design techniques. Although Simula-67 [Dahl et al., 1967] is generally regarded as the first object-oriented programming language, most object-oriented languages, such as Smalltalk-80 [Goldberg and Robson, 1983], C++ [Stroustrup, 1986], and Eiffel [Meyer, 1988], did not become popular until the early 1980's. More recent definitions of object-oriented programming languages appear in the descriptions of C++ [Stroustrup, 1997] and Java [Arnold et al., 1997]. Widespread inter- est in object-oriented programming languages was followed by research involving the development of object-oriented design techniques, the most prevalent of which were

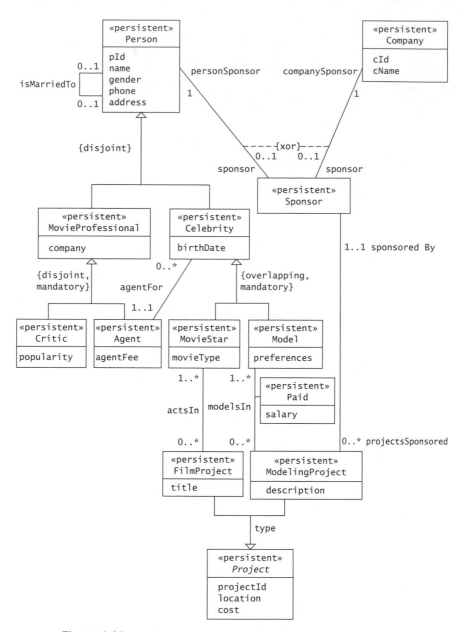

Figure 2.28   UML Class Diagram of the HOLLYWOOD ENTERPRISE

James Rumbaugh's Object Management Technique [Rumbaugh et al., 1991], Ivar Jacobson's Object-Oriented Software Engineering Notation [Jacobson et al., 1992], and Grady Booch's Object-Oriented Analysis and Design Technique [Booch, 1994]. Eventually, the work of Rumbaugh, Jacobson, and Booch converged when all three joined the Rational Software Corporation in the mid-1990's, leading to the creation of UML. In 1996, the specification of UML was submitted to the Object Management Group [OMG, 2002] in response to a request for proposals for a standardized approach to object-oriented modeling. UML was subsequently adopted as a standard by the OMG in 1997 and has continued to evolve since that time. The specification of UML is maintained by OMG and can be found at the Web site of OMG-UML [2001]. Other useful sources of reference for UML class diagrams are Rumbaugh et al., [1999], Fowler and Scott [1999], Muller [1999], and Schmuller [1999].

The SCHOOL DATABASE ENTERPRISE used in the exercises of this section originally appeared in Urban et al., [2000].

Chapter 3

The SQL Standard: Advanced Relational Features

Synopsis

This chapter presents features of the SQL standard that are relevant to the database implementation and application development issues addressed in the remaining chapters of this book. The chapter begins with a review of the SQL Data Definition Language (DDL) and the different types of constraints that can be expressed in the schema design. The review also includes the use of views for abstraction and assertions for the statement of general application constraints. The remainder of the chapter then presents more advanced features of the SQL standard, including the use of SQL-invoked routines, persistent stored modules, and triggers, as well as an overview of different techniques for programmatic access to relational databases.

Assumed Knowledge

- Fundamentals of the Relational Data Model

- Fundamentals of the SQL Query Language

Case Study

- Relational Design of the SCHOOL DATABASE ENTERPRISE (Chapter 9)

In the database design process, a conceptual data model must ultimately be transformed into an implementation-specific database design. Relational database technology provides one of the most widely used implementation frameworks for constructing database applications, with the SQL standard defining a common basis for the definition, access, and use of relational data. This standard, governed by the American National Standards Institute (ANSI) and the International Standards Organization (ISO), is a broad language that includes sublanguages for data definition, data queries and manipulation, integrity constraints, view definition, functions and procedures, stored procedures, transaction control, triggers, the programmatic use of SQL, and user authorization. Before delving into the details of conceptual-to-relational database design in Chapter 4, this chapter provides a closer look at the features of the SQL standard that are relevant to the design of relational database applications.

Assuming that the reader is already familiar with the fundamental concepts of the relational model and relational query languages (relational algebra, relational calculus, and the SQL query language), the chapter begins with a review of basic data definition and data manipulation in SQL, with a specific focus on the expression of constraints in the data definition process. The remainder of the chapter then focuses on advanced features of SQL that are a prerequisite to the topics in the chapters that follow. Views and assertions are presented in support of the conceptual-to-relational mapping procedures addressed in Chapter 4. The use of SQL-invoked procedures and persistent stored modules for developing the behavioral aspects of a database application, as well as the utilization of triggers for active capability, are covered as a precursor to discussing the object-relational features of SQL in Chapter 8. In addition, features such as embedded SQL and dynamic SQL are addressed, which are complementary to the coverage of Web-based issues in Chapter 5.

3.1   Review of Data Definition
and Data Manipulation

Defining and populating a relational schema in SQL requires the use of the *Data Definition Language (DDL)* and the *Data Manipulation Language (DML)*, with the optional use of *views* for abstraction and *assertions* for integrity constraints. This section reviews these relevant aspects of schema definition and manipulation, providing the foundation for a detailed examination of conceptual-to-relational database mapping in Chapter 4. The book assumes that readers are already familiar with using the `select` statement for data retrieval in SQL, as well as with the relational algebra and relational calculus on which the SQL query language is based. Readers who are unfamiliar with the SQL query language should consult the references at the end of the chapter for more detailed coverage of the `select` statement.

Throughout this chapter, syntax diagrams will be used to present relevant features of the SQL standard. The syntax diagrams use the following notational conventions:

< > denotes the names of syntactic elements;

[ ] denotes optional syntax;

{ } denotes mandatory syntax;

| denotes a choice of syntax;

... denotes repeatable syntax;

::= separates a syntactic element from its definition.

The syntax diagrams provide a high-level sketch of the SQL standard. Words in the diagrams that represent syntactic elements for names, labels, values, queries, and conditional expressions are not fully defined. Readers should refer to the SQL standards documents for the complete definition of the language.

3.1.1 Data Definition Language

Figure 3.1 presents the high-level syntax for data definition in SQL. As illustrated in the figure, basic data definition requires the specification of *tables*, *columns*, and *constraints*. Each table must consist of one or more columns. Each column within a table has a data type as specified in Table 3.1 and a possible specification of a default value. With the exception of *constructed* types, all of the types in the table are relevant for schema definition as discussed in this chapter. The constructed types provide advanced type definition features, such as user-defined types, array types, references to object types, and row types (similar to record and struct types in programming languages). Constructed types will be used in Chapter 8 for the definition of object-relational schemas.

Integrity Constraints

Recall that integrity constraints are used in schema definition to define the semantic meaning of the data stored in a database. Within any given state of the database, all constraints must be satisfied to ensure the correctness of the data. Constraints in SQL

Create Table Syntax:

```
create table  <table_name> (<table_element_list>)
<table_element_list> ::= <table_element> [{,<table_element>}...]
<table_element> ::= <column_definition> | <table_constraint>
<column_definition> ::= <column_name> <data_type>
  [default <default_value>] [<column_constraint>...]
```

Column Constraint Syntax:

```
<column_constraint> ::= [constraint <constraint_name>]
  not null | primary key | unique | <check_constraint> |
    <column_reference>
<check_constraint> ::= check (<boolean_valued_expression>)
<column_reference> ::= references <referenced_table_name>
  [(referenced_column_name)]
  [<update>] [<delete>]
```

Table Constraint Syntax:

```
<table_constraint> ::= [constraint <constraint_name>]
  <primary_key_constraint> | <unique_constraint> |
    <referential_constraint> | <check_constraint>
<primary_key_constraint> ::= primary key (<column_name>
  [{,<column_name>}...])
<unique_constraint> ::= unique (<column_name> [{,<column_name>}...])
<referential_constraint> ::= foreign key (<referencing_column_name>
  [{,<referencing_column_name>}...]) <references_specification>
<references_specification> ::= references <referenced_table_name>
  [(<referenced_column_name> [{,<referenced_column_name>}...])]
    [<update>] [<delete>]
<update> ::= on update <action>
<delete> ::= on delete <action>
<action> ::= no action | cascade | set null | set default
```

Figure 3.1 SQL Syntax for Data Definition

TABLE 3.1 Data Types in SQL

Category	Data Types
Character String	`char, varchar, nchar, nchar varying, clob` (character large object), `nclob`
Number	`int, integer, smallint, numeric, decimal, float, real, double precision`
Temporal	`date, time, timestamp, interval`
Boolean	`boolean (true, false,` or `unknown)`
Constructed	user-defined type (UDT) reference type row type collection type
Binary String	`blob` (binary large object)
Bit String	`bit, bit varying`

can be expressed either as part of the table definition or as separate assertions over table definitions (See Section 3.1.4.).

As shown in the syntax of Figure 3.1, constraints within a table definition can be expressed as either *column constraints* or *table constraints*. Column constraints provide a way to state constraints for each individual column specification. As an alternative syntax, the same constraints can be specified as table constraints following the definition of the table columns. A constraint *must* be expressed in the form of a table constraint if it involves multiple columns within the table.

The column and table constraints that can be specified include the following:

- The `not null` constraint specifies that the value of a column can never contain a null value.

- The `primary key` constraint defines a column or a set of columns as the primary key of the relation. The primary key is used to uniquely identify each tuple in a relation. As a result, no two tuples can have the same primary key value. A primary key can never contain a null value.

- The `unique` constraint defines a single column value or a combination of column values to be unique, meaning that no two tuples can have the same value for the column or combination of columns involved in the constraint definition. When a relation has several candidate keys, one of them is identified as the primary key. The remaining candidate keys are specified as `unique`.

- The `check` constraint defines restrictions, also known as *domain* constraints, on column values. Check constraints can also be used to constrain relationships between multiple columns of the same table.

- The `foreign key` constraint defines the notion of *referential integrity* between a foreign key in one table and a primary key in a separate (or possibly the same) table. Referential integrity through the foreign key constraint is fundamental to the definition of the relational model, constraining the value of the foreign key (composed of one or more columns) to be either null or equal to the value of a primary key that it references. A foreign key must have the same data type as the primary key to which it is related.

The `foreign key` constraint includes the specification of actions that can be taken by the database system to ensure that referential integrity is preserved when tuples are updated or deleted. The actions that can be specified are as follows:

- `no action`. This option, the default, will prevent an `update` or `delete` if referential integrity will be violated by the operation.

- `cascade`. An `update` or `delete` of a tuple in the referenced table will cause the database system to update or delete all of the matching rows in the referencing table.

- `set null`. An `update` or `delete` of a tuple in the referenced table will cause the database system to set the foreign key to null for matching rows in the referencing table. This action cannot be used with the `not null` constraint on the foreign key.

- `set default`. An `update` or `delete` of a tuple in the referenced table will cause the database system to set the foreign key to the default value for matching rows in the referencing table.

The DDL of the SCHOOL DATABASE ENTERPRISE from Figure 2.16 is presented in Figure 3.2 as a specific example of data definition in SQL. A discussion of the mapping of an object-oriented conceptual schema to the relational model is deferred to Chapter 4. Figure 3.2 is used in the remainder of this chapter to illustrate more advanced features of SQL involving the use of SQL-invoked routines, persistent stored modules, triggers, embedded SQL, and dynamic SQL.

Recall that the SCHOOL DATABASE ENTERPRISE captures information about students, the clubs in which they are involved, and the departments in which they major. The database also captures information about faculty members, the clubs they advise, and the departments in which they work. In addition, information is stored about departments and the chair of each department.

In Figure 3.2, all single-attribute `primary key` constraints and all `not null` constraints are expressed as column constraints. Since the key of the `clubs` table is composite, the definition of the primary key is expressed in the form of a table constraint. The `check` constraints of the schema are also expressed as table constraints. The first `check` constraint is on the `rank` attribute of the `faculty` table, defining the valid rank values for each tuple in the table. The second `check` constraint is on the `student` table, defining valid values for the `status` attribute of each student. In the case of `status` and `rank`, each attribute is also defined as `not null`. As a result, each attribute is *required* to contain one of the values specified in the `check` clause.

Foreign key constraints are specified as table constraints at the end of each table definition. The `facultyDeptFk` constraint in `faculty` does not specify an `on delete` option in the foreign key definition, thus defaulting to the `no action` option. As a result, a tuple in `department` cannot be deleted as long as there is a tuple in `faculty` that references the department. The `facultyPIdFk` constraint in `faculty` is handled in the

```
create table department
(code  varchar(3)   primary key,
 name  varchar(40)  not null,
 chair varchar(11));

create table person
(pId        varchar(11)  primary key,
 dob        date         not null,
 firstName  varchar(20)  not null,
 lastName   varchar(20)  not null);

create table faculty
(pId   varchar(11)  primary key,
 rank  varchar(10)  not null,
 dept  varchar(3)   not null,
 constraint rankValue check (rank in ('Assistant', 'Associate',
   'Full', 'Emeritus')),
 constraint facultyPIdFk foreign key (pId) references person (pId),
 constraint facultyDeptFk foreign key (dept)
   references department (code));

alter table department
 add constraint departmentChairFk foreign key(chair)
 references faculty(pId) on delete set null;

create table student
(pId    varchar(11)   primary key,
 status varchar(10)   not null,
 major  varchar(3)    not null,
 constraint statusValue check (status in ('Freshman', 'Sophomore',
   'Junior', 'Senior', 'Graduate')),
 constraint studentPIdFk foreign key (pId) references person(pId),
 constraint studentMajorFk foreign key (major)
   references department (code));

create table campusClub
(cId       varchar(10)   primary key,
 name      varchar(50)   not null,
 phone     varchar(12),
 location  varchar(40),
 advisor   varchar(11),
 constraint campusClubAdvisorFk foreign key(advisor)
   references faculty(pId) on delete set null);

create table clubs
(pId varchar(11) not null,
 cId varchar(10) not null,
 constraint clubsPk primary key(pId, cId),
 constraint clubsPIdFk foreign key (pId)
   references student(pId) on delete cascade,
 constraint clubsCIdFk foreign key (cId)
   references campusClub(cId) on delete cascade);
```

Figure 3.2   DDL for the SCHOOL DATABASE ENTERPRISE

same manner. The `clubsPIdFk` and `clubsCIdFk` constraints in the `clubs` table use the `on delete cascade` option. Both of these foreign key constraints will cause a tuple in `clubs` to be deleted if the referenced tuple is deleted. Using the `clubsPIdFk` constraint, for example, deleting a student tuple will invoke the deletion of all tuples in `clubs` that refer to the deleted student, thus removing the student from all clubs to which he or she belonged.

The DDL in Figure 3.2 indicates that the `Person` hierarchy from Figure 2.16 is mapped to a relational schema by means of three relations: `person`, `student`, and `faculty`. These relations correspond, respectively, to the `Person`, `Student`, and `Faculty` classes from Figure 2.16. The `pId` attribute from the `Faculty` class is used as a common attribute in each relation to support the simulation of inheritance using views. This relational representation of a class hierarchy is one of three possible representations. Chapter 4 provides a more detailed discussion of each mapping alternative for class hierarchies and the manner in which views can be used to enhance the mapping process.

Updating Table Definitions

The DDL of SQL includes statements that modify and delete table definitions. Figure 3.3 presents the syntax for the `alter table` and `drop table` statements of the DDL. The `alter table` statement can be used to add or drop column definitions, column constraints, or table constraints from a table definition. As an example, consider again the SCHOOL DATABASE ENTERPRISE. The following statement adds a new column named

Alter Table Syntax:

```
alter table <table_name> <alter_table_action>
<alter_table_action> ::=
    add [column] <column_definition>
    /* Add a column */
  | drop [column] <column_name> {restrict | cascade}
    /* Drop a column */
  | alter [column] <column_name> set default <default_value>
    /* Set default value */
  | alter [column] <column_name> drop default
    /* Drop default value */
  | add <table_constraint>
    /* Add constraint */
  | drop constraint <constraint_name> {restrict | cascade}
    /* Drop constraint */
```

Drop Table Syntax:

```
drop <table_name> <drop_behavior>
<drop_behavior> ::=
    restrict /* The table won't be dropped if the table is */
             /* referenced by another table. */
  | cascade  /* The referencing table will also be dropped. */
```

Figure 3.3 Syntax for the `alter table` and `drop table` Statements

gradePointAverage to the Student table and modifies the status attribute to define a default value:

```
alter table student
     add gradePointAverage numeric
     alter status set default = 'Freshman';
```

The removal of a column or a constraint can include the restrict or cascade option. When a column is removed, the restrict option can be used to indicate that the column can be removed only if there is no other schema component that refers to the column. The cascade specification will drop any schema component that references the removed column.

In the case of *cyclic* and *recursive* table references, the alter table statement must be used to define the schema incrementally. As an example of a cyclic table reference, consider the case where table x has a foreign key reference refY to the key of table y, table y has a foreign key reference refZ to the key of table z, and table z has a foreign key reference refX to the key of table x. It might be tempting at first to specify the schema as follows:

```
create table z
(keyOfZ           varchar(3),
 refX             varchar(3) references x(keyOfX));
create table y
(keyOfY           varchar(3),
 refZ             varchar(3) references z(keyOfZ));
create table x
(keyOfX           varchar(3),
 refY             varchar(3) references y(keyOfY));
```

In the compilation of the schema, however, table z cannot refer to table x before table x has been defined. To remedy this problem, the column reference for refX in table z must be added separately after tables x, y, and z are defined:

```
create table z
(keyOfZ           varchar(3));
create table y
(keyOfY           varchar(3),
 refZ             varchar(3) references z(keyOfZ));
create table x
(keyOfX           varchar(3),
 refY             varchar(3) references y(keyOfY));
alter table z
 add refX         varchar(3) references x(keyOfX);
```

In the DDL in Figure 3.2, defining chair as a foreign key in department requires the use of the alter table statement because of the cyclic references between department and faculty in Figure 2.16. The alter table statement in Figure 3.2 defines the departmentChairFk foreign key constraint for the department table after the faculty table is defined.

The drop table statement is used to delete a table definition and all of its data from the database. For example, the following statement deletes the student table only if student is not referenced by any other schema components:

```
drop table student restrict;
```

In comparison, the following statement deletes the student table and any other schema components that refer to student:

```
drop table student cascade;
```

3.1.2 Data Manipulation Language: Inserting, Deleting, and Updating Data

The DML of SQL includes statements that insert, delete, and update data within a database. Figure 3.4 presents the syntax for each statement form.

The insert statement can be used to insert an individual tuple or a set of tuples into a relation. In the most basic form of the statement, a single tuple is inserted by listing the values of each column in parentheses:

```
insert into department
     values ('cse', 'Computer Science and Engineering', 'FA111221111');
```

In the preceding statement, a value must be provided for every column of the table in the order in which the columns are specified in the table definition. A value of null can be specified for columns with unknown values. In the alternative form of the statement, the column names of the table can be identified explicitly:

```
insert into department(code, name, chair)
     values ('cse', 'Computer Science and Engineering', 'FA111221111');
```

It is only necessary to specify the names of columns for which values are being inserted. Column names that are not explicitly specified will be assigned the value null if no default value has been specified.

Insert Syntax:

```
insert into <table_name> [(<column_name> [{,<column_name>}...])]
   <inserted_values>
<inserted_values> ::= <SQL_query> | values (<value_list>)
<value_list> ::= <value> [{,<value>}...]
```

Delete Syntax:

```
delete from <table_name> [where <search_condition>]
```

Update Syntax:

```
update <table_name> set <set_clause> [{,<set_clause>}...]
   [where <search_condition>]
<set_clause> ::= <column_name> = <row_value_designator>
<row_value_designator> ::= <value_expression> | null | default |
   <SQL_query>
```

Figure 3.4 Syntax for the insert, delete, and update Statements

As indicated in the syntax of Figure 3.4, a set of tuples can be inserted into a table by embedding a query in the `insert` statement. In this case, the `from` clause of the query cannot refer to the table of the `insert` statement. The number and types of values returned by the query must also match the columns specified in the `insert` statement.

The `delete` statement will delete tuples that satisfy the condition specified in the `where` clause of the `delete` statement. In the following statement, any student who is a member of 'ClubMed' will be deleted:

```
delete from student where pId in
    (select cl.pId
     from clubs cl, campusClub cc
     where cc.name = 'ClubMed' and cc.cId = cl.cId);
```

The `update` statement is used to update the column values of every tuple that satisfies the condition specified in the `where` clause of the statement. The statement presented next can be used to promote all faculty named 'Joe' to the rank of full professor. Any tuple in `faculty` that satisfies the condition in the `where` clause will be modified as specified in the `set` clause:

```
update faculty
    set rank = 'full professor'
    where name = 'Joe';
```

More than one attribute can be set in an `update` statement. The condition of the `update` statement must also be restricted to attributes of the table being updated.

3.1.3 Views

An additional aspect of data definition in SQL involves the specification of views. A view in SQL is a *derived table*. Derived tables are not physically stored in the database, but are dynamically calculated from queries that are executed on demand. Views can be employed to restrict user access to different parts of the database. In large schemas, views are useful as a form of abstraction and also to simplify the portion of the schema that a user must access. Views can also be used to ease the expression of complex queries. The syntax for the `create view` statement is shown in Figure 3.5.

As an example of a view over the SCHOOL DATABASE ENTERPRISE, suppose that a specific group of users needs to see faculty names, ranks, and the names of the departments in which the faculty members work. For security reasons, this group of users should not be able to access the full database. In this case, a `facultyInfo` view can

```
create [recursive] view <view_name>
 [(<column_name> [{,<column_name>}...])]
 as <SQL_query>;
```

Figure 3.5 Syntax for the `create view` Statement

be used to provide the relevant information. Notice that a join is performed between the faculty and person tables to simulate the inheritance of attributes from the Person class:

```
create view facultyInfo
    select d.name as dName, p.firstName as fName, p.lastName as lName,
        f.rank as rank
    from   person p, faculty f, department d
    where  f.pId = p.pId and f.dept = d.code;
```

Users can then retrieve the information by accessing the view without being concerned about inheritance issues. The view can also be used to restrict users from seeing more personal information such as the pId or the dob. The following query sorts the results of facultyInfo in ascending order by department name, last name, first name, and rank:

```
select * from facultyInfo
order by dName asc, lName asc, fName asc, rank asc;
```

Unlike stored tables, views cannot be freely updated, because of the ambiguity that can be created in the modification process by the query that defines the view. The view update problem has been a subject of research for many years and is still relevant to current work involving the use of materialized views (i.e., temporarily stored view results) in data warehousing. The SQL standard defines additional syntax that can be used to create updatable views. The reader should refer to that standard for further details about updatable views.

An interesting new feature of SQL involves the use of *recursive views*. In general, a recursive query is a query in which a relation is joined with itself an indefinite number of times. The standard example is that of calculating one's heritage. (Find your mother, your mother's mother (i.e., your grandmother), your mother's mother's mother (i.e., your great-grandmother), etc.) A similar example involves identifying a chain of supervisors in a work environment. Recursive views have been added to SQL to provide a means for deriving recursive values.

To illustrate a recursive view, consider relations that capture information about employees and immediate supervisors:

```
create table employee
(eId       varchar(10),
 lName     varchar(10),
 fName     varchar(10)); /* employee information */
create table immediateSupervisor
(eId       varchar(10)
 immSupId  varchar(10)) ; /* employee and immediate supervisor */
```

The keyword recursive in the view definition presented next indicates that the union operation should be executed recursively to calculate the employee chain of command. The first select initializes the supervisor view with the relationship between an employee and the employee's immediate supervisor, renaming the columns to eId and supId as specified in the header of the recursive view definition. The second select clause joins the supervisor view with the immediateSupervisor table to find the next level of the supervisory hierarchy. The recursive keyword indicates that the recursive select using supervisor is executed until the management hierarchy is exhausted:

```
create recursive view supervisor(eId, supId) as
    select * from immediateSupervisor
    union
    select s.eId, m.immSupId
    from supervisor s join immediateSupervisor m on s.supId = m.eId;
```

3.1.4 Assertions

In addition to allowing the expression of column and table constraints, SQL provides a create assertion statement for the expression of more general constraints:

```
create assertion <constraint_name>
  check (search_condition);
```

Unlike column and table constraints, an assertion is not attached to any specific table definition. Assertions are typically used to express constraints that involve more than one table. An example of such a constraint in the SCHOOL DATABASE ENTERPRISE is that a faculty member can be the chair of only the department for which the faculty member works. This is a constraint that affects the faculty *and* department tables. Instead of expressing the constraint as a table constraint on one or both of the tables, it is more appropriate to express it as a stand-alone assertion:

```
create assertion chairDepartment
    check (not exists
        (select * from faculty, department
          where faculty.pId=department.chair and
          not (faculty.dept=department.code)));
```

The condition in the check clause must return true or unknown for the constraint to be satisfied. In general, the search condition can be any conditional expression over the database; often, the expression contains the keyword exists. Some restrictions apply to the construction of conditional expressions as outlined in the SQL standard. For example, the expression cannot contain host variables, SQL parameter names, or system functions that return values such as the current date or time.

Some constraints can be expressed either as assertions or as table constraints. The database designer, however, must ultimately decide on the most appropriate form to use, based on the subtle distinction between the two forms of constraint expression. Assertions are checked once at the end of each SQL statement. Table constraints are checked at the end of an SQL statement *for every row* in the table. To illustrate the difference, let us consider a classic example. If there is a constraint over the SCHOOL DATABASE ENTERPRISE asserting that the department table must always contain at least one tuple, then the following table constraint will be satisfied even when the department table is empty, which is obviously not the desired result (this is due to the fact that the constraint is checked *only if there are rows in the table*):

```
create table department
(...
    constraint departmentIsNotEmpty
            check ((select count(*) from department) > 0));
```

Such a constraint is more appropriately expressed by means of a stand-alone assertion. The following assertion guarantees that `department` is never empty:

```
create assertion departmentIsNotEmpty
    check ((select count(*) from department) > 0);
```

When using assertions, the database designer must be careful about the fact that an assertion will be satisfied even if the condition returns `unknown`. For example, consider a constraint stating that the average of a specific column of a table must be greater than 10:

```
create assertion AvgConstraint
    check ((select avg(someColumn) from someTable) > 10);
```

If there are no tuples in the table, the `avg` function will return a null value, which will result in an `unknown` condition and a satisfied constraint. The database designer must determine whether enforcing the constraint will return the desired result when the constraint references empty tables.

Although assertions and table constraints are normally checked at the end of an SQL statement, constraints can also be deferred until the commit point of a transaction. (Readers should refer to the SQL standard for further details about deferred constraints.)

3.1.5 Checkpoint: DDL, DML, Views, and Assertions

Specifying an application with the SQL standard involves the specification of data definition using the DDL. The DDL supports the specification of tables, where each table is composed of one or more columns with specific types. The DDL also provides statements that modify the schema definition.

Database constraints can be specified at the column or table level and include the specification of keys, unique values, default values, domain values, null values, and referential integrity. Figure 3.6 presents the DDL of the ABSTRACT ENTERPRISE from Figures 1.2 and 2.23. The DDL illustrates the use of column constraints for the specification of `primary key`, `unique`, and `not null` constraints. The default value for `attrOfC` is also specified as a column constraint. The primary key of `ab` and the primary key of `multiC`, however, must be expressed as table constraints, since the primary key of each relation is a composite key. In this example, all `foreign key` and domain constraints are specified by using table constraints with specific constraint names, such as `bKeyOfCFk` in table b and `attrOfCValue` in table c. Since class B has a recursive reference to itself through the bb relationship, a recursive reference is added to the table definition for b via the `alter table` statement after the initial definition of table b.

```
create table c
(keyOfC  varchar(20) primary key,
 attrOfC varchar(20) default 'C1',
 constraint attrOfCValue check (attrOfC in ('C1','C2')));


create table multiC
(keyOfC          varchar(20),
 multiValuedAttr varchar(20),
 constraint multiCKeyOfCFk foreign key(keyOfC) references c(keyOfC),
 constraint multiCPk primary key (keyOfC, multiValuedAttr));


create table b
(keyOfB        varchar(20) primary key,
 attrOfB       varchar(20),
 keyOfC        varchar(20) unique not null,
 parentKeyOfB varchar(20),
 constraint bKeyOfCFk foreign key (keyOfC) references c(keyOfC)
     on delete cascade);


alter table b
 add constraint recursiveRef foreign key (parentKeyOfB)
     references b(keyOfB) on delete set null;


create table a
(keyOfA   varchar(20) primary key,
 attrOfA   varchar(20),
 attrA1    varchar(20),
 attrA2    varchar(20),
 attrA3    varchar(20),
 keyOfB    varchar(20) not null,
 attrOfBA varchar(20),
 constraint aKeyOfBFk foreign key (keyOfB) references b(keyOfB));


create table weak
(keyOfA     varchar(20),
 partialKey varchar(20),
 attrOfWk   varchar(20),
 constraint weakKeyOfAFk foreign key (keyOfA) references a(keyOfA)
   on delete cascade,
 constraint weakPk primary key (keyOfA, partialKey));


create table ab
(keyOfA   varchar(20),
 keyOfB   varchar(20),
 attrOfAB varchar(20),
 constraint abKeyOfAFk foreign key (keyOfA) references a(keyOfA)
   on delete cascade,
 constraint abKeyOfBFk foreign key (keyOfB) references b(keyOfB)
   on delete cascade,
 constraint abPk primary key (keyOfA, keyOfB));
```

Figure 3.6   DDL for the ABSTRACT ENTERPRISE

More general constraints are specified through the use of the check clause in table definitions or through the use of stand-alone assertions. Assertions are typically used when the constraint involves more than one table.

The data definition can be enhanced through the use of views, which provide both a form of abstraction and a security mechanism to restrict the data that users can see. The data in a database can be manipulated through the use of the DML, which allows the data to be queried, inserted, deleted, and modified.

Chapter 4 provides more specific details on how to generate a relational schema from the EER and UML conceptual data models.

Exercises

1. Figure 3.7 presents the DDL of the Eclectic Online Shopping Enterprise from Figure 1.1, where as many constraints as possible are expressed as column constraints. Why are the primary keys of lineItems and inventoryItem expressed as table constraints instead of column constraints? Create an equivalent version of the DDL that expresses all constraints as table constraints with specific constraint names.

2. Use Figure 3.7 to develop the following views:

   (a) A view showing the firstName and lastName of customers that have shopping carts.

   (b) A view showing the code, itemNum, categoryId, and qtyInStock of inventory items that need to be reordered. An inventory item needs to be reordered if the quantity in stock is below 25.

   (c) A view showing the loginName, firstName, lastName, orderCartId, and totalPrice of each order.

   (d) A view showing the loginName, firstName, lastName, and total of all orders placed by each customer. (*Hint*: You can use the view created in the previous problem to express this view.)

3. Using Figure 3.7, develop the following assertions:

   (a) Even though a customer can be related to many instances of orderCartInfo, a customer can have at most one shopping cart.

   (b) An inventory item can appear as a line item only once on any order. For example, suppose an order contains 10 thing-a-ma-bobs. To add 5 more thing-a-ma-bobs to the order, the quantity should be adjusted instead of creating a new line item for 5 thing-a-ma-bobs.

   (c) For each unique itemNum, there cannot be two inventory items with a different code having the same color and size.

4. Use Figure 3.7 to develop the following DML statements:

   (a) Delete all customers that have no order cart information.

```
create table customerInfo
(loginName        varchar(10) primary key,
 password         varchar(15) not null,
 firstName        varchar(40) not null,
 lastName         varchar(20) not null,
 email            varchar(20) not null,
 cStreet          varchar(20) not null,
 cCity            varchar(20) not null,
 cState           varchar(2)  not null,
 cZip             varchar(6)  not null);

create table orderCartInfo
(orderCartId      varchar(11) primary key,
 type             varchar(1)  not null check (type in ('S', 'O')),
 oYear            int         not null,
 oMonth           int         not null,
 oDay             int         not null,
 customerId       varchar(10) not null references
                     customerInfo(loginName) on delete cascade);

create table category
(categoryId       varchar(10) primary key,
 description      varchar(50));

create table itemType
(itemNum          varchar(10)  primary key,
 name             varchar(20)  not null,
 picture          varchar(50),
 price            float        not null,
 belongsTo        varchar(10)  not null references category(categoryId)
                    on delete cascade);

create table inventoryItem
(itemNum          varchar(10)   not null references itemType(itemNum)
                    on delete cascade,
 code             varchar(20)   not null,
 qtyInstock       float         not null,
 itemColor        varchar(15),
 itemSize         float,
 primary key (itemNum, code));

create table lineItems
(orderCartId      varchar(10)  not null,
 itemNum          varchar(10)  not null references itemType(itemNum)
                    on delete cascade,
 code             varchar(20)  not null references itemType(code)
                    on delete cascade,
 qtyOrdered       float        not null,
 orderPrice       float        not null,
 primary key (orderCartId, itemNum, code));
```

Figure 3.7 DDL for the ECLECTIC ONLINE SHOPPING ENTERPRISE

(b) Delete all items that have never appeared on an order.

(c) Update the password of the customer with the loginName of "JSmith" to "xyz123".

(d) For all item types in the category with categoryId = "c1", increase price by 10 percent.

5. The following is an abbreviated version of a relational schema for the MUSIC AGENCY ENTERPRISE from Exercise 4 in Checkpoint 1.1.3:

```
recordingLabels(labelId, labelName, location)
cdTitles(cdCode, cdTitle, numberSold, year, labelId, groupCode)
songTitles(songCode, songTitle)
composedOf(cdCode, songCode, trackNumber)
musicalGroups(groupCode, groupName)
artists(artistId, firstName, lastName, yearBorn)
member(artistId, groupCode, fromDate, toDate)
writtenBy(songCode, artistId)
yearY(year)
topSongs(year, songCode)
topCDs(year, cdCode)
```

Each of the preceding lines defines the relation name, with the attributes of the relation enclosed in parentheses. The primary key of each relation is underlined. If the underline includes two or more attributes, then the attributes collectively represent a composite key. An attribute with the same name as a primary key in another relation represents a foreign key. For example, labelId in the relation cdTitles is a foreign key that references the primary key labelId in the relation recordingLabels. If you need a review of how a conceptual model maps to a relational schema, you may want to read Chapter 4 first before doing this exercise.

Develop a DDL for the foregoing relations. Use appropriate types for each attribute and define all primary keys. Define all foreign key constraints with an appropriate update or delete action. Use a check constraint to specify that the fromDate in member must be an older date than the toDate for representing the period for membership in a group. Use additional check constraints where appropriate to define domain values. Which attributes require the not null constraint? Why?

6. Create the following views over the DDL for the MUSIC AGENCY ENTERPRISE in Exercise 5:

(a) A view showing the groupCode, groupName, and total number of CD titles produced by each musical group.

(b) A view showing the year and songTitle of the number-one-rated song for the last 10 years.

(c) A view showing the cdTitle and the numberSold for each CD produced by the recording label with the labelName of "Star Music".

7. Create the following assertions for the MUSIC AGENCY ENTERPRISE in Exercise 5:

   (a) An artist can be a member of many musical groups, but can be a member of only one group at a time. The current group of an artist is indicated by a null value for `toDate`.

   (b) A musical group cannot record CD titles with more than one recording label in the same year.

8. Create the following DML statements for the MUSIC AGENCY ENTERPRISE in Exercise 5:

   (a) Delete all artists that have never been a member of any group and have never written any songs.

   (b) Terminate Johnny Star's membership with the group named "The Rockets". (Use today's date as the termination date.)

   (c) Using today's date as the starting date, add Johnny Star to the group named "The Punkers".

9. With any commercial relational database available at your site, use the DDLs of the SCHOOL DATABASE ENTERPRISE, the ECLECTIC ONLINE SHOPPING ENTERPRISE, and the MUSIC AGENCY ENTERPRISE to create a database for each application. This exercise will require studying the user manuals for the specific system that you use. (See Chapter 9 for a case study using Oracle.) Create insert statements to populate each database. For each application, experiment with the views, assertions, and DML statements in the exercises of this section. Did you find any differences between the standard and the commercial system? (*Hint*: some commercial database products may not fully support assertions.)

3.2   SQL-Invoked Routines

SQL-invoked routines, also known as *stored procedures*, are the SQL approach to creating *procedures* and *functions* that can be invoked from SQL code. Procedures and functions in the SQL standard have the same meaning that you would expect from procedures and functions in any programming language. There is a third type of SQL-invoked routine, known as a *method*, but methods will not be addressed until the coverage of user-defined types in Chapter 8.

SQL-invoked routines can be of two different types: *SQL routines*, which are written in SQL, and *external routines*, which are written in an external programming language, such as Java, C++, or Fortran. Deciding whether to write a routine in SQL or an external language is purely up to the application developer. Writing a routine in an external language allows the developer to make use of existing code. The use of external code also promotes portability between database systems, since routines are written in a language that is independent of any specific SQL database product. In addition, external routines may be necessary in the case of procedures or functions that require the efficient computation of complex tasks. By contrast, external routines can lead to the *impedance mismatch* problem, since the data types in SQL (such as date, time, blob, or clob from Table 3.1) do not match the data types expected by external programming languages. The cardinality and type of SQL query results (i.e., multiple rows of columns) is also a mismatch with the type of data expected as parameters in traditional programming language procedures and functions. To resolve the impedance mismatch problem, SQL routines can be used. SQL routines also avoid the context switch overhead that exists with the creation of new SQL sessions for the execution of external routines. Context switch time can degrade the performance of an application.

Figure 3.8 presents the syntax of SQL procedures and functions, as well as the syntax for calling SQL procedures. A procedure has a name, a list of parameters, and a routine body. Parameters for a procedure can be either in, out, or inout parameters. The routine body consists of a single SQL statement, such as a select, insert, update, or delete statement. For example, the deleteStudentsInClub procedure deletes all students that are members of a specific club, where the club is specified as a parameter to the procedure:

```
create procedure deleteStudentsInClub (in clubName varchar(50))
delete from student where pId in
      (select cl.pId
       from clubs cl, campusClub cc
       where cc.name = clubName and cc.cId = cl.cId);
```

A procedure is invoked by using the call statement within SQL code:

```
call deleteStudentsInClub('ClubMed');
call deleteStudentsInClub('Chess Club');
```

In comparison, a function has a name, a list of parameters, a routine body, and a return data type. The parameters of a function are, by default, in parameters. As a result, the parameter type is not specified for function parameters. As with procedures, the routine body is a single SQL statement. The return type specifies the type of data that will be

SQL Procedure Syntax:

```
   create procedure <routine_name> ([parameter [{, parameter}...]])
      <routine_body>
   <parameter> ::= [{in | out | inout}] [<parameter_name>] <data_type>
   <routine_body> ::= <SQL_statement>
```

SQL Function Syntax:

```
   create function <routine_name> ([parameter [{, parameter}...]])
      returns <data_type>
      <routine_body>
   <parameter> ::= [<parameter_name>] <data_type>
   <routine_body> ::= return <value_expression> | null
```

Call Syntax:

```
call <routine_name> ([<SQL_argument_name> [{,<SQL_argument_name>}...]])
```

Figure 3.8 Syntax for SQL Procedures and Functions

returned as a result of executing the function. For example, the getName function returns the concatenated name of a person:

```
create function getName(in pId varchar) returns varchar
return (
    select lastName + ',' + firstName
    from person
    where person.pId = pId);
```

Functions are used in-line with SQL statements to return a value. The following example illustrates the use of the getName function to embed the concatenated name in a temporary table, where the student identifier is passed as a parameter to the function:

```
insert into tempTable(studentName) values(getName('ST111223333'));
```

With external routines, the routine body is specified as follows, where the external name of the routine and the language type are declared to the SQL environment:

```
<routine body > ::=
external [ name <external_routine_name> ]
<language {ADA | C | COBOL | FORTRAN | MUMPS | PASCAL | PLI | SQL}>
```

An external routine is called in the same manner as an SQL procedure or function, although special precautions may have to be taken with respect to parameter types due to the impedance mismatch problem. Readers should consult the SQL standard for more detailed coverage of the data type mismatch problem between SQL and external routine parameters.

3.3 Persistent Stored Modules

Persistent Stored Modules (PSMs) are an optional feature of the SQL standard that enhance SQL routines with procedural concepts typically found in high-level programming languages. Very few commercial database systems have implemented PSM fully. An example of a language that resembles PSM is the PL/SQL language of Oracle, which will be presented as a case study in Chapter 9. This section focuses on the features of the SQL standard that add computational completeness to the language through the use of compound SQL statements, the declaration of variables, assignments to variables, and control flow statements.

Compound Statements

The use of a single SQL statement in SQL routines may seem somewhat restrictive. In PSM, routine bodies can be expanded into *compound statements* through the use of the begin..end statement. For example, recall that the SCHOOL DATABASE ENTERPRISE in Figure 2.16 specifies the use of the total specialization constraint on the Person hierarchy. Every hierarchy also requires enforcement of the ISA constraint. In the DDL of Figure 3.2, the Person, Student, and Faculty classes are mapped to three separate relations with a common pId attribute. Because of the total specialization constraint, creating a row in the person table also requires creating a row in either the student or faculty table. Likewise, because of the ISA constraint, creating a row in the student or faculty table requires creating a row in the person table. To enforce total specialization and the ISA constraint, the insertStudent procedure with a compound statement is created for insertion into the student table. A similar procedure can be created for insertion into the faculty table:

```
create procedure insertStudent (in pId varchar, in dob date,
     in fName varchar,
     in lName varchar, in status varchar, in major varchar)
begin
     insert into person values(pId, dob, fName, lName);
     insert into student values(pId, status, major);
end
```

In a similar manner, a compound statement can be used to enforce the ISA and total specialization constraints when deleting rows from the tables that represent the hierarchy. The deleteStudent procedure ensures that a row will not be deleted from the student table without deleting the corresponding row from the person table. The atomic option has been added to the compound statement. When this option is not used, each statement within the compound statement will commit individually. When the atomic option is added, the entire procedure does not commit until all statements in the compound statement execute successfully. If one statement fails, the entire procedure will fail. The atomic option is used as follows:

```
create procedure deleteStudent (in pId varchar)
begin atomic
     delete student S where S.pId = pId;
     delete person P where P.pId = pId;
end;
```

Variables

PSM also enhances SQL routines with the use of variable declarations and assignment statements. The following statements declare the variables deptCode and deptName:

```
declare deptCode varchar(3);
declare deptName varchar(50);
```

The variables can then be used in assignment statements and SQL statements. The following code sequence adds the words "and Engineering" to the name of the department with a code of "CSE":

```
set deptCode = 'CSE';
select name into deptName from department where code = deptCode;
set deptName = deptName + 'and Engineering';
update department set name = deptName where code = deptCode;
```

Result Sets and Cursors

The result of a query in SQL is referred to as a *result set*. To support control flow statements in SQL, a cursor is a feature of PSM that supports the process of iterating through the rows of a result set. A cursor is basically a pointer that is used to examine each row of a result set. Four statements are associated with the use of cursors: the declare statement, the open statement, the fetch statement, and the close statement. Figure 3.9 shows the syntax for each statement.

As a simple, noniterating example of using cursors, consider a revised version of the getName function:

```
create function getName(in pId varchar) returns varchar
begin
     declare name varchar;
     declare cc cursor for
     select lastName + ',' + firstName
     from person
     where person.pId=pId;
     open cc;
     fetch cc into name;
     close cc;
     return name;
end
```

The getName function declares the cursor cc to be associated with the select statement for retrieving the name of a person with a specific pId. The query is not executed until the open cc statement. At this point, the cursor is initialized, pointing before the first row of the query result, which, in the current case, should contain only one row. The fetch statement then positions the cursor to a specific row and assigns the value of the cursor query to the name variable. In general, the fetch statement can be used to point to the first, last, prior, or next row, as indicated in the syntax of Figure 3.9. The close statement deletes the result set of the query.

Declare Cursor Syntax:

```
declare <cursor_name> cursor  for <SQL_query>
```

Open Syntax:

```
open <cursor_name> [cascade <on | off>]
```

Fetch Syntax:

```
fetch [[ first | last | prior | next ] from] <cursor_name> into
    <variable_name> [{,<variable_name>}...]
```

Close Syntax:

```
close <cursor_name>
```

Figure 3.9   Syntax for Cursor-Related Statements

Control Flow Statements

Cursors are fundamental to the operation of the different types of looping statements supported by PSM. Figure 3.10 presents the syntax for the `for` statement, the `while` statement, the `loop` statement, and the `repeat` statement. Each of these statements is used in a manner similar to the way corresponding statements are used in most high-level programming languages.

The `for` statement is the only looping statement with an implicit use of cursors. The next example iterates through rows of the `person` table, inserting concatenated names into a temporary table. Notice that the declaration of the cursor is embedded in the `for` statement syntax. The `open`, `fetch`, and `close` statements are not explicitly stated, since they are built into the semantics of the `for` statement.

```
declare name varchar;
for rec as cc cursor for select * from person;
do
    select cc.lastName + ',' + firstNname into name;
    insert into tempTable(personName) values(name);
end for
```

As a more complete example, the `deleteClub` procedure uses a `for` statement to delete a club from the `campubClub` table along with information about its club membership from the `clubs` table. The `where current of` clause deletes the row currently pointed to by the specified cursor.

Loop Syntax:

```
[<statement_label>]
loop
    <SQL_statement>...
end loop [<statement_label>];
```

While Syntax:

```
[<statement_label>]
while <search_condition> do
    <SQL_statement>...
end while [<statement_label>];
```

Repeat Syntax:

```
[<statement_label>]
repeat
    <SQL_statement>... until <search_condition>
end repeat [<statement_label>];
```

For Syntax:

```
for <loop_variable_name> as <cursor_name> cursor for <SQL_query>
    do <SQL_statement>...
end for;
```

Figure 3.10 Syntax for Looping Control Statements

Case Syntax:

```
case
    when <search_condition> then <SQL_statement>...
    [when <search_condition> then <SQL_statement>......]
    [else <SQL_statement>...]
end case
```

If-then-elseif Syntax:

```
if <search_condition> then <SQL_statement>...
    elseif <search_condition> then <SQL_statement>...
    [elseif <search_condition> then <SQL_statement>......]
    [else <SQL_statement>...]
end if
```

Figure 3.11   Syntax for Branching Statements

```
create procedure deleteClub(in clubId varchar)
begin
    for rec as clubCursor cursor for
        select * from clubs where cId = clubId;
    do
        delete from clubs where current of clubCursor;
    end for;
    delete from campusClub where cId = clubId;
end;
```

Control statements in PSM also allow branching logic. Figure 3.11 presents the syntax for the `case` statement and the `if-then-elseif` statement. The `updateStudentStatus` procedure illustrates the use of a `case` statement within a `for` loop to update each student's status to the next higher level. (Seniors are deleted, assuming that they graduate). The `sStatus` variable is used in the `case` statement to determine which `update` or `delete` statement to execute:

```
create procedure updateStudentStatus()
begin
declare sStatus varchar(10);
for rec as studentC cursor for select * from student
do
    select status into sStatus from student where pId = rec.pId;
    case when (sStatus ='senior') then call deleteStudent(rec.pId);
        when (sStatus ='junior') then update student
            set status='senior';
        when (sStatus ='sophomore') then update student
            set status='junior';
        when (sStatus ='freshmen') then update student
            set status='sophomore';
    end case;
end for;
end;
```

The same procedure is rewritten below using the `if-then-elseif` statement to achieve the same logic:

```
create procedure updateStudentStatus()
begin
declare sStatus varchar(10);
for rec as studentC cursor for select * from student
do
      select status into sStatus from student where pId = rec.pId;
      if (sStatus ='senior') then call deleteStudent(rec.pId);
          elseif (sStatus ='junior') then update student
            set status='senior';
          elseif (sStatus ='sophomore') then update student
            set status='junior';
          elseif (sStatus ='freshmen') then update student
            set status='sophomore';
      end if;
end for;
end;
```

The `while` statement provides a looping construct that requires explicit use of the cursor statements. As shown in the next revised version of the `updateStudentStatus` procedure, the cursor must be explicitly declared, opened, fetched, and closed. The `while` statement will continue to loop until its condition evaluates to false. The condition uses a counter i that is counting up to the number of rows in the `student` table.

```
create procedure updateStudentStatus()
begin
    declare sPId varchar(11);
    declare sStatus varchar(10);
    declare sCount int;
    declare i int = 0;
    declare studentC cursor for select pId, status from student;
    select count(*) into sCount from student;
    set i = 0; open studentC;
    while(i < sCount) do
        fetch next from studentC into sPId, sStatus;
        case when (sStatus = 'senior') then ...
        ...
        end case;
        set i = i + 1;
    end while;
    close studentC;
end;
```

Another example of looping is found in the `repeat` statement. The following code uses an `until` clause to test the terminating condition for the loop and deletes all clubs with identifiers in the range from 1 to 10:

```
x = 1;
repeat
    delete from campusClub where cId = x;
    set x = x + 1;
    until x > 10;
end repeat;
```

The loop statement can be used to implement the same logic. The loop statement has no built-in condition to test for termination. The leave statement is used to exit from the loop.

```
clubsDeleteLoop:
x = 1;
loop
    delete from campusClub where cId = x;
    set x = x + 1;
    if x > 10 then leave clubsDeleteLoop;
    end if;
end loop clubsDeleteLoop;
```

3.4   Active Capability with Triggers

Triggers are an interesting feature of the SQL standard that add *active capability* to relational database systems. Triggers are based on the notion of *event–condition–action* rules, also known as *active rules*, from research in the area of active database systems. An active database system provides application developers the capability to monitor the occurrence of specific types of events that occur in a database. Such events are typically data modification events, but can also include the invocation of procedures and functions or the occurrence of events based on the system clock (e.g., at 3:00 P.M. every Monday through Friday). When an event occurs, an active rule allows a condition to be evaluated. If the condition is true, then the action of the rule is executed. Active rules have been investigated as a means of correcting constraint violations, to enforce business rules, to manage log files, to alert users about situations of interest, or, in general, to provide a way of responding to exceptional conditions that occur in the database. The advantage of active rules is that they afford a means of separating the logic for responding to special events from the main logic of the application.

Trigger Terminology

Before examining triggers in detail, it is important to understand the terminology associated with the use of triggers. A trigger is always defined on a *subject table*. The trigger is *activated* (or *fired*) when a *triggering event* occurs on the subject table. The triggering event is either an insert, delete, or update statement that causes a change to the state of the subject table. The statement that executes the triggering event is referred to as the *triggering SQL statement*. A *triggered SQL statement* is executed in response to a triggering event. An optional *when condition* can be included in the trigger definition so that the triggered SQL statement is executed only in response to the event when the specified condition is true, thus following the event–condition–action model of active database rules.

The syntax for the create trigger statement is shown in Figure 3.12. The syntax illustrates three other important features to the specification of a relational trigger: the timing of the triggering event (before or after), the type of trigger (row or statement), and the referencing clause for the use of *transition* tables. A before trigger

```
create trigger <trigger_name>
{before | after} { insert | delete |
  update [of <column_name> [{,<column_name>}...]] }
on <table_name> [referencing <old_or_new_values_alias_list>]
  [for each {row | statement}] [when (search_condition)]
  <triggered_SQL_statement>
<old_or_new_values_alias_list> ::=
  [old [row] [as] old values <correlation_name>]
  [new [row] [as] new values<correlation_name>]
  [old table [as] <old_values_table_name>]
  [new table [as] <new_values_table_name>]
<triggered_SQL_statement> ::= <SQL_statement> |
  begin atomic <SQL_statement>...end
```

Figure 3.12 Syntax for the `create trigger` Statement

indicates that the triggered SQL statement is executed before the execution of the triggering event, whereas an `after` trigger will execute the triggered SQL statement after the completion of the triggering event. The trigger type indicates the number of times the triggered SQL statement is executed in response to the triggering event. In the case of a row trigger, the triggered SQL statement is executed once *for every row affected by the event*. For a `statement` trigger, the triggered SQL statement is executed *only once* after the completion of the triggering event. As a result, statement triggers can be used only together with the `after` specification for the timing of the event. Many triggers can be written either as row triggers or as statement triggers. The choice between the use of a row trigger or a statement trigger also depends on the type of action to be performed.

To illustrate the trigger features discussed so far, consider the `afterUpdateRank` trigger. This trigger is used to give a 10-percent raise to any faculty member who is promoted from assistant professor to associate professor. The triggering event is an `update` statement on the faculty table. The triggered `set` statement is executed once for every faculty member who is promoted.

```
create trigger afterUpdateRank
after update on faculty referencing
            new row as newFac
            old row as oldFac
for each row when (oldFac.rank = 'Assistant' and
    newFac.rank = 'Associate')
set newFac.salary = oldFac.salary * 1.1;
```

An example of a triggering SQL statement for the `afterUpdateRank` trigger is the following `update` statement:

```
update faculty
set rank = 'Associate'
where rank = 'Assistant';
```

The `update` statement on `faculty` can affect more than one row in the faculty table. If five assistant professors are promoted to associate professor, then the `set` statement will be executed five times. The change to salary can be stated as part of the update state-ment, but there are advantages to implementing the change within a trigger. The trigger afterUpdateRank represents a business rule about salary increases. If the percentage changes, the rule can be updated once in the trigger instead of in every occurrence of the update statement. The rule can also be eliminated and replaced with a different rule that prevents changes to the salary during periods when the budget does not permit salary increases.

Transition Tables

The referencing clause in the afterUpdateRank trigger illustrates the use of transition tables in SQL. During an update to a table, a relational database temporarily maintains the old and new values of the rows being updated. An insert statement has new values only for the rows being added to the table. Likewise, a delete statement has old values only for the rows being deleted. An update statement has old and new values, where an old value contains the value of a row before it is changed and a new value represents the value of a row after it is changed. If a trigger needs to refer to the name of the subject table or to the names of columns in the subject table, the trigger must always use the referencing clause to define references to the old or new values. According to the syntax, the referencing clause can be used to define old or new references at the row level or at the table level, where an old table is the set of all old rows and a new table is the set of all new rows. If a trigger action time is before, a referencing clause may not define old or new aliases at the table level.

The afterUpdateRank trigger uses old and new row references in the when clause to detect a change to the appropriate attribute. A new row reference is used in the set statement to assign the pay raise.

Since no specific column is specified for the triggering event on the faculty table, the afterUpdateRank trigger will be activated for an update to any column of the faculty table, even if the rank attribute is not modified. To avoid unnecessary activation of the trigger, the triggering event can be revised to explicitly specify the modified attribute that will activate the trigger.

```
create trigger afterUpdateRank
after update of rank on faculty ...
```

Using Triggers

As an example of how a trigger can be used to maintain application constraints, recall the constraint that a faculty member can be the chair of a department only if the faculty member works in the department. Rather than expressing the constraint with an assertion, the constraint can be maintained through the use of triggers. The afterUpdateFaculty-Dept trigger is used to set the department chair value to null if the chair of the department decides to work in a different department.

```
create trigger afterUpdateFacultyDept
after update of dept on faculty
     referencing old row as oldRow
                 new row as newRow
```

```
for each row when (oldRow.dept <> newRow.dept and
    oldRow.pId in (select chair
                   from department
                   where code = oldRow.dept))
update department set chair = null where chair = oldRow.pId;
```

The use of a before trigger is illustrated in the beforeDeleteClubs trigger. This trigger is used to enter rows that are deleted from the clubs table into the clubHistory log table to maintain a log of all past members of each club. Because of the before option, the entries are made into the clubHistory table before each row is deleted.

```
create trigger beforeDeleteClubs
before delete on clubs referencing old row as oldRow
for each row
insert into clubHistory (oldRow.cId, oldRow.pId);
```

A trigger can also be used to alert the club advisor of members who are deleted, as well as to print a log report of deleted members. The afterDeleteClubs trigger performs this function with a statement trigger, where the action is executed only once after completion of the delete statement. A reference is created to the old table (the set of old values for the deleted rows) to retrieve the identifiers of the clubs affected by the delete operation. Procedures are then invoked to send email and print the reports.

```
create trigger afterDeleteClubs
after delete on clubs referencing old table as oldTable
for each statement
begin atomic
    for rec as oldCursor cursor for select oldTable.cId from oldTable
    do
            call sendDeleteAlertToClubAdvisor(rec.cId);
            call printDeleteMemberLogReport(rec.cId);
    end for;
end;
```

The afterDeleteClubs trigger also illustrates additional features of the triggered SQL statement. According to the syntax in Figure 3.12, the triggered SQL statement is either a single statement or a compound statement. A compound statement must include the atomic keyword, to indicate that the triggered action is an all-or-nothing activity. If any statement in the triggered action fails, then the entire trigger will fail. If a trigger fails, the triggering event will also fail. A system that conforms to the specifications for PSM can use any of the PSM statements in the triggered action.

A classic problem with the use of triggers is the termination problem. For example, what happens if rule A triggers rule B, rule B triggers rule C, and rule C triggers rule A? Here, a cycle with the potential for infinite rule triggering has been created in the trigger execution sequence. Commercial database systems should provide some mechanism to ensure that infinite rule cycles do not occur. A common technique is to detect whether the same column has been changed more than once in a cycle. If this condition is detected, an execution error is generated.

3.5   Embedded SQL

Section 3.2 addressed an approach for executing external procedures and functions from SQL code by using invoked routines. Another scenario for interaction between SQL and application programming languages is to execute SQL statements from within a host programming language. One of the original techniques defined by the SQL standard for achieving this interaction is *embedded SQL*, which requires the use of a preprocessor that analyzes the native host programming language code to separate the embedded SQL statements from the programming language source code. The SQL statements are delivered to the database for execution, while the source code is then compiled, with appropriate code inserted to execute the SQL statements from the source code. Languages that support the use of embedded SQL include Ada, C, COBOL, Fortran, MUMPS, Pascal, and PL/I. With the increased use of the Java programming language, a slightly different version of embedded SQL, known as SQLJ, has been defined for use with Java. This section presents an overview of embedded SQL as described in the SQL standard.

In a language that supports embedded SQL, every SQL statement must be preceded by the `exec sql` phrase:

```
exec sql select * from faculty;
```

Host language variables that are needed by SQL statements must be declared between the `exec sql begin declare section` and `exec sql end declare section` statements. The following example illustrates the declaration and use of host variables in the C programming language (users of embedded SQL should consult the programming language of their choice for specific guidelines with respect to type compatibility between host variables and SQL):

```
exec sql begin declare section;
    char code[3];
    char name[40];
exec sql end declare section;

strcpy(code, "CSE");
strcpy(name, "Computer Science & Engineering");
exec sql insert into department values(:code, :name);
```

A feature of SQL that contributes to the impedance mismatch problem between SQL and programming languages is that an SQL query returns a result set (a set of rows). To address this mismatch between SQL and programming language data types, cursors can be used in embedded SQL in the same manner as described for use in PSM. In the sequence of C code shown next, the `personCursor` is declared and opened. The `fetch` statement, preceded with `exec sql`, is then used in a loop to iterate through the rows of the result. The number of iterations is determined by a query that counts the number of rows in the `person` table. This example also illustrates the use of statements to connect and disconnect from the database that is being accessed.

```
exec sql begin declare section;
char[12] pId; char[21] dob; char[21] firstName; char[21] lastName;
    int numRows;
```

```
exec sql end declare section;
int i;
void main(){
exec sql connect to schoolDB user guestUser;
exec sql declare personCursor for select * from person;
exec sql select count(*) into numRows from person;
exec sql open personCursor;
for(i = 0; i < numRows; i++)
   {exec sql fetch personCursor into :pId, :dob,:firstName,:lastName;
    printf("%s, %s, %s, %s", pId, dob, firstName, lastName);}
exec sql close personCursor;
exec sql disconnect schoolDB; }
```

In general, it is advisable to account for SQL exceptions that may occur during the execution of SQL statements. Exceptions are identified through the use of a whenever statement. In the following example, if the select statement raises an exception, the whenever statement causes the program to branch to code that will handle the exception:

```
exec sql select ...
exec sql whenever sqlexception go to exceptionlabel;
```

Users of embedded SQL should refer to the SQL standard for all of the different types of exceptions that can be recognized in the whenever statement.

3.6 Dynamic SQL

Embedded SQL, as described in the previous section, is also called *static SQL*, where all SQL statements to be executed from a host programming language are known in advance. An advantage of static SQL is that the SQL statements are compiled and optimized during preprocessing, thus helping to improve the execution of an application. It may not be possible in all cases, however, to know the exact queries to be executed when the application code is written. In many modern Web-based applications, for example, it is useful to allow users to dynamically construct queries to be executed, with the users either directly entering SQL queries or constructing queries within the code based on input from the user. *Dynamic SQL* is a part of the SQL standard that addresses this approach to using SQL within application code.

The advantage of dynamic SQL is flexibility, because the queries to be executed are determined at execution time. Queries can also be parameterized. The disadvantage of dynamic SQL is that performance may deteriorate, since the compilation and optimization of queries is moved to execution time. For example, suppose that the School Orientation club allows only freshmen to become members. When a student's status changes to something other than freshman, a query can be used to delete the nonfreshman members of the club. With dynamic SQL, the query is stored in a string variable. The execute immediate statement is used to compile, optimize, and execute the query. The compilation and optimization process will be repeated every time the following sequence of code is executed:

```
string sqlStatement = "delete from clubs where
    clubs.cId in (select cId from campusClub
```

```
          where cname = 'School Orientation')
          and clubs.pId in (select pId from student where status
                  <> 'freshman')";
exec sql execute immediate :sqlStatement;
```

By contrast, with the `prepare` and `execute` statements, it is possible to perform the compilation and optimization process once and then execute the optimized version of the query. The same example of deleting nonfreshman members of a club is shown next. The club name has been parameterized, with a ? for the club name. In this revised example, the `prepare` statement is used to compile the query. The `execute` statement then executes a stored, optimized version of the query. The `using` clause identifies the variable that provides the parameterized value for the query.

```
string clubName;
string sqlStatement = "delete from clubs where
      clubs.cId in (select cId from campusClub where cname = ?)
      and clubs.pId in (select pId from student where status
                  <> 'freshman'";
                          .
                          .
                          .
exec sql prepare :sqlStatement;

clubName = "School Orientation";
exec sql execute :sqlStatement using :clubName;

clubName = "Computer Science Freshman";
exec sql execute :sqlStatement using :clubName;
```

There are many other details associated with the use of dynamic SQL, including other features for the description of queries and for the use of cursors. Many of these features are also similar to the Call Level Interface of the SQL standard.

3.7 Call-Level Interface

The *Call-Level Interface* (*CLI*) provides a more dynamic approach to communication with a database than that afforded by embedded SQL and dynamic SQL. The advantage of CLI is that it does not require the use of a preprocessor. The interface between the programming language and the database occurs through the use of an *application programming interface* (*API*) designed for interaction with relational databases. A program that uses CLI can therefore dynamically communicate with several database systems and is not specifically compiled for communication with a single database system, as with embedded SQL. Another advantage of the CLI is that it supports the ability to query the metadata of the database.

CLI originated with the development of the Open Database Connectivity (ODBC) API for database access in the early 1990s. ODBC was initially developed by several database vendors and quickly adopted by Microsoft. A formal consortium of database vendors, known as the SQL Access Group (SAG), continued to refine ODBC, with further refinement performed by the X/Open consortium of hardware vendors and by ISO. The

CLI has now been published as part of the SQL standard. Microsoft has subsequently aligned its ODBC interface with CLI, although some differences do exist that are specific to Windows environments.

Rather than elaborate on CLI in this chapter, we will present a CLI-like approach to interaction with database systems in Chapter 5 through the coverage of Java Database Connectivity (JDBC), an API that can be used by Java programs for dynamic interaction with relational database systems.

3.8   Checkpoint

This chapter has reviewed data definition and data manipulation in the SQL standard and presented several advanced features of the standard. The advanced features focus on issues that are relevant to application development, such as the use of SQL-invoked routines for writing procedures and functions in SQL or in an external programming language. The persistent stored module features provide programming-language-like extensions to SQL, including the use of compound statements, variables, and control flow statements that support looping and branching. Triggers provide an active capability to database applications— a built-in mechanism for automatically responding to database update events. Commercial database vendors offer varying levels of support for persistent stored modules and triggers.

A different approach for application access to an SQL database includes the use of embedded SQL, where SQL statements are included in application code through the use of a preprocessor for the programming language. Embedded SQL can be either static (queries are known at compile time) or dynamic (queries are determined at run time). More recent approaches to application development make use of the call-level interface features of the SQL standard, wherein SQL statements are executed by calling an API for interfacing with a relational database.

Later chapters in the book will make use of the SQL features covered in this chapter. Chapter 4 demonstrates the use of constraints, views, and assertions in the mapping of conceptual models to relational schema designs. Chapter 5 demonstrates a call-level interface feature through the use of JDBC for accessing databases from Java programs. Chapter 8 illustrates the use of SQL-invoked routines through the use of methods in the object-relational features of the SQL standard. Oracle relational and object-relational case studies present the Oracle version of persistent stored modules (PL/SQL) and triggers in Chapter 9.

Exercises

1. Develop the following SQL routines and triggers, using the DDL of the ECLECTIC ONLINE SHOPPING ENTERPRISE in Figure 3.7:

   (a) Write a parameterized function to return the `totalPrice` of a specific `orderCartId`. Recall that the total price is calculated from the line items on the order.

   (b) Assume that there is a relation named `oldOrderCartInfo` with the same structure as `orderCartInfo`. The relation `oldOrderCartInfo` is used to archive aging order information. Write a procedure to copy rows in `order-CartInfo` that were created before 2005 into `oldOrderCartInfo`. All rows copied should then be deleted from `orderCartInfo`. Write a version of the procedure for each of the different looping control statements supported by the SQL standard.

(c) Write a procedure to increase the price of each item type. If the current price is less than or equal to $10, then increase the price by 5 percent. If the current price is greater than $10, but less than or equal to $50, increase the price by 10 percent. If the current price is greater than $50, increase the price by 15 percent. Write different versions of the procedure to illustrate the use of the `case` and `if-then-elseif` statements.

(d) Write a trigger that will alert customers when the price of an item they have purchased in the past has decreased. (They may want to order more at a lower price!) Assume the existence of an external routine that will accept as parameters the customer's first name, last name, and email address, along with the item name and price. The external routine will take care of sending the email message. Write the trigger first as a row trigger. Then revise the trigger as a statement trigger.

(e) Write a trigger that will prevent a customer from ordering an item when the quantity ordered is greater than the quantity on hand.

(f) Write a trigger that will prevent the deletion of an inventory item that appears as a line item on a past order or shopping cart.

2. Develop the following SQL routine and trigger, using the DDL of the MUSIC AGENCY ENTERPRISE that you developed in Exercise 5 in Checkpoint 3.1.5:

(a) Given a `groupCode` of a musical group as a parameter, write a function that will calculate the total number of CDs sold for all CDs ever recorded by the musical group.

(b) Write a trigger that will notify the recording label when sales for a CD that is not in the list of top 10 CDs for the current year exceed 5 million copies. Assume the existence of an external procedure that will locate the email address and send the email message. The procedure will accept as parameters the `labelId`, `cdTitle`, and `numberSold`. Write the trigger as a row trigger and as a statement trigger.

3. If you have access to a commercial relational database system, create a database for the ECLECTIC ONLINE SHOPPING ENTERPRISE as specified in Exercise 5 in Checkpoint 3.1.5. Use embedded SQL in a language supported by your system to develop a program for printing the invoice of a shopping cart for a customer. Given a login name and password, the program should authenticate the user. If the user has a shopping cart, the program should print the user's name and contact information, followed by line items on the shopping cart. Each line item of the invoice should show the item number, code, color, size, and quantity ordered. Print the total price of the shopping cart at the end of the invoice.

4. If you have access to a commercial relational database system, create a database for the MUSIC AGENCY ENTERPRISE as specified in Exercise 1 in Checkpoint 3.1.5. Use embedded SQL in a language supported by your system to develop a program for printing the title of a specific CD together with a list of the track numbers and song titles for each song on the CD. The list should be sorted into ascending order by track number.

3.9 Bibliographic References

Following the original definition of the relational data model by E. F. Codd in 1970 [Codd 1970], IBM initiated the definition of a database language known as SEQUEL (Structured English QUEry Language). SEQUEL was developed as part of the System R database research project at IBM. After several revisions of the language, the name SEQUEL was changed to Structured Query Language (SQL). By the early 1980s, Oracle Corporation (then known as Relational Software, Inc.) and IBM produced the first commercial relational database products based on SQL.

Because of the growing influence of SQL, the language officially became a standard in 1986, when the American National Standards Institute (ANSI) and the International Standards Organization (ISO) published the standard as SQL-86. SQL was revised again in 1989 as SQL-89, defining embedded SQL and features for the expression of integrity constraints. A major revision of the standard appeared again in 1992 as SQL-92, with features for joined tables and assertions. The SQL:1999 version provided support for object-relational features, triggers, and recursive queries, as well as additional changes that affected the use of transactions, stored procedures, and programmatic access to relational databases. The format of the name (SQL:1999 rather than SQL-99) was also changed for compliance with year-2000 compatibility issues and to conform to ISO naming conventions, thus reflecting the increasing international recognition of the standard. The most recent version of the standard is SQL:2003, which introduces features for the support of XML [Eisenberg et al., 2004].

The most comprehensive reference works treating the SQL standard are Gulutzan and Pelzer [1999], and Melton and Simon [2001]. Melton [1998] also provides more detailed coverage of persistent stored modules, as well as examining the relationship between the SQL standard and Java technology [Melton and Eisenberg, 2000]. The complete SQL standards documents can be ordered by contacting ANSI or ISO.

Triggers in the SQL standard are not as expressive as some of the active rule languages that have been addressed in active database research projects, but triggers do provide similar active capabilities to commercial relational database systems. Database vendors have been implementing the concept of triggers since the release of the SQL-92 standard, even though the specifications for triggers were not actually included in the standard until the release of SQL:1999. As a result, many commercial products do not directly conform to the standard. Surveys on active database research can be found in Widom and Ceri [1996] and Paton and Diaz [1999].

For introductory coverage of the relational data model and relational query languages, readers should consult Kifer et al., [2005], Elmasri and Navathe [2003], Dietrich [2001],

Garcia-Molina et al., [2002], Silberschatz et al., [2002], Ramakrishnan and Gehrke [2003], and Ullman and Widom [2002]. Background on the view update problem is addressed in Dayal and Bernstein [1978], Bancilhon [1981], and Cosmadakis and Papadimitriou [1984]. Further readings on recursive views can be found in the context of deductive database systems [Ramakrishnan and Ullman, 1995].

Chapter 4

Mapping Object-Oriented Conceptual Models to the Relational Data Model

Synopsis

The EER and UML object-oriented conceptual models represent the semantics of a database enterprise. This chapter uses side-by-side illustrations of similar concepts from EER and UML diagrams to present the mapping of the conceptual level to the relational data model for implementation. The presentation includes coverage of maintaining the inherent constraints of the conceptual models.

Assumed Knowledge

- Enhanced Entity Relationship (EER) Diagrams (Chapter 1)

- Unified Modeling Language (UML) Conceptual Class Diagrams (Chapter 2)

- The SQL Standard: Advanced Relational Features (Chapter 3)

Implementation Examples on Web

- Relational Implementation of the Hollywood Enterprise

Case Study

- Relational Design of the School Database Enterprise (Chapter 9)

The EER and UML diagrams are excellent tools for modeling a database enterprise at a conceptual level. The modeled data and constraints must be mapped to an implementation data model to realize the database application. This chapter covers the mapping of these object-oriented conceptual models to the relational data model. The mapping coverage emphasizes the importance of maintaining the constraints in the relational data model that are inherent in the object-oriented conceptual models.

The ABSTRACT ENTERPRISE and the HOLLYWOOD ENTERPRISE presented in Chapters 1 and 2 form the basis of the mapping discussion. The presentation emphasizes the mapping of similar modeling concepts from EER and UML diagrams, providing side-by-side illustrations of the corresponding concepts being mapped to the relational data model.

4.1   Notation and Terminology

The mapping of a conceptual model to the relational data model requires using the SQL standard to define relational tables and views for data representation, together with constraints that enforce application semantics. Chapter 3 provides a review of these concepts. Tables and views are different forms of relations. The distinction is that a table is a relation that is explicitly stored in the database, while a view is a relation that is derived with the use of a query specification.

When an object-oriented conceptual model is mapped to a relational schema, some components of the conceptual model will be mapped to tables, while other components will be mapped to views. The term *extensional schema* refers to the relations that are defined with the `create table` statement, whereas the term *intensional schema* refers to the view definitions. For brevity of presentation, this chapter introduces a notation to summarize the specification of the extensional schema. A table definition is summarized by giving the name of the table, listing the attribute names, underlining the attributes that form a candidate key of the table, and listing the table constraints. As a convention, table and attribute names start with a lowercase letter. As an example, consider the following notation:

```
tableName(keyAttribute, attr1, attr2, foreignKeyAttr)
     foreign key (foreignKeyAttr) references
         primaryKeyTable(primaryKeyAttr)
```

This schema shows a table named `tableName` with four attributes: `keyAttribute`, `attr1`, `attr2`, and `foreignKeyAttr`. The `keyAttribute` is a candidate key for the table. Recall that a candidate key in the EER model is an attribute (simple or composite) that uniquely identifies an instance of the class. A candidate key has a similar meaning in this notation introduced to summarize table definitions. The value of a candidate key in a table uniquely identifies a tuple in the table. The `foreignKeyAttr` is an attribute that references the value of a primary key in another table. Therefore, a referential integrity table constraint is listed as part of the summary definition to capture this constraint in the schema. Since there is only one candidate key for `tableName`, the candidate key `keyAttribute` is also the primary key. An explicit primary key table constraint will be used only when a table has more than one candidate key.

If there are multiple candidate keys for a table, each candidate key will be underlined. For example,

```
tableMultipleCandidateKeys(candidateKey1, anyAttr, candidateKey2)
     primary key (candidateKey1)
     unique (candidateKey2)
```

indicates that the table named `tableMultipleCandidateKeys` has two candidate keys: `candidateKey1` and `candidateKey2`. Each candidate key uniquely identifies a tuple in the table. Therefore, an explicit primary key table constraint indicates which candidate key is considered the primary key for uniquely identifying a row in the table. A `unique` constraint enforces the uniqueness of `candidateKey2`.

If a table has a composite candidate key, then the line underscores all of the attributes that are part of the candidate key. For example,

`tableCompositeCandidateKey(`< u>`partOfCandidateKey1, partOfCandidateKey2`</u>`,`
    `anyAttr)`

indicates that the table named `tableCompositeCandidateKey` has one candidate key that consists of two attributes: `partOfCandidateKey1` and `partOfCandidateKey2`. The value of both attributes is required to uniquely identify a tuple in the table.

This syntax for describing a table definition is an abbreviation of the SQL DDL described in Chapter 3 and is used as an abstraction to facilitate the presentation of mapping object-oriented conceptual models to the relational data model. This summary syntax is used only for the extensional schema. The view definitions for the intensional schema consist of queries, which must be specified explicitly.

4.2 Classes

The first step in mapping a conceptual model to the relational data model involves the mapping of classes. This section covers classes that are not part of a class hierarchy; the mapping of class hierarchies is deferred to Section 4.4.

The relational representation of classes having simple, composite, derived, and multi-valued attributes is illustrated with the use of the ABSTRACT ENTERPRISE given as an EER diagram in Figure 1.2 and as a UML diagram in Figure 2.23. A comparison view of the EER and UML diagrams for each component of the ABSTRACT ENTERPRISE will be used as each component is mapped to the relational data model. To facilitate the identification and differentiation of a class from its corresponding table, a class is mapped to a table that is named based on a lowercase version of its associated class name.

Consider class A shown in Figure 4.1. This class has simple attributes (`keyOfA`, `attrOfA`), a composite attribute (`compositeOfA`), and a derived attribute (`derivedAttr`).

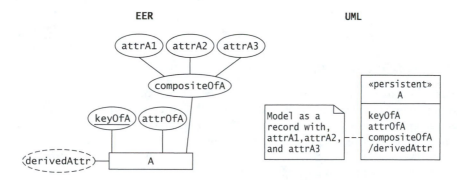

Figure 4.1 EER and UML Diagrams for Class A of the ABSTRACT ENTERPRISE

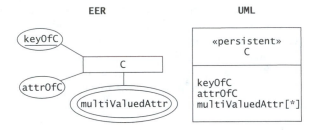

Figure 4.2 EER and UML Diagrams for Class C of the ABSTRACT ENTERPRISE

Class A is mapped to a table that contains its simple attributes. Since the relational data model does not allow structured types, the composite attribute (compositeOfA) cannot be directly included. However, the simple components (attrA1, attrA2, attrA3) of the composite attribute are included in the corresponding table:

a(<u>keyOfA</u>, attrOfA, attrA1, attrA2, attrA3)

The table for A does not include the derived attribute for A. One alternative is to define a view for A that retrieves the stored attributes and computes the value of the derived attribute (derivedAttr) in the view definition. Another alternative is to explicitly store the value of the derived attribute in the table for A and update its value by using triggers when the value on which it depends changes:

a(<u>keyOfA</u>, attrOfA, attrA1, attrA2, attrA3, derivedAttr)

A classical example of a derived attribute is a person's age, which is computed on the basis of the current date and the person's birthdate.

Class C shown in Figure 4.2 has simple attributes (keyOfC, attrOfC) and a multi-valued attribute (multiValuedAttr). Class C is mapped to a table of the same name containing its simple attributes. Since the relational data model allows only simple types for attributes, the multivalued attribute must be mapped to its own table along with the key of the class. The key of the corresponding table (multiC) is a composite key consisting of the key of the class and the multivalued attribute. Note that a referential integrity constraint must hold between the foreign key and the primary key that it references:

c(<u>keyOfC</u>, attrOfC)
multiC(<u>keyOfC, multiValuedAttr</u>)
        foreign key (keyOfC) references c(keyOfC)

4.3 Associations

The associations of a UML class diagram and the relationships of an EER diagram provide important semantics about the relationships that exist between the entities involved in an enterprise model. These semantics affect the mapping of the conceptual model to relational tables and also determine the constraints that must be expressed to enforce the intended meaning of the associations. This section presents relational mapping considerations for associations. Binary associations can be mapped using either a *bidirectional* or *unidirectional* approach. In a bidirectional mapping, the resulting relational tables can be used to traverse the association in either direction. In a unidirectional association, the mapping supports traversal of the association only in one direction. Although the EER model does not make a distinction between the bidirectional and unidirectional mappings, UML diagrams use navigation to explicitly specify the unidirectional approach.

Mapping techniques must also consider recursive binary associations, n-ary associations, weak entities, class hierarchies, shared subclasses, and categories. All of these features are supported by the EER and the UML modeling techniques. The UML conceptual class diagrams support additional semantics on associations, such as aggregation and composition, but these semantics do not change the basic mapping of the associations. In all cases, participation and multiplicity constraints play an important role in the specification of constraints on associations. The following sections elaborate on association mappings, beginning with mapping techniques for bidirectional binary associations.

4.3.1 Bidirectional Binary Associations

The bidirectional mapping of binary associations creates a table for the binary association that can be used to traverse the association in either direction. There is an alternative unidirectional technique for mapping binary associations that have a 1:1 or 1:N cardinality ratio. The unidirectional mapping approach is presented in detail in Section 4.3.5, along with a comparison of the bidirectional and unidirectional mapping techniques for binary associations. This section describes the bidirectional mapping approach for a binary association, illustrating the mapping of M:N, 1:N, and 1:1 associations with examples of relationships from the ABSTRACT ENTERPRISE. A detailed discussion of the enforcement of the association's participation and multiplicity constraints on the resulting schema is deferred to Section 4.3.2.

Using a bidirectional mapping approach, a binary association is mapped to a table, where the attributes of the table include the primary key attributes of the related classes and any descriptive attributes of the association. Since the resulting table representing the binary association contains two foreign keys referencing the primary key attributes of the classes involved in the association, referential integrity constraints must be introduced for each foreign key. The key of the resulting table depends on the multiplicity of the association and the semantics of the enterprise.

The ab association shown in Figure 4.3 represents an M:N relationship between classes A and B. Following the bidirectional mapping heuristic, the association is mapped to a table containing the key of A (keyOfA), the key of B (keyOfB), and the descriptive attribute of the relationship (attrOfAB). Since ab is an M:N relationship, the key of the table ab is a composite key. If the semantics of the application allow multiple values of attrOfAB for a given (keyOfA, keyOfB) pair, then the key of the ab table is a composite key consisting of the attributes keyOfA, keyOfB, and attrOfAB. If there is exactly one value of attrOfAB for a given (keyOfA, keyOfB) pair, then the primary key of the ab table is (keyOfA, keyOfB), as shown in the following schema:

```
a(keyOfA, attrOfA, attrA1, attrA2, attrA3)
b(keyOfB, attrOfB)
ab(keyOfA, keyOfB, attrOfAB)
        foreign key (keyOfA) references a(keyOfA),
        foreign key (keyOfB) references b(keyOfB)
```

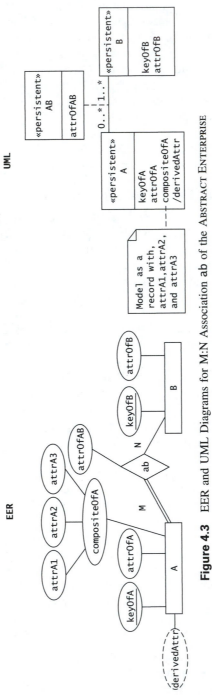

Figure 4.3 EER and UML Diagrams for M:N Association ab of the ABSTRACT ENTERPRISE

The ba association of Figure 4.4 is an example of a 1:N relationship between classes B and A. The mapping of the ba association results in a table named ba containing the attributes keyOfA, keyOfB, and attrOfBA. Since an instance of A is related to exactly one B, the keyOfA forms the primary key of the ba table. The keyOfA and keyOfB attributes are each foreign keys of the ba table. Since an instance of A must be related to an instance of B, there is an additional constraint requiring that the value of the keyOfB attribute is not null.

```
a(keyOfA, attrOfA, attrA1, attrA2, attrA3)
b(keyOfB, attrOfB)
ba(keyOfA, keyOfB, attrOfBA)
        foreign key (keyOfA) references a(keyOfA),
        foreign key (keyOfB) references b(keyOfB),
        constraint notNullB not null (keyOfB)
```

This additional not null constraint is not needed on the table representing the ab association, since the keyOfA and keyOfB attributes are part of the primary key. The value of primary key attributes cannot be null.

The bc association shown in Figure 4.5 illustrates a 1:1 relationship between classes B and C. Since the bc association does not have any descriptive attributes, its corresponding bc table contains only the keyOfB and keyOfC attributes. Each attribute is a candidate key of the bc table based on the 1:1 cardinality ratio, and each attribute is a foreign key. Since B has total participation in the association, indicating that an instance of B must be related to exactly one instance of C, the attribute keyOfB is chosen as the primary key of the bc table. Since keyOfC is a candidate key, additional table constraints are specified to enforce the existence and uniqueness of the attribute:

```
b(keyOfB, attrOfB)
c(keyOfC, attrOfC)
bc(keyOfB, keyOfC)
        primary key (keyOfB),
        foreign key (keyOfB) references b(keyOfB),
        foreign key (keyOfC) references c(keyOfC),
        constraint notNullCandidateKey not null (keyOfC),
        constraint candidateKeyConstraint unique (keyOfC)
```

4.3.2 Participation and Multiplicity Constraints

The participation and multiplicity constraints of the EER and UML conceptual models provide semantics regarding the participation of a class in an association. In the 1:1 bc association shown in Figure 4.5, class B has total participation in the association, requiring the participation of an instance of class B in the bc association. In the EER diagram, the double line linking class B to the relationship bc indicates total participation. In the UML diagram, the multiplicity of 1..1 on the bc association indicates that an instance of B must be related to a minimum of one and a maximum of one instance of C.

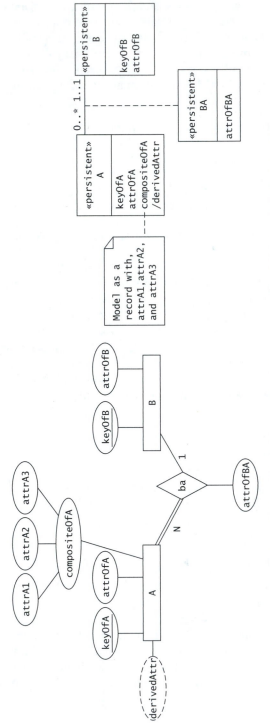

Figure 4.4 EER and UML Diagrams for 1:N Association ba of the ABSTRACT ENTERPRISE

110

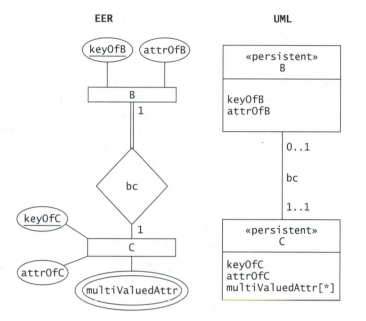

Figure 4.5 EER and UML Diagrams for 1:1 Association bc of the ABSTRACT ENTERPRISE

In the definition of the bc table, the `foreign key` and not null constraints on the keyOfC require that a B appearing in the bc table be related to exactly one C. However, these constraints do not check whether there is a tuple in the bc table for each tuple in the b table. A schema-level integrity constraint can be used to verify the total participation constraint. For example, the assertion `totalBinC` verifies the total participation constraint of B in the bc association, checking that there does not exist a B that does not participate in the bc association (i.e., checking that all B's participate in the bc association).

```
create assertion totalBinBC
    check (not exists
    (select *
     from    b
     where   b.keyOfB not in
             (select bc.keyOfB
              from bc)));
```

Similar schema-level constraints must be specified for the total participation of A in the ab association of Figure 4.3 and the ba association of Figure 4.4.

The capability of specifying general schema-level constraints is a powerful tool. However, not all implementations of SQL allow for `check` constraints across multiple tables. An alternative approach to constraint checking is the use of views to find integrity constraint violations. The view `notTotalBinBC` finds instances of B that do not participate in the bc association:

```
create view notTotalBinBC as
    select  *
```

```
from      b
where     b.keyOfB not in
          (select bc.keyOfB
           from bc);
```

The min..max multiplicities of UML diagrams and the (min,max) pairs of EER diagrams give specific requirements on the minimum and maximum number of times that an instance of a class participates in an association instance. Consider the abstract EER diagram of Figure 4.6. The (2,4) pair annotating the edge between class D and the relationship de indicates that an instance of class D participates a minimum of two times and a maximum of four times in an instance of the de relationship. Assume that the class D is mapped to a relational table d containing the primary key keyOfD and that the table de represents the relationship instance containing a composite primary key (keyOfD, keyOfE). The view countDinDE counts the number of times an instance of D participates in the de association. The second operand in the union is required to return a zero count when an instance of D is not participating in the de association:

```
create view countDinDE(keyOfD, countInDE) as
    (select  keyOfD, count(*)
     from     de
     group bykeyOfD)
    union
    (select  keyOfD, 0
     from     d
     where    d.keyOfD not in (select de.keyOfD from de))
```

The assertion DinDE verifies the multiplicity constraints using the defined countDinDE view:

```
create assertion DinDE
    check (not exists
    (select    *
     from       countDinDE
     where      countInDE < 2 or countInDE > 4));
```

4.3.3 Recursive Associations

When a (binary) association relates a class to itself, the association is called a *recursive* association. A canonical example of a recursive binary association is the employee–supervisor relationship, since an employee's supervisor is an employee. Recursive associations are mapped in the same manner as any other binary association. A table is created with the primary keys of both classes related by the association. Since the primary keys

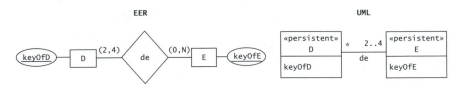

Figure 4.6 EER and UML Diagrams Illustrating Minimum and Maximum Constraints

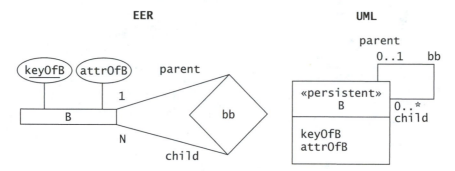

Figure 4.7 EER and UML Diagrams for the Recursive Association bb of the ABSTRACT ENTERPRISE

are the same in a recursive association, the names of the attributes in the table representing the association must be renamed to include the role name of the attribute.

As an example, consider the abstract recursive association given in Figure 4.7, which relates the class B to itself via the bb association. The role name `parent` is given to the one side of the association, and the `child` role name labels the many side. The table bb that corresponds to the recursive association contains the primary key of B (keyOfB) twice: `childKeyOfB` and `parentKeyOfB`. The primary key of the table bb corresponds to the child role in the association (`childKeyOfB`), since a parent can have many children, but a child has one parent:

```
b(keyOfB, attrOfB)
bb(childKeyOfB, parentKeyOfB)
    foreign key (childKeyOfB) references b(keyOfB),
    foreign key (parentKeyOfB) references b(keyOfB)
```

4.3.4 N-ary Associations

The most common form of an association is a binary association, which relates two entities. However, associations involving more than two entities are possible as well. The same mapping approach for binary associations is applicable to associations of degree higher than two. The attributes that form the primary key of each entity involved in the association is included in the resulting table. Any descriptive attributes of the association itself are also included. The candidate key of the table depends on the semantics of the enterprise.

Recall the nonbinary `finance` relationship between Car, Person, and Bank shown in Figure 4.8. The ternary `finance` relationship represents a car dealership application wherein a person buys a car that is financed by a specific bank. The `finance` table representing the ternary association includes the key attributes of all three entities involved in the relationship (`inventoryId`, `pId`, and `bankId`) and the descriptive attribute of the association (`loanAmount`). The cardinality ratios or multiplicities of the association indicate that the car's `inventoryId` forms a key for the table, since a car from the dealer's inventory can be sold only once:

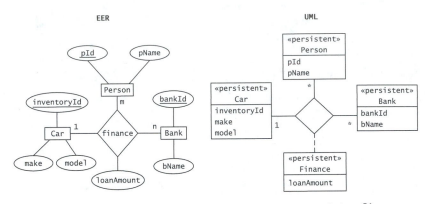

Figure 4.8 EER and UML Diagrams for the Ternary Association `finance`

```
finance(inventoryId, pId, bankId, loanAmount)
     foreign key (inventoryId) references car(inventoryId),
     foreign key (pId) references person(pId),
     foreign key (bankId) references bank(bankId)
```

4.3.5 Navigation of Unidirectional Binary Associations

The bidirectional approach to mapping binary associations presented in Section 4.3.1 created a table to represent the relationship containing the primary key attributes of both classes involved in the association. The resulting table provides a mechanism to traverse the association, given either of the primary keys of the objects involved in the association. UML diagrams support the concept of navigability, which allows the designer to restrict the association to be unidirectional. A unidirectional association indicates that the implementation of the association is stored in only one direction.

Although M:N associations are inherently bidirectional, 1:N and 1:1 associations can be unidirectional and have an alternative mapping approach that does not require creating another table for the association. The alternative mapping strategy stores the primary key of the one side of the association and any descriptive attributes of the association itself in the table representing the class on the other side of the association.

Consider the UML diagram in Figure 4.9, representing a revision of the 1:N association ba over the ABSTRACT ENTERPRISE to be unidirectional from A to B. The unidirectional mapping of the 1:N ba association results in two tables instead of three. Since an instance of A is related to exactly one instance of B, the primary key of the related B (keyOfB) and the descriptive attribute of the ba association (attrOfBA) are included in the table for A. Since A has total participation in the ba association, the keyOfB attribute is constrained to be not null:

```
b(keyOfB, attrOfB)
a(keyOfA, attrOfA, attrA1, attrA2, attrA3, keyOfB, attrOfBA)
        foreign key (keyOfB) references b(keyOfB),
        constraint totalParticipationAinBA not null (keyOfB)
```

A comparison of the bidirectional and unidirectional schema designs for the mapping of the 1:N ba association is warranted. Since A has total participation in the relationship,

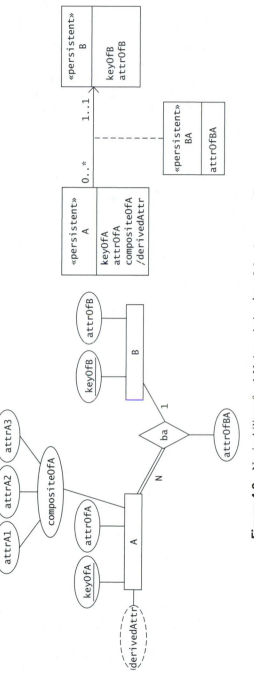

Figure 4.9 Navigability of a 1:N Association ba of the ABSTRACT ENTERPRISE

115

the unidirectional mapping that includes the keyOfB and the attrOfBA in the a table is preferred for performance reasons. When a tuple from the a table is retrieved, the information regarding its ba association is accessed at the same time. When the ba association is stored in its own table with the bidirectional mapping approach, the a table and the ba table must be joined to retrieve the same information.

If A did not have total participation in the ba association, then the unidirectional mapping approach results in null values for the keyOfB and attrOfBA attributes for any instances of A that are not related by the ba association to an instance of B. With the lack of the total participation constraint, the choice of the unidirectional or the bidirectional approach should be based on the application's requirements and the resulting space-time tradeoff.

When A has total participation in the ba association, the unidirectional approach has another performance advantage during database inserts, updates, and deletes. When the ba association is stored as part of the a table, the total participation constraint of A in the ba association is verifiable by means of a table-level constraint specifying that the keyOfB attribute value cannot be null. When the ba association is stored in its own table, a schema-level constraint is required to enforce the total participation. A table-level constraint is more efficient to enforce than a schema-level constraint.

Another point to notice is that the navigability of an association in the relational data model is not truly affected by the alternative mapping approaches. In both designs, there is a table that contains the primary key attributes of the associated values. The navigability of associations on the resulting schema design is more evident in object-oriented and object-relational approaches, as illustrated in Chapters 7 and 8.

The UML diagram in Figure 4.10 shows a unidirectional representation of the 1:1 bc association over the ABSTRACT ENTERPRISE. Since B has total participation in the association, the primary key attributes of C are included in the table for B:

```
c(keyOfC, attrOfC)
b(keyOfB, attrOfB, keyOfC)
        primary key (keyOfB),
        foreign key (keyOfC) references c(keyOfC),
        constraint notNullCandidateKey not null (keyOfC),
        constraint candidateKeyConstraint unique (keyOfC)
```

Since B has total participation in the bc association, the unidirectional mapping of the 1:1 bc association shares the same advantages as the unidirectional mapping of the 1:N ba association: the key of the related instance of C is automatically retrieved as part of the tuple for an instance of B, and the total participation of B in the bc association is enforced using the not null table constraint. When neither class has total participation in a 1:1 association, the bidirectional approach is preferred. Without the total participation constraint, there is no clear choice for the direction of the unidirectional association, which results in null values for any instances that do not participate in the 1:1 association.

4.3.6 Weak Entities and Identifying Relationships

The classes that have been mapped up to this point have had a primary key, allowing the unique identification of an instance across the entire database. Recall that a weak entity

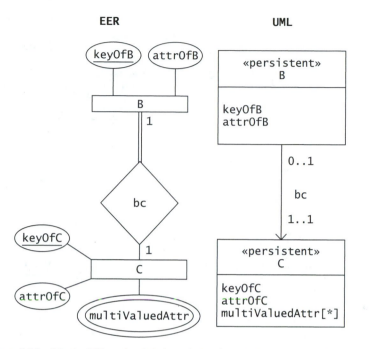

Figure 4.10 Navigability of a 1:1 Association bc of the ABSTRACT ENTERPRISE

in an EER diagram is existence dependent on its identifying owner to form a partial key that uniquely identifies the weak entity in the context of that owner. To create a unique identifier for the weak entity, the partial key is combined with the primary key of its identifying owner. A weak entity has total participation in the identifying relationship that links the weak entity to its identifying owner. Figure 4.11 shows the Weak entity of the ABSTRACT ENTERPRISE. In the EER diagram, the weak entity Weak is denoted by a double rectangle that is linked to its identifying relationship by a double line. The identifying relationship dependsOn is designated by a double diamond. In the UML diagram, Weak is represented using a qualified association.

The mapping of a weak entity creates a table for that entity with its attributes and the primary key attributes of its identifying owner. The table weak has a composite primary key consisting of the key of its identifying owner (keyOfA) and its partialKey. A referential integrity constraint verifies the validity of the key of the identifying owner:

a(keyOfA, attrOfA, attrA1, attrA2, attrA3)
weak(keyOfA, partialKey, attrOfWeak)
         foreign key (keyOfA) references a(keyOfA)

When an EER diagram is mapped to a relational schema, identifying relationships are not explicitly mapped to a relation, since the semantics of the identifying relationship are captured in the mapping of the weak entity itself. Consider as a counterexample the explicit mapping of the dependsOn identifying relationship to its own table. Following the bidirectional mapping approach for binary associations, the dependsOn table would

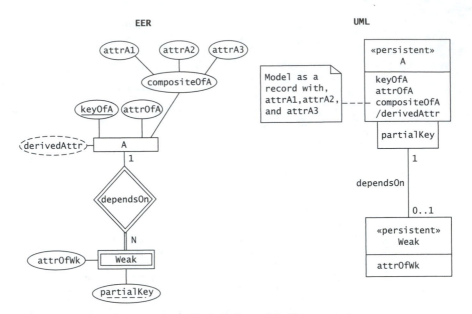

Figure 4.11   An EER Diagram for a Weak Entity and Its Representation as
a Qualified Association in UML

include the primary key attributes of the identifying owner (A) and the weak entity (Weak).
The values of the keyOfA and identifyingKeyOfA attributes would have to be the same.
This resulting dependsOn table is redundant in the relational schema, since the weak table
already captures the identifying owner in the primary key:

```
dependsOn(keyOfA, partialKey, identifyingKeyOfA)
        foreign key (keyOfA) references a(keyOfA),
        foreign key (identifyingKeyOfA) references a(keyOfA)
```

4.3.7   Checkpoint: Classes and Associations

Table 4.1 summarizes the heuristics for mapping classes and associations to a relational
schema. For each type of component, Table 4.1 shows whether a table is created and gives
the attributes with candidate key specification for the corresponding table. Figure 4.12
provides the complete relational schema for the ABSTRACT ENTERPRISE, using a unidirectional representation for the navigation of associations as shown in the revised
UML diagram in Figure 4.13. The corresponding EER diagram is given in Figure 1.2.

Exercises

1. Use the bidirectional mapping approach to define a relational schema for the
   ABSTRACT ENTERPRISE shown in Figure 1.2. Compare the resulting schema with
   the unidirectional schema given in Figure 4.12.

TABLE 4.1 Summary of Relational Mapping Heuristics for Classes and Associations

Component	Table	Attributes	Candidate Key
class C	c	simple attributes of C and the simple components of composite attributes	key of C
multivalued attribute m of C	m	primary key of class C and the attribute m	composite key consisting of the primary key of C in combination with the attribute m
bidirectional (M:N) or n-ary association a	a	primary key of each class involved in the association and the descriptive attributes of a	depends on the multiplicity of a and the semantics of the enterprise
unidirectional association a or bidirectional (1:N and 1:1)	–	add the primary key of the one side of the association as a foreign key on the other side of the association, along with the descriptive attributes of a	candidate key of existing table (in the case of a 1:1 association, the foreign key is also a candidate key)
weak entity W	w	primary key of identifying owner class O and the simple attributes of W	composite key consisting of the primary key of O in combination with the partial key of W

2. Generate a relational schema for the GET FIT HEALTH CLUB ENTERPRISE described in Exercise 2 of Checkpoint 1.1.3. Identify any assumptions made in the process of mapping the object-oriented conceptual schema to a relational schema. Write schema-level constraints to enforce constraints of the enterprise that are not inherently specified in the table definitions. Are there any remaining constraints that are not specified by table or schema-level constraints?

3. Repeat Exercise 2 for the MEDICAL PRACTICE ENTERPRISE described in Exercise 3 in Checkpoint 1.1.3.

4. Repeat Exercise 2 for the MUSIC AGENCY ENTERPRISE described in Exercise 4 in Checkpoint 1.1.3.

4.4 Class Hierarchies

Object-oriented conceptual models, such as EER and UML diagrams, provide inherent support for class hierarchies, including the inheritance of properties and behavior. The

```
c(keyOfC, attrOfC)
multiC(keyOfC, multiValuedAttr)
        foreign key (keyOfC) references c(keyOfC)
b(keyOfB, attrOfB, keyOfC, parentKeyOfB)
        primary key (keyOfB),
        foreign key (keyOfC) references c(keyOfC)
        constraint notNullCandidateKey not null (keyOfC),
        constraint candidateKeyConstraint unique (keyOfC)
        /* use alter table to establish recursive reference */
        foreign key (parentKeyOfB) references b(keyOfB)
a(keyOfA, attrOfA, attrA1, attrA2, attrA3, keyOfB, attrOfBA)
        foreign key (keyOfB) references b(keyOfB),
        constraint totalParticipation not null (keyOfB)
ab(keyOfA, keyOfB, attrOfAB)
        foreign key (keyOfA) references a(keyOfA)
        foreign key (keyOfB) references b(keyOfB)
weak(keyOfA, partialKey, attrOfWk)
        foreign key (keyOfA) references a(keyOfA)
```

Figure 4.12 Relational Schema of ABSTRACT ENTERPRISE Using Unidirectional Navigability

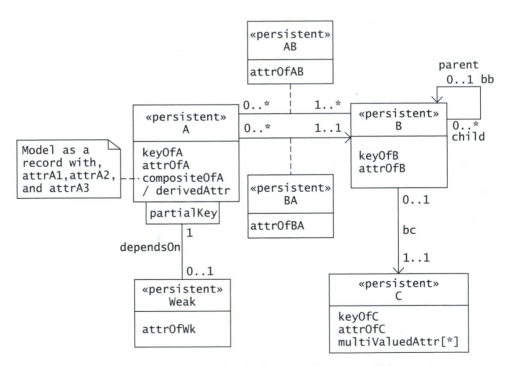

Figure 4.13 A Revised UML Diagram for the ABSTRACT ENTERPRISE Using Unidirectional Navigability

relational data model provides the concept of a table, which does not inherently support class hierarchies. However, through the use of both the extensional and intensional schemas of the relational data model, class hierarchies can be supported. There are three main approaches for mapping class hierarchies to tables:

1. Creating a table for each class

2. Creating a table for subclasses only

3. Flattening the hierarchy

The relational schema must represent both the specialized and inherited properties of a class. For each approach, a class is realized by a relation named by using a lowercase version of the class name, where a relation is either a stored table or a view. Therefore, the relational schema consists of a specification of the extensional schema of stored tables, the intensional schema of views, and the constraints that hold on the relations. The name of a table that is created to assist with the definition of a class will use a suffix to differentiate it from the relation for the class. This section uses the class hierarchies of the HOLLYWOOD ENTERPRISE (see Figures 1.16 and 2.28) to illustrate the alternative mapping approaches presented in sections 4.4.1 through 4.4.3. A detailed discussion of the enforcement of the specialization constraints over the resulting relational schema is deferred to Section 4.4.4.

4.4.1 Creating a Table for Each Class

One mapping approach for class hierarchies creates a table for each class in the class hierarchy, including superclasses and subclasses. The table for the superclass contains its attributes. The attributes of the table defined for the subclass include the primary key attributes of its superclass and the specialized attributes of the subclass. A view is defined for the subclass that performs an equijoin of the subclass and superclass tables to include both the inherited and specialized attributes of the subclass.

Consider, as an example, the specialization of `Person` into the subclasses `Movie-Professional` and `Celebrity` in the HOLLYWOOD ENTERPRISE. The extensional schema in the relational data model contains a table for `Person` and a table for each of the subclasses: `MovieProfessional` and `Celebrity`. The table names for the subclasses use the suffix EDB to indicate that the table represents the properties of the subclass that are stored in the extensional database. The primary key and referential integrity constraints specified in the extensional schema enforce the ISA constraint by ensuring that every `pId` in the `movieProfessionalEDB` and `celebrityEDB` tables is a valid `pId` in the `person` table:

```
person(pId, gender, name, isMarriedTo, phone, address)
movieProfessionalEDB(pId, company)
        foreign key (pId) references person(pId)
celebrityEDB(pId, agentPId, birthDate)
        foreign key (pId) references person(pId)
```

A referential integrity constraint to restrict the value of the `agentPId` attribute to be a valid `pId` for an `agent` is shown in the full extensional schema of Figure 4.14.

The relation names that correspond to the subclasses must refer to a relation that provides all of the attributes for a subclass, including its inherited attributes. The movieProfessional and celebrity relations are defined with the use of views to include the inherited attributes of the Person superclass:

```
create view movieProfessional as
    select   P.pId, P.gender, P.name, P.isMarriedTo, P.phone,
             P.address, M.company
    from     person P, movieProfessionalEDB M
    where    P.pId = M.pId;
create view celebrity as
    select   P.pId, P.gender, P.name, P.isMarriedTo, P.phone,
             P.address, C.agentPId, C.birthDate
    from     person P, celebrityEDB C
    where    P.pId = C.pId;
```

A complete representation of the class hierarchies for the HOLLYWOOD ENTERPRISE, using the mapping approach in which a table is created for each class, is given in Figures 4.14 and 4.15. The guiding design principle creates a relation for each class that includes both the specialized and inherited attributes. Figure 4.14 presents the extensional schema, where the suffix EDB designates the table for a subclass that stores the key

```
person(pId, gender, name, isMarriedTo, phone, address)
movieProfessionalEDB(pId, company)
        foreign key (pId) references person(pId)
criticEDB(pId, popularity)
        foreign key (pId) references movieProfessionalEDB(pId)
agentEDB(pId, agentFee)
        foreign key (pId) references movieProfessionalEDB(pId)
celebrityEDB(pId, agentPId, birthDate)
        foreign key (pId) references person(pId)
        foreign key (agentPId) references agentEDB(pId)
movieStarEDB(pId, movieType)
        foreign key (pId) references celebrityEDB(pId)
modelEDB(pId, preferences)
        foreign key (pId) references celebrityEDB(pId)
project(projectId, cost, type, location)
filmProjectEDB(projectId, title)
        foreign key (projectId) references project(projectId)
modelingProjectEDB(projectId, description)
        foreign key (projectId) references project(projectId)
actsIn(movieStarPId, filmProjectId)
        foreign key (movieStarPId) references movieStarEDB(pId)
        foreign key (filmProjectId)
          references filmProjectEBD(projectId)
modelsIn(modelPId, modelingProjectId, paid)
        foreign key (modelPId) references modelEBD(pId)
        foreign key (modelingProjectId)
          references modelingProjectEDB(projectId)
```

Figure 4.14 Extensional Schema for Class Hierarchies of the HOLLYWOOD ENTERPRISE

```
create view movieProfessional as
      select    P.pId, P.gender, P.name, P.isMarriedTo, P.phone,
                P.address, M.company
      from      person P natural join movieProfessionalEDB M;
create view critic as
      select    M.pId, M.gender, M.name, M.isMarriedTo, M.phone,
                M.address, M.company, C.popularity
      from      movieProfessional M natural join criticEDB C;
create view agent as
      select    M.pId, M.gender, M.name, M.isMarriedTo, M.phone,
                M.address, M.company, A.agentFee
      from      movieProfessional M natural join agentEDB A;
create view celebrity as
      select    P.pId, P.gender, P.name, P.isMarriedTo, P.phone,
                P.address, C.agent PId C.birthDate
      from      person P natural join celebrityEDB C;
create view movieStar as
      select    C.pId, C.gender, C.name, C.isMarriedTo, C.phone,
                C.address, C.agentPId, C.birthDate, M. movieType
      from      celebrity C natural join movieStarEDB M;
create view model as
      select    C.pId, C.gender, C.name, C.isMarriedTo, C.phone,
                C.address, C.agentPId, C.birthDate, M.preferences
      from      celebrity C natural join modelEDB M;
create view filmProject as
      select    P.projectId, P.location, P.cost, P.type, F.title
      from      project P natural join filmProjectEDB F
      where     P.type = 'F';
create view modelingProject as
      select    P.projectId, P.location, P.cost, P.type, M.description
      from      project P natural join modelingProjectEDB M
      where     P.type = 'M';
```

Figure 4.15   Intensional Schema for Class Hierarchies of the HOLLYWOOD ENTERPRISE

of its superclass and its specialized attributes. Figure 4.15 provides the view definitions
that comprise the intensional schema, assuming the extensional schema of Figure 4.14.
The view definitions provide the relations that correspond to each subclass, including
the inherited attributes. The relational schema of the HOLLYWOOD ENTERPRISE shown in
Figures 4.14 and 4.15 represents the mapping of classes, associations, and class hierarchies. The mapping of the Sponsor category (and its association with ModelingProject)
is deferred to Section 4.6.

4.4.2   Creating a Table for Subclasses Only

Another approach to mapping a class hierarchy to a relational schema creates a table for
each subclass in the class hierarchy. In this approach, the table for each subclass includes
both the specialized and inherited attributes. The relation for a superclass is defined
by using a view as a generalization of its subclasses. The view defining the superclass
inherently supports the ISA constraint.

Consider the specialization of `Project` into a `FilmProject` or a `ModelingProject`. Since the table for a subclass includes all of the attributes of the subclass, including the inherited ones, the names of the tables for the subclasses are `filmProject` and `modelingProject`:

```
filmProject(projectId, title, cost, type, location)
modelingProject(projectId, description, cost, type, location)
```

The relation for the `Project` superclass is defined by a view that is a union of the inherited attributes from the `filmProject` and `modelingProject` tables. Therefore, the ISA constraint of the hierarchy, indicating that a `FilmProject` is a `Project` and a `ModelingProject` is a `Project`, is inherently supported by the intensional schema:

```
create view project as
      select    projectId, cost, type, location
      from      filmProject
      union
      select    projectId, cost, type, location
      from      modelingProject;
```

In mapping a class hierarchy via the approach in which a table is created for subclasses only, there are several issues to consider. One is that this mapping approach cannot support a partial specialization, since there is no explicit representation of the superclass in the extensional database. Another issue is based on specializations that are not disjoint. If the specialization is overlapping, then the inherited attributes are stored redundantly in each subclass. As a result, this mapping approach should be used for specializations that are both disjoint and total. A disjoint and total specialization is common in the mapping of abstract classes from UML, since an abstract class is a class that cannot be directly instantiated. The concrete subclasses are mapped as part of the extensional relational database, and the abstract class is defined intensionally with the use of a view.

4.4.3 Flattening the Hierarchy

The third approach to mapping a class hierarchy into a relational schema is to *flatten the hierarchy* into a single table. The table includes the attributes of the superclass and each subclass and also includes type fields to indicate the subclasses to which a tuple belongs. Thus, the ISA constraint is inherently supported. If a tuple in the table does not belong to a subclass, then the corresponding specific attributes of the specialization have null values. This approach is not recommended if there are many attributes for the specialized subclasses.

Again, consider the mapping of the `MovieProfessional` specialization into `Critic` and `Agent` subclasses. Throughout all mapping approaches, a relation name that corresponds to a class represents the specialized and inherited attributes of the class. Mapping the `MovieProfessional` hierarchy into a flattened table requires the introduction of a table in the extensional database to maintain all attributes of the hierarchy. In this example, the suffix `Hierarchy` indicates that the stored table `mpCriticAgent-Hierarchy` represents the entire hierarchy. The `pId` attribute describes the primary key for the relation. The `company` attribute is the only specialized attribute of a `Movie-Professional`. The `popularity` attribute is a specialized attribute of `Critic`, and the agentFee attribute is a specialized property of an Agent. The subtype attribute indicates whether the MovieProfessional is a Critic or an Agent:

mpCriticAgentHierarchy(pId, company, popularity, agentFee, subtype)

The intensional schema provides the mapping for each class from the MovieProfessional hierarchy. These views assume that there exists a relation named person that describes the attributes of the Person class. Therefore, the relations for the MovieProfessional, Critic, and Agent classes must include the inherited attributes from Person:

```
create view movieProfessional as
        select  P.pId, P.gender, P.name, P.address, P.isMarriedTo,
                P.phone, H.company
        from    person P natural join mpCriticAgentHierarchy H;
create view critic as
        select  M.pId, M.gender, M.name, M.address, M.isMarriedTo,
                M.phone, M. company, H.popularity
        from    movieProfessional M join
                    mpCriticAgentHierarchy H on M.pId = H.pId
        where   H.subtype = 'c';
create view agent as
        select  M.pId, M.gender, M.name, M.address, M.isMarriedTo,
                M.phone, M. company, H.agentFee
        from    movieProfessional M join
                    mpCriticAgentHierarchy H on M.pId = H.pId
        where   H.subtype = 'a';
```

Since the specialization of MovieProfessional into the Critic and Agent subclasses is disjoint, the specification of the corresponding subclasses uses a single type indicator (subtype). Multiple type indicators specify overlapping subclasses. Consider the Celebrity specialization into the overlapping subclasses of MovieStar and Model. Again, the suffix Hierarchy is appended to the table name, representing the fact that the celebrityHierarchy table is a flattening of the Celebrity hierarchy. The pId attribute forms the primary key of the resulting table. The birthDate and agentPId attributes are the specialized properties for a Celebrity. A MovieStar has an additional attribute for movieType, and a Model has an additional attribute for preferences. The Boolean attributes movieStar and model indicate membership of the Celebrity in the corresponding subclass:

celebrityHierarchy(pId, birthDate, agentPId, movieStar, movieType, model, preferences)

The intensional schema defines relations for Celebrity, MovieStar, and Model, assuming an existing person relation that describes the attributes of the Person class. Since Celebrity is a subclass of Person and the MovieStar and Model are subclasses of Celebrity, they all inherit the attributes of Person:

```
create view celebrity as
        select  P.pId, P.gender, P.name, P.address, P.isMarriedTo,
                P.phone, H.birthDate, H.agentPId
        from    person P natural join celebrityHierarchy H;
```

```
create view movieStar as
        select  C.pId, C.gender, C.name, C.address, C.isMarriedTo,
                C.phone, C.birthDate, C.agentPId, H.movieType
        from    celebrity C join celebrityHierarchy H on C.pId = H.pId
        where   H.movieStar;
create view model as
        select  C.pId, C.gender, C.name, C.address, C.isMarriedTo,
                C.phone, C.birthDate, C.agentPId, H.preferences
        from    celebrity C join celebrityHierarchy H on C.pId = H.pId
        where   H.model;
```

Attribute-defined subclasses are inherently supported by using a single type indicator when flattening the hierarchy. Consider again the attribute-defined specialization of `Project` into a `FilmProject` or a `ModelingProject`. When the hierarchy is flattened, the extensional schema consists of one table named `projectHierarchy`. Again, the `Hierarchy` suffix indicates that this table represents the flattened hierarchy and not the `Project` class itself. All projects have the attributes `projectId`, `location`, `cost`, and `type`, where the `type` field indicates the type of the project. A `FilmProject` has a specialized attribute `title`, and the attribute `description` is a specialized attribute of `ModelingProject`.

`projectHierarchy(`<u>`projectId`</u>`, location, cost, type, title, description)`

The intensional schema provides a relation for each class (`Project`, `FilmProject`, and `ModelingProject`) in the hierarchy, using a view definition to provide the appropriate attributes:

```
create view project as
        select    H.projectId, H.location, H.cost, H.type
        from      projectHierarchy H;
create view filmProject as
        select    H.projectId, H.location, H.cost, H.type, H.title
        from      projectHierarchy H
        where     H.type = 'F';
create view modelingProject as
        select    H.projectId, H.location, H.cost, H.type,
                  H.description
        from      projectHierarchy H
        where     H.type = 'M';
```

4.4.4   Specialization Constraints

As illustrated in Chapters 1 and 2, the EER and UML conceptual models, respectively, provide inherent support for several specialization constraints: the disjoint constraint, the completeness constraint, and the attribute-defined constraint. The disjoint constraint specifies whether the subclasses in the resulting specialization are disjoint or overlapping. The completeness constraint indicates whether the specialization is total or partial. A total specialization requires that the superclass participate in the specialization into one of its subclasses. The attribute-defined specialization constraint requires that the value of an attribute on which the specialization is defined be of the appropriate value for the subclass. These specialization constraints are not inherently supported by the relational model, but can be specified using schema-level integrity constraints.

The guiding principle in the design of the relational schema is that a class is realized by a relation named by using a lowercase version of the class name. The relation for the class includes both the specialized and inherited attributes of the class. Whether a relation is defined as a stored table or a view is transparent in the constraint specifications.

Consider the specification of the disjoint constraint disjointPersonSpecialization asserting the disjoint specialization of Person into MovieProfessional and Celebrity. The disjoint constraint is violated if the pId of a Person represents both a MovieProfessional and a Celebrity:

```
create assertion disjointPersonSpecialization as
    check (not exists
    (select   *
     from     person P
     where    P.pId in (select M.pId from movieProfessional M) and
              P.pId in (select C.pId from celebrity C)));
```

In the Hollywood Enterprise, a MovieProfessional has a total specialization into a Critic or Agent, requiring that a MovieProfessional be either a Critic or an Agent. The total specialization constraint is violated if the pId of a MovieProfessional does not appear in the relations for Critic or Agent:

```
create assertion totalMovieProfessionalSpecialization as
    check (not exists
    (select   *
     from     movieProfessional M
     where    M.pId not in
              (select C.pId from critic C union
               select A.pId from agent A)));
```

The attribute-defined specialization constraint requires that the value of the attribute type of a Project be either 'F', for a FilmProject, or 'M', for a ModelingProject:

```
create assertion attrDefinedFilmProjectSpecialization as
    check (not exists
    (select   *
     from     project P
     where    (P.projectId in (select F.projectId from filmProject F)
              and P.type <> 'F') or
              (P.projectId not in (select F.projectId from
              filmProject F) and P.type = 'F')));
```

The attribute-defined specialization constraint is violated if the projectId attribute is considered a FilmProject and the type attribute is not 'F' or if the type attribute is 'F' and the projectId attribute does not represent a FilmProject. A companion constraint must also be included to verify the value of the type attribute for a ModelingProject.

A summary of the specialization constraints for the alternative approaches to mapping class hierarchies is given in Figure 4.16. A checkmark indicates that the mapping approach can satisfy the constraint, whereas an X indicates that the mapping approach should not be used for the indicated specialization constraint. A comment in parentheses provides a brief indication of how the approach supports or fails to support the specialization constraint. A summary of the specialization constraints supported by each approach as indicated in Figure 4.16 follows:

- *Creating a table for each class*. This mapping approach allows for the support of disjoint or overlapping specializations, total or partial specializations, and attribute-defined specializations.

- *Creating a table for subclasses only*. This approach supports disjoint and total specializations, including attribute-defined specializations. Overlapping specializations would result in redundancy of the inherited attributes of the superclass, which are stored in the table for each subclass. A partial specialization is not supported because the superclass is represented as a union of the inherited attributes stored in the tables for the subclasses.

- *Flattening the hierarchy*. This mapping design also allows for the support of disjoint or overlapping specializations, total or partial specializations, and attribute-defined specializations. A single type indicator represents a disjoint specialization, since the attribute is single valued. Overlapping specializations are represented by multiple type indicators. Partial specializations are allowed. If the superclass does not belong to a subclass, then the values of the specialized attributes are null.

4.4.5 Checkpoint: Class Hierarchies

Table 4.2 provides a summary of the approaches to mapping class hierarchies by using the simple abstract hierarchy shown in Figure 4.17 consisting of a superclass S and two subclasses S1 and S2. The extensional database (EDB) row provides a summary of the table definitions. The intensional database (IDB) row gives a summary of the view definitions.

Figure 4.18 provides a template of the SQL assertion statements needed to support the specification of the specialization constraints for disjoint specializations, total specializations, and attribute-defined specializations. The template assumes that the class S with primary key keyOfS has a specialization into two subclasses: S1 and S2. The attribute-defined specialization constraint requires a constraint for each subclass. Figure 4.18 shows

Mapping Approach	Disjoint Constraint		Completeness Constraint		Attribute-defined Constraint
	Disjoint	Overlapping	Total	Partial	
Table for each class	✓	✓	✓	✓	✓
Table for each subclass	✓	✗ (redundancy)	✓	✗ (no superclass)	✓
Flattening the hierarchy	✓ (single type indicator)	✓ (multiple type indicators)	✓	✓ (null values)	✓

Figure 4.16 Summary of Support for Specialization Constraints for Mapping Class Hierarchies

TABLE 4.2 Summary of Relational Mapping Heuristics for Class Hierarchies

Create a table for each class	
EDB	`s(keyOfS, attrOfS)`
	`s1EDB(keyOfS, attrOfS1)` `  foreign key (keyOfS) references s(keyOfS)`
	`s2EDB(keyOfS, attrOfS2)` `  foreign key (keyOfS) references s(keyOfS)`
IDB	`create view s1 as select * from s natural join s1EDB`
	`create view s2 as select * from s natural join s2EDB`
Create a table for subclasses only	
EDB	`s1(keyOfS, attrOfS, attrOfS1)`
	`s2(keyOfS, attrOfS, attrOfS2)`
IDB	`create view s as (select keyOfS, attrOfS from s1)` `   union (select keyOfS, attrOfS from s2)`
Flattening the hierarchy (single type indicator)	
EDB	`sHierarchy(keyOfS, attrOfS, attrOfS1, attrOfS2, type)`
IDB	`create view s as select keyOfS, attrOfS from sHierarchy`

	`create view s1 as`
	`  select keyOfS, attrOfS, attrOfS1`
	`  from  sHierarchy`
	`  where type='S1'`

	`create view s2 as`
	`  select keyOfS, attrOfS, attrOfS2`
	`  from  sHierarchy`
	`  where type='S2'`

Flattening the hierarchy (multiple type indicators)	
EDB	`sHierarchy(keyOfS, attrOfS, typeS1, attrOfS1, typeS2,` `attrOfS2)`

IDB	`create view s1 as`
	`  select keyOfS, attrOfS, attrOfS1`
	`  from  sHierarchy`
	`  where typeS1=TRUE`

	`create view s2 as`
	`  select keyOfS, attrOfS, attrOfS2`
	`  from  sHierarchy`
	`  where typeS2=TRUE`

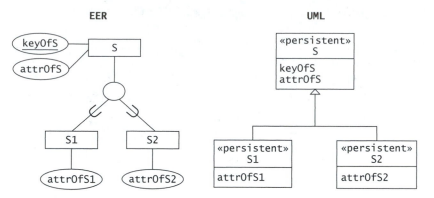

Figure 4.17   EER and UML Diagrams for a Simple Class Hierarchy

```
create assertion disjointSpecialization as
    check (not exists
    (select  *
     from    s
     where   s.keyOfS in (select s1.keyOfS from s1) and
             s.keyOfS in (select s2.keyOfS from s2)));

create assertion totalSpecialization as
    check (not exists
    (select  *
     from    s
     where   s.keyOfS not in
             (select s1.keyOfS from s1
             union
             select s2.keyOfS from s2)));

create assertion attrDefinedSpecializationS1 as
    check (not exists
    (select  *
     from     s
     where    (s.keyOfS in (select s1.keyOfS from s1) and
                 s.type <> 'S1') or
              (s.keyOfS not in (select s1.keyOfS from s1) and
                 s.type = 'S1')));
```

Figure 4.18   SQL Assertion Specification Template for Specialization Constraints

the attribute-defined specialization constraint for the S1 subclass. The companion constraint for the S2 subclass is not shown.

Exercises

1. Using the mapping of the HOLLYWOOD ENTERPRISE given in Figures 4.14 and 4.15, write schema-level integrity constraints to check for *all* specialization constraints as given in Figures 1.16 and 2.28.

2. Using the mapping approach that creates a table for subclasses only, represent the HOLLYWOOD ENTERPRISE (see Figures 1.16 and 2.28) as a relational database

schema. Use the design principle that creates a relation for each class of the hierarchy, where the relation contains both the specialized and inherited attributes of the class. Identify any advantages or disadvantages of the resulting schema compared with the HOLLYWOOD ENTERPRISE relational schema given in Figures 4.14 and 4.15, which uses the mapping approach that creates a table for each class.

3. Using the mapping approach that flattens the hierarchy, represent the HOLLYWOOD ENTERPRISE (see Figures 1.16 and 2.28) as a relational database schema. Use the design principle that creates a relation for each class of the hierarchy, where the relation contains both the specialized and inherited attributes of the class. Identify any advantages or disadvantages of the resulting schema compared with the HOLLYWOOD ENTERPRISE relational schema given in Figures 4.14 and 4.15, which uses the mapping approach that creates a table for each class.

4.5 Shared Subclasses

A shared subclass is a class that has more than one superclass organized in a specialization lattice. Figure 4.19 illustrates an example of the StarModel shared subclass that is both a MovieStar and a Model. If the superclasses have a common ancestor, then the shared subclass has the same key attribute, and several of the mapping approaches of the class hierarchy are possible. For example, consider mapping the Celebrity class hierarchy, using the table for each class approach. The extensional database consists of a table for each class:

```
person(pId, gender, name, isMarriedTo, phone, address)
celebrityEDB(pId, birthDate)
```

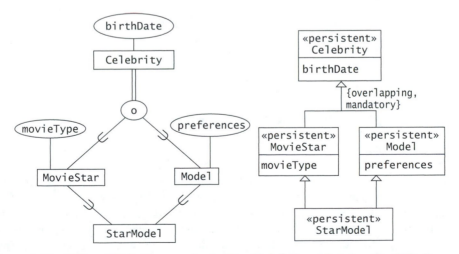

Figure 4.19 EER and UML Diagrams for the StarModel Shared Subclass. The EER diagram is from "Database Models," by S. Urban, in *Encyclopedia of Electrical and Electronics Engineering*, John G. Webster (ed.); copyright © 1999 John G. Webster. This material is used by permission of John Wiley & Sons, Inc.

```
movieStarEDB(pId, movieType)
modelEDB(pId, preferences)
starModelEDB(pId)
```

To support the appropriate inherited attributes, the intensional schema defines views for
`Celebrity`, `MovieStar`, `Model`, and `StarModel`. For brevity, only the `StarModel` view
is shown:

```
create view starModel as
          select    C.pId, C.gender, C.name, C.isMarriedTo, C.phone,
                    C.address C.birthDate, MS.movieType, M.preferences
          from      (((starModelEDB S natural join modelEDB M)
                    natural join movieStarEDB MS)
                    natural join celebrity C);
```

If the hierarchy is flattened, then the extensional schema consists of the `celebrity-
Hierarchy` table:

```
celebrityHierarchy(pId, birthDate, movieStar, movieType, model,
   preferences)
```

The intensional schema defines the `starModel` view on the basis of both Boolean
attributes `movieStar` and `model` being `TRUE`. Note that this view assumes that the
relation `celebrity` is already defined, containing all of the attributes describing the
`Celebrity` class:

```
create view starModel as
          select    C.pId, C.gender, C.name, C.isMarriedTo, C.phone,
                    C.address, C.birthDate, H.movieType, H.preferences
          from      celebrity C join celebrityHierarchy H on C.pId = H.pId
          where     H.movieStar and H.model;
```

Since the mapping approach that creates a table only for subclasses requires a disjoint
and total specialization, this mapping approach is not applicable to shared subclasses,
which are inherently overlapping and partial specializations.

4.6 Categories

A category in the EER or the xor constraint in UML requires the introduction of a
surrogate key attribute for mapping to the relational data model. The surrogate key
represents a mechanism for the database system to generate a unique value for a category,
which models a union of two or more different types of classes having different primary
key attributes. For the `Sponsor` category of Figure 1.15 and the `Sponsor` xor constraint
of Figure 2.22, a table is created for the `Sponsor` category containing the surrogate
key attribute `sponsorCode`. The `sponsorCode` surrogate key is also an attribute of each
of the tables for the superclasses `Person` and `Company`. Since there is only one sponsor
for a modeling project, the surrogate key `sponsorCode` is included in the `modeling-
ProjectEDB` table to identify the sponsor of the project:

```
sponsor (sponsorCode)
person (pId, name, phone, gender, address, sponsorCode)
```

```
        foreign key (sponsorCode) references sponsor(sponsorCode)
company (cId, cName, sponsorCode)
        foreign key (sponsorCode) references sponsor(sponsorCode)
modelingProjectEDB (projectId, description, sponsorCode)
        foreign key (projectId) references project (projectId)
        foreign key (sponsorCode) references sponsor(sponsorCode)
```

Because a category represents the union of its superclasses, a schema-level assertion enforces the requirement that the surrogate key appear in one of the superclasses:

```
create assertion sponsorCategoryUnion
check (not exists
        (select   *
         from     sponsor S
         where    S.sponsorCode not in
                  (select   P.sponsorCode
                   from     person P
                   union
                   select   C.sponsorCode
                   from     company C)));
```

A category is also an exclusive-or of its superclasses, as shown in the UML diagram of Figure 2.22. Another schema-level constraint for a category checks that a surrogate key value is not in more than one superclass:

```
create assertion sponsorCategoryXor
check (not exists
        (select   *
         from     sponsor S
         where    S.sponsorCode in
                  (select   P.sponsorCode
                   from     person P
                   intersect
                   select   C.sponsorCode
                   from     company C)));
```

If a category is constrained to be total, then every instance of each superclass must participate in the categorization and must be an instance of the category subclass. To enforce the total categorization constraint, add a constraint requiring that the surrogate key attribute in each superclass table is not null.

```
sponsor (sponsorCode)

person (pId, name, phone, gender, address, sponsorCode)
        foreign key (sponsorCode) references sponsor(sponsorCode)
        constraint totalPerson not null (sponsorCode)
company (cId, cName, sponsorCode)
        foreign key (sponsorCode) references sponsor(sponsorCode)
        constraint totalCompany not null (sponsorCode)
```

4.7   Checkpoint

The mapping of the semantic constructs of the EER and UML conceptual models to the relational data model consists of three parts: an extensional schema of stored tables (including column- and table-level constraints), an intensional schema of view definitions, and the schema-level constraints that provide the semantic checking of the relations.

The mapping of classes, attributes, and associations emphasizes how the constraints inherent in the conceptual model can be realized in the corresponding mapping to the relational data model. Some constraints can be specified inherently as table-level constraints in the definition of the relational schema by the use of primary key, foreign key, not null, and unique specifications. Other constraints require schema-level specifications that create an assertion to check the constraint.

There are three approaches to mapping class hierarchies to a relational schema:

1. Creating a table for each class

2. Creating a table for subclasses only

3. Flattening the hierarchy.

The guiding design principle of the mapping of the class hierarchies maps a class to a relation named by using a lowercase version of the class name. This relation contains all the attributes that describe the class, including both specialized and inherited attributes. The relation for a class can be defined as a table as part of the extensional schema, or as a view as part of the intensional schema. The naming convention for class relations allows the reuse of the templates for verifying specialization constraints (disjoint, total, and attribute defined) across all three mapping approaches.

The mapping of categories requires several schema-level constraints to enforce the constraints inherent in a categorization as the (exclusive) union of its superclasses.

Exercises

1. Some implementations of SQL do not support general schema-level constraints involving multiple tables. Write the corresponding view definitions for the specialization constraint templates shown in Figure 4.18.

2. Review the characteristics of the FICTITIOUS BANK ENTERPRISE described in Exercise 2 in Checkpoint 1.2.5. Choose one of the mapping approaches to create a relational schema that corresponds to the semantics of the enterprise. Justify the mapping approach taken, and identify how the semantics of the enterprise are captured in the resulting relational schema.

3. Map the HORSE RACING ENTERPRISE described in Exercise 1 in Checkpoint 1.4 to a relational schema. Since there are several class hierarchies, choose which mapping approach best suits each hierarchy, based on the constraints of the enterprise. Verify that your resulting schema captures the semantics of the enterprise. Identify the constraints that are inherent in the specification of the relational schema, and identify the constraints that must be explicitly checked with schema-level integrity constraints.

4. Assume the Sponsor category in Figure 1.15 a is changed to be a total category. Define a schema-level constraint using an assertion statement that supports the total categorization constraint.

4.8 Bibliographic References

The *extensional* and *intensional* database terminology is from the research area of deductive databases, which investigates logic programming languages as database query languages [Ramakrishnan and Ullman, 1995]. Most deductive database prototypes use facts to store the extensional database and rules to define the intensional database. The mapping of object-oriented conceptual data models to the relational data model given in this chapter is a synergy of the myriad approaches presented in the deductive database literature, other database textbooks [e.g., Elmasri and Navathe, 2003], and semantic data modeling research.

Chapter 5

JDBC and Web Access to Relational Databases

Synopsis

A call-level interface (CLI) provides an application programming interface (API) to access a relational database from a programming language. Web pages typically interact with relational databases by using a CLI. This chapter presents the JDBC API as a sample CLI from the Java programming language to a relational database.

Assumed Knowledge

- The SQL Standard: Advanced Relational Features (Chapter 3)

- Fundamentals of the Java Programming Language

Implementation Examples on Web

- METAWEBDB:

    Java Servlets and Java Server Pages (JSP) with JDBC

    ASP.NET with ADO.NET

- ECLECTIC ONLINE SHOPPING:

    ASP.NET with ADO.NET

    JSP with JDBC

The Web has changed the way we live. Access to global information is at our fingertips 24 hours a day, 7 days a week. Web pages that contain fixed content are known as *static* Web pages. However, today it is common to use the Web to shop and pay bills online and to share photos with family and friends. These common interactions require *dynamic*

Web pages, which do not have fixed content, but are more interactive, displaying content based on information from resources such as a database or user input. In database-driven dynamic Web pages, the Web browser interacts with an underlying database to return the personalized Web pages.

This chapter introduces the recognized three-tiered architecture for Web-based applications with database access and briefly discusses the technologies for interacting with databases for the generation of dynamic Web pages. The chapter's focus is on the JDBC API, which is the recognized mechanism for Java programs to interact dynamically with relational databases. Recall that Chapter 3 alluded to the JDBC API as an example of a CLI to relational databases, rather than discussing the CLI of the SQL standard in detail. The JDBC API also includes the ability to query the metadata of the database.

5.1 Overview and Architecture

The recognized architecture for Web-based applications with database access is a three-tiered architecture, as shown in Figure 5.1, which is specialized for the JDBC API. The Web browser is the top presentation layer, and the data store is the bottom layer. The middle tier is the application that interfaces with the Web browser and the database. The application includes the business logic or rules of the semantics of the application.

The three-tiered architecture provides independence between the levels of the Web-based application. The presentation of the information on the Web page can change without affecting the data store. The database used in the data store tier can change without impacting the presentation layer. The middle tier provides the communication between the layers. When the application server is written in Java, the JDBC API provides a recognized interface for interacting with relational databases. The JDBC API will be examined in detail later in the chapter. The next section briefly discusses alternative technologies for interacting with a data store to generate dynamic Web pages. The technology for communicating between the presentation layer and the application server is beyond the scope of this book.

5.2 Database-Driven Dynamic Web Pages

A database-driven dynamic Web page has dynamic content based on information from an underlying data store. A typical application for a database-driven dynamic Web page is online shopping, whereby information on the current availability and pricing of products is retrieved from a database. Online paying of bills is another example of an application that displays dynamic content personalized for the user, based on the data from his or her account. This section briefly discusses a few approaches to generating database-driven dynamic Web pages.

The use of the Common Gateway Interface (CGI) for interfacing to external applications is one of the first approaches to displaying dynamic content on Web pages. With CGI, the Web browser calls a program that is typically written in a scripting language or a general-purpose programming language. The Web server creates a process for the

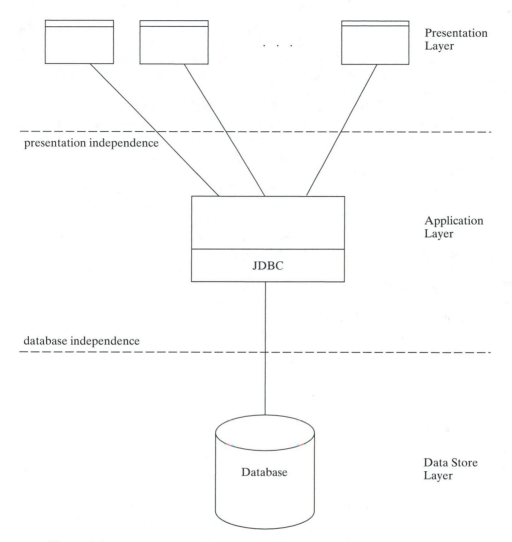

Figure 5.1   Three-tiered Architecture for Web-based Database Access with JDBC

execution of that program, sending any input to the program with standard input or environment variables. The program typically uses embedded SQL to access the database via the given input and generates a response in HTML, which is displayed in the Web browser at the requesting site. CGI is an established technology, but it suffers from the drawback that a process is created for each request, resulting in numerous processes running on the Web server.

Another solution to dynamic Web pages is Microsoft's Active Server Pages (ASP), which uses scripting languages embedded in the HTML to create a dynamic Web page. The scripts are invoked and access the underlying database through calls to ActiveX Data Objects (ADO) via Microsoft's Open Database Connectivity (ODBC), which is a standard database access mechanism that uses a driver to manage the interaction between the database and the application. Although ASP is widely supported on Windows operating systems, there is limited support in other server environments. Another disadvantage is that the use of ASP technology requires the integration of several programming paradigms, such as the scripting languages and ODBC.

The latest rendition of ASP in the .NET framework, called ASP.NET, solves some of the shortcomings of ASP. The .NET framework enhances ASP support on non-Microsoft platforms, since the .NET framework uses a virtual-machine concept, which is similar to that of Java. ASP.NET accesses ADO in the .NET framework, called ADO.NET. ADO.NET supports a rich API for accessing the database.

Java Server Pages (JSP) represents another solution for dynamically generating Web content. The JSP integrates Java code and HTML in one file, where the JDBC API can be used in the Java code to access the underlying database. The Web server executes Java code in the JSP file and responds with the resulting HTML code to be displayed on the client's browser. Java Servlets, which provide platform-independent, server-side Java programs that integrate and extend the capabilities of the Web server, can be used to control the execution of the Web application.

There are various technologies for the generation of database-driven dynamic Web pages. This section has briefly discussed only some of these technologies. The next section provides a description of the JDBC API, the recognized mechanism for Java programs to interact dynamically with an underlying relational data store. The JDBC API is representative of the types of interactions that the various technologies require to interface with relational databases.

5.3   The JDBC API

JDBC is designed to take advantage of existing interfaces with relational databases, such as ODBC and the SQL standard's CLI. The goal of this section is to provide the reader with a conceptual introduction to the JDBC API for connecting Java programs to relational databases. The main JDBC API is contained in the `java.sql` package from Sun Microsystems. The reader is encouraged to explore further references on the JDBC API, listed at the end of the chapter.

5.3.1   Connecting to the Database

JDBC requires a software driver that allows a Java program to communicate with a database. Since such a program can communicate with multiple databases at the same time, JDBC uses a `DriverManager` class to manage the available JDBC drivers for the system. Figure 5.2 displays a snippet of code that illustrates loading the default driver provided with Java and establishing a connection to a data source. The `forName()` static method of the class `Class` loads the default driver, named `sun.jdbc.odbc.JdbcOdbcDriver`. The `getConnection()` method of the `DriverManager` class establishes a connection to the database. The JDBC `url` consists of the name of the driver, concatenated with the name of the database. In general, a URL, which stands for *Uniform Resource Locator*, is a global address for a resource on the Web.

```
/* dbName is the registered name of the ODBC data source */
String url = "jdbc:odbc:" + dbName ;
try {
    /* Load the default jdbc-odbc driver */
    Class.forName("sun.jdbc.odbc.JdbcOdbcDriver");
    /* Open a connection to the odbc data source */
    Connection dbConnection = DriverManager.getConnection(url);
}
```

Figure 5.2 Connecting to a Database

The Connection interface represents a session with the database. The statements issued to the database are, by default, automatically committed. The setAutoCommit() method allows the database programmer to change the default commit behavior. When autocommit mode is off, each statement must be explicitly committed or rolled back, based on the execution of the statement using the commit() or rollback() method of the Connection object.

5.3.2 Querying the Database

Once a connection to the database is established, the Connection object provides methods for creating the desired objects representing an SQL statement that is sent to the database to be executed. There are three types of objects for querying the database: Statement, PreparedStatement, and CallableStatement. Each object is created in the context of a database session, using the following methods of a Connection object:

- Statement createStatement()
  A Statement object allows for the execution of SQL statements without any parameters.

- PreparedStatement prepareStatement(String sql)
  A PreparedStatement precompiles the SQL query with input parameters. The value of the input parameters are set via methods of the PreparedStatement interface.

- CallableStatement prepareCall(String sql)
  A CallableStatement allows for SQL queries, using stored procedures with input and output parameters. In addition to setting the value of the input parameters, the type of the output parameters must be registered.

Each of the types of statements will be discussed, and detailed examples will be provided for the SCHOOL DATABASE ENTERPRISE defined with SQL in Figure 3.2.

Statement

A Statement object represents a simple SQL statement that will be sent to the database to be executed. The executeQuery() method of the Statement object sends the parameter SQL query to the database for execution and returns the result of the query in a ResultSet:

```
ResultSet executeQuery(String sql);
```

```
Statement stmt = dbConnection.createStatement();
ResultSet rs = null;
rs = stmt.executeQuery("select cId, name from campusClub");
while rs.next()
{
System.out.println(rs.getString("cId"), rs.getString("name"));
}
rs.close();
```

Figure 5.3 Executing a `Statement`

The `next()` method of the `ResultSet` traverses through the tuples. The data stored in a `ResultSet` object are retrieved through the use of `get` methods that allow access to the various columns of the current row, using the column name:

TTTT get*TTTT*(String columnName)

Here, *TTTT* represents the name of a type. The types given in java.sql.Types include BIGINT, BINARY, BIT, CHAR, DATE, DECIMAL, DOUBLE, FLOAT, INTEGER, LONGVARBINARY, LONGVARCHAR, NULL, NUMERIC, OTHER, REAL, SMALLINT, TIME, TIMESTAMP, TINYINT, VARBINARY, and VARCHAR. Each `get` method is overloaded to retrieve the column by using its position in the result set:

TTTT get*TTTT*(int columnIndex)

When the processing of the result set is complete, the `close()` method of the `ResultSet` object closes the result set, immediately releasing its resources.

Figure 5.3 shows a snippet of Java code that illustrates the execution of a query by using a simple statement. A `Statement` object, named `stmt`, is created in the context of the current database session with the `createStatement()` method of the `dbConnection`. The `rs ResultSet` is initialized to `null`. The `executeQuery()` method sends the query to find the id and name of the campus clubs in the database, assigning the result to `rs`. For each row of the result set, the appropriate `get` method retrieves the value of the column of the result, using the name of the attribute. When all campus clubs are displayed, the `close()` method releases the resources held by the result set.

PreparedStatement

A `PreparedStatement` is an interface that extends `Statement` and allows for the execution of precompiled SQL statements with input parameters. By precompiling the SQL code, the query plan is generated once by the database and is reused upon subsequent calls to the statement, with different values of input parameters. A `PreparedStatement` is created by using the `prepareStatement()` method of the `Connection` object, which specifies the SQL query as a parameter. Question marks (?) are placeholders for the input parameters in the SQL query string to `prepareStatement()`. The value of the input parameters are then specified with `set` methods of the appropriate type, where the input parameter is specified with the use of the `parameterIndex` argument and the `parameterValue` argument provides the value of the parameter.

void set*TTTT*(int parameterIndex, *TTTT* parameterValue)

```
String getAdvisorQuery =
          "select f.pId, f.lastName, f.firstName, f.dept"+
          "from faculty f, campusClub c"+
          "where c.advisor = f.pId and c.cId = ?";
PreparedStatement pstmt =
  dbConnection.prepareStatement (getAdvisorQuery);
/* Assume that the following code is executed in a loop */
/* where clubId contains the Campus Club Id of interest */
    pstmt.setString(1, clubId);
    ResultSet rs = pstmt.executeQuery();
    while(rs.next())
    {
        System.out.println("Campus Club:", clubId);
        System.out.println("Faculty Advisor: + rs.getString(2));
        System.out.println("Advisor's Department: + rs.getString(4));
    }
    rs.close();
```

Figure 5.4 Executing a `Prepared Statement`

The `executeQuery()` method of the `PreparedStatement` sends the SQL statement to the database for execution and returns the database result set:

```
ResultSet executeQuery();
```

Figure 5.4 illustrates the initialization, call and processing of a `PreparedStatement` that finds the faculty advisor and the advisor's department for a given campus club in the database. Since a `PreparedStatement` is useful when a similar query is called multiple times with different input parameters, this example assumes that the query is within a looping construct into which the user inputs a club of interest. The input parameter is set to the value of the user input. After executing the prepared statement, the code displays the faculty advisor's last name and department.

CallableStatement

A `CallableStatement` provides the capability to call stored procedures with input and output parameters. A `CallableStatement` is an interface that extends the interface given by a `PreparedStatement`. As with a `PreparedStatement`, any input parameter values must be `set` before the statement is executed. For a `CallableStatement`, the types of the output parameters must also be registered before execution and the value of the parameters must be retrieved after the query is executed. The types of the output parameters are registered through the `registerOutParameter()` method of a `CallableStatement`:

```
void registerOutParameter(int parameterIndex, int sqlType)
```

The values of the output parameters are retrieved via the appropriate `getTTTT()` method of the interface for a `CallableStatement`, where *TTTT* represents the type of the output parameter:

```
TTTT getTTTT(int parameterIndex)
```

```
CallableStatement cs =
  dbConnection.prepareCall("Call getAdvisor(?, ?, ?, ?)" );
/* Set the value of the first (IN) parameter */
cs.setString(1, "ACM"); /* id of the Campus Club */
/* Register the type of the second (OUT) parameter as VARCHAR */
cs.registerOutParameter(2, Types.VARCHAR); /* id of faculty advisor */
/* Register the type of the third (OUT) parameter as VARCHAR */
cs.registerOutParameter(3, Types.VARCHAR); /* advisor's department */
/* Register the type of the fourth OUT parameter as INTEGER */
cs.registerOutParameter(4, Types.INTEGER); /* number of members */
/* Execute the CallableStatement */
cs.execute();
/* Display the values of the output parameters */
System.out.println("Campus Club: ACM");
System.out.println(" Faculty Advisor: "+ cs.getString(2));
System.out.println(" Advisor's Department:" + cs.getString(3));
System.out.println(" Number of Members:" + cs.getInt(4));
```

Figure 5.5 Executing a `Callable Statement`

Assume that there is a procedure defined over the SCHOOL DATABASE ENTERPRISE called `getAdvisor`, which, when given the identifier of a campus club, returns the identifier of the faculty advisor, the advisor's department, and the number of students that are currently members of the club. Figure 5.5 shows a snippet of Java code that calls the `getAdvisor` procedure with a `CallableStatement`. The `prepareCall()` method of the `dbConnection` object creates an instance of a `CallableStatement` `cs` that is a call to the `getAdvisor` procedure. The value of the first parameter, which is the input corresponding to the identifier of the campus club, is set by using the `setString()` method. The types of the output parameters are registered via the `registerOutParameter()` method. The second parameter is an output parameter that is a string (VARCHAR) representing the faculty advisor. The advisor's department is also a string (VARCHAR) and is given by the third parameter of the procedure. The fourth parameter is of type INTEGER and returns the number of student members in the club. Since this `CallableStatement` is calling a stored procedure, there is no result set associated with the execution of the statement. The JDBC API provides an `execute()` method for executing a `Statement` that does not return a result set. Therefore, the `execute()` method executes the `CallableStatement`. The values of the faculty advisor and department are retrieved with the use of `getString()`, and the `getInt()` method returns the number of student members.

5.3.3   Updating the Database

The previous section examined how to query a database by using JDBC. This section focuses on updating the database, which not only includes insertions (e.g., `insert`), modifications (e.g., `update`) and deletions (e.g., `delete`) with respect to the data stored in the database, but also covers additions (e.g., `create table`), changes (e.g., `alter table`), and removals (e.g., `drop table`) at the schema level. The method `executeUpdate()` appears in the interface for `Statement`, `PreparedStatement`, and `CallableStatement`:

```
int executeUpdate(String sql)
```

The `executeUpdate()` method executes the SQL statement, returning the number of rows affected. This statement must be an `insert`, `update`, or `delete` statement or an SQL statement that does not return any values, such as a DDL statement. The various SQL statement interfaces also provide a generic `execute()` method for executing either a query or an update.

Figure 5.6 illustrates some of the data manipulation examples discussed in Chapter 3 that are called with the use of the JDBC API. As an example of a DDL statement, consider the creation of the `facultyInfo` view that returns faculty names, ranks, and names of the departments in which faculty members work. The `insert` statement inserts "Computer Science Department" into the `department` table, and the rank of the faculty whose first name is "Joe" is updated to "Full" professor. The `delete` statement deletes the names of the students who are members of "Club Med".

5.3.4 Metadata

Metadata is a term that means data about data. When an SQL DDL specification is compiled, the resulting description of the database schema is stored as metadata in the database. The JDBC API provides the capability to retrieve the metadata about the database schema as a result set.

As a motivating example for the use of metadata, consider an application that can connect to a relational database via a CLI with a Web-based user interface. Let's call this application METAWEBDB. The METAWEBDB application provides the user with the capability to issue ad hoc queries and data manipulation statements over the database

```
String createView = "create view facultyInfo as "
    + "select d.name as dName, p.firstName as fName,"
    + "p.lastName as lName, f.rank as rank"
    + "from person p, faculty f, department d "
    + "where f.pId = p.pId and f.dept = d.code";
Statement createStmt = dbConnection.createStatement();
int createResult = createStmt.executeUpdate(createView);

String insertCSE = "insert into department"+
    "values ('cse', 'Computer Science Department')";
Statement insertStmt = dbConnection.createStatement();
int insertResult = insertStmt.executeUpdate(insertCSE);

String updateRank = "update faculty "
    + "set rank = 'Full'"
    + "where firstName = 'Joe'" ;
Statement updateStmt = dbConnection.createStatement();
int updateResult = updateStmt.executeUpdate(updateRank);

String deleteClubMed = "delete from student where pId in "
    + "(select cl.pId from clubs cl, campusClub cc "
    + "where cc.name = 'Club Med' and cc.cId = cl.cId)";
Statement deleteStmt = dbConnection.createStatement();
int deleteResult = deleteStmt.executeUpdate(deleteClubMed);
```

Figure 5.6 Examples of the `executeUpdate()` Method

and displays the schema and instance of the database in another browser window. This section illustrates the metadata features of the JDBC API in the context of the METAWEBDB application. For the purposes of the current exposition, METAJDBC refers to an implementation of the METAWEBDB application that uses JDBC to access the relational database.

DatabaseMetaData

In establishing a connection with a database via JDBC, the name of the database is part of the `url` parameter of the `DriverManager`'s `getConnection` method. The user can input the name of the database on a Web form. The METAJDBC application can then establish the connection with the database using this name. To retrieve the metadata about the database schema, the `getMetaData()` method of the `Connection` object returns an instance of type `DatabaseMetaData`:

```
DatabaseMetaData getMetaData()
```

The `DatabaseMetaData` class has numerous methods to support the dynamic investigation of the schema of the underlying database. This exposition focuses on the methods needed to implement the METAJDBC sample application.

`DatabaseMetaData` has methods that the `MetaJDBC` application can use to determine the tables and the names and types of the attributes. The `getTables` method has four parameters that are used to filter the tables returned:

```
ResultSet getTables(String catalog, String schemaPattern,
   String tableNamePattern, String[] types)
```

Typically, in referring to a database schema, the assumption is that there is one schema defining the necessary relations, constraints, domains, and privileges. The SQL standard allows the specification of multiple schemas in a database by schema name and the naming of a catalog, which is a collection of database schemas. Referential integrity constraints can be defined between relations in the schemas in the same catalog. The METAJDBC application assumes that there is one catalog and one schema associated with the database being accessed.

Figure 5.7 illustrates a Java code template that corresponds to the database metadata feature of the METAJDBC application. The `getTables()` method call uses `null` for all four parameters to retrieve all tables associated with the database. Each table description includes the following attributes: TABLE_CAT, TABLE_SCHEM, TABLE_NAME, and TABLE_TYPE. Since METAJDBC displays only the metadata for user-defined tables, the TABLE_TYPE value is checked. If the type is "TABLE", then the table's columns and types are retrieved. Examples of other TABLE_TYPE values include "VIEW" and "SYSTEM TABLE".

The `getColumns()` method retrieves the columns of a table, filtered by parameters for the database catalog, schema, table, and column:

```
ResultSet getColumns(String catalog, String schemaPattern, String
   tableNamePattern, String columnNamePattern)
```

```
DatabaseMetaData dbmd;
ResultSet dbmdTables = null;
ResultSet dbmdTableColumns = null;
dbmd = dbConnection.getMetaData();
dbmdTables = dbmd.getTables(null, null, null, null);
while (dbmdTables.next())
{
     tableName = dbmdTables.getString("TABLE_NAME");
     tableType = dbmdTables.getString("TABLE_TYPE");
     /* checks if it's a user-defined table */
     if (tableType.equals("TABLE"))
     ...
     /* Get the column names in the ResultSet */
     dbmdTableColumns = dbmd.getColumns(null,null,tableName,null);
     while (dbmdTableColumns.next())
     { /* get the attribute names */
       columnName = dbmdTableColumns.getString("COLUMN_NAME") ;
     }
}
```

Figure 5.7 Illustrating DatabaseMetaData

The METAJDBC application code shown in Figure 5.7 retrieves the columns for the user-defined table given as the third parameter. The dbmdTableColumns result set contains the column description for each column in the table. The column description contains various entries, including COLUMN_NAME and TYPE_NAME.

Once the schema of the database is displayed, another useful functionality can be added to the METAJDBC application to display the contents of a table. The instance of a table can be easily returned by using executeQuery("select * from " + tableName) and iterating through the result set.

ResultSetMetaData

Once the metadata of the database are available, the user of the METAJDBC application can pose ad hoc data manipulation statements. Figure 5.8 shows a snippet of code illustrating how the METAJDBC example can display the results of the ad hoc query posed. The query is executed with the executeQuery() method and its result set assigned to the variable rs. The getMetaData() method for a result set returns a ResultSet-MetaData object. The getColumnCount() method returns the number of columns in the

```
rs = stmt.executeQuery(query);
ResultSetMetaData rsmd = rs.getMetaData();
int numCols = rsmd.getColumnCount();
for ( int i = 1; i <= numCols; i++)
{    /* Get the column names and their types using
       rsmd.getColumnLabel(i) and rsmd.getColumnTypeName(i) */
}
while(rs.next())
{    /* Iterate through the ResultSet and display results */
}
```

Figure 5.8 Illustrating ResultSetMetaData

result of the query. The names and types of the columns can be found by using the `getColumnLabel()` and `getColumnTypeName()` methods available in the `ResultSet-MetaData` API. This information can be displayed as headers for the query results, which are then processed and displayed.

The execution of `insert`, `update`, and `delete` statements uses the `executeUpdate()` method, since these data manipulation statements do not return a result set. Recall that the `executeUpdate()` method returns an integer giving the number of rows affected by the data manipulation statement.

The METAJDBC application can return a confirmation of the number of rows affected by the execution of the specified data manipulation statement. The user can then browse the table instances to confirm that the change has taken place as expected.

5.4   Checkpoint

Web database applications typically use a three-tiered architecture, which separates the top presentation layer, the middle application server layer, and the bottom data store layer. This architecture allows for independence of both presentation and data storage.

There are several technologies available for generating dynamic Web pages that interact with an underlying database. The JDBC API is a recognized call-level interface, which allows Java programs to communicate with relational databases. Table 5.1 summarizes the main JDBC API presented in the chapter. Table 5.2 provides a brief summary of the metadata JDBC API used in the discussion of the METAJDBC application.

Exercises

1. Look at the JDBC API (see bibliographic references) for the `getColumns()` method of the `DatabaseMetaData` interface. Examine the other columns contained in a column description. Which columns correspond to column constraints in the DDL? Explain how.

2. Look at the JDBC API (see bibliographic references) for the `ParameterMetaData` interface, which was introduced in JDBC 3.0. Describe at least three methods for the `ParameterMetaData` interface, and explain how these methods dynamically discover relevant information regarding parameters.

3. This book's Web site has two implementations of the METAWEBDB application, one using JSP and Java Servlets, the other using ASP.NET. Download and install each implementation, and compare and contrast the technologies.

4. An Access implementation of the EMPLOYEE TRAINING ENTERPRISE from Dietrich [2001] is available at the author's Web site, `http://www.eas.asu.edu/~winrdbi/author/`. Write a Java program that uses the JDBC API to answer the sample queries from that book concerning the Access database.

5. Choose an implementation of an enterprise in a relational database that is available to you. Use the JDBC API to write a Java program to display the metadata of that database.

TABLE 5.1 Chapter Summary of the JDBC API

Interface *Connection*	
Statement	createStatement()
PreparedStatement	prepareStatement(String sql)
CallableStatement	prepareCall(String sql)
DatabaseMetaData	getMetaData()
Interface *Statement*	
ResultSet	executeQuery(String sql)
int	executeUpdate(String sql)
boolean	execute(String sql)
void	close()
Interface *ResultSet*	
TTTT	get*TTTT*(String columnName)
TTTT	get*TTTT*(int columnIndex)
void	close()
ResultSetMetaData	getMetaData()
Interface *PreparedStatement* extends *Statement*	
void	set*TTTT*(int parameterIndex, *TTTT* parameterValue)
Interface *CallableStatement* extends *PreparedStatement*	
TTTT	get*TTTT*(int i)
TTTT	get*TTTT*(String parameterName)
void	registerOutParameter(int parameterIndex, int sqlType)

TABLE 5.2 Chapter Summary of the JDBC MetaData API

Interface *DatabaseMetaData*	
ResultSet	getTables(String catalog, String schemaPattern, String tableNamePattern, String[] types)
ResultSet	getColumns(String catalog, String schemaPattern, String tableNamePattern, String columnNamePattern)
Interface *ResultSetMetaData*	
int	getColumnCount()
String	getColumnName(int column)
String	getColumnTypeName(int column)

5.5   Bibliographic References

There are numerous technologies available for generating dynamic Web pages [Deitel et al., 2002]. The JDBC API is an example of a call-level interface that provides dynamic database access from Java. The METAJDBC application is based on the JDBC demonstration software described in Dietrich et al., [2002]. The online documentation for the JDBC API is available from Sun's JDBC Web site, `http://java.sun.com/products/jdbc/`. Look for the java.sql package under the documentation link. There are numerous books covering JDBC. A practical guide to JDBC for Java programmers is given in Speegle [2002]. Database programming perspectives for JDBC can be found in Hamilton et al., [1995], Reese [2000], and Taylor [2003]. Melton and Eisenberg [2000] provide a perspective of SQL and Java, including both JDBC and the SQLJ specification for database access from Java programs. The JDBC API provides dynamic access from Java, whereas the SQLJ specification allows the embedding of SQL statements in Java programs.

Chapter 6

XML and Databases

Synopsis

XML is a flexible markup language that has become a universal representation for data and the semantics of data. This chapter introduces XML and its relationship to relational databases. The specification of the schema of an XML document is covered by exploring both Document Type Definitions (DTDs) and XML Schema. The chapter also covers the exchange of data between XML-enabled relational databases.

Assumed Knowledge

- The SQL Standard: Advanced Relational Features (Chapter 3)

Implementation Examples on Web

- Data Exchange Examples using Sample Employee Data

The HyperText Markup Language (HTML) is the primary language used to write Web pages. HTML contains begin and end tags that a Web browser interprets for directions on how to display the text within the tags. HTML has a fixed collection of tags to use. The Extensible Markup Language (XML) is a markup language that is flexible, since it allows user-defined tags. XML was originally developed for the representation of documents. Due to its simplicity and ease of use, XML is a universal language for representing both data and the semantics of data.

Before the introduction of XML, delimited text files were one of the preferred methods for exchanging textual data. In a delimited text file, the fields are separated or delimited by a designated symbol, such as a comma or colon. Various software products provide a mechanism to import delimited text files. However, the process requires knowledge of the contents and order of the fields in the file. XML is now the preferred method for data interchange. XML provides a textual representation of data, along with a representation of the meaning of the data.

XML is also widely used in configuration files for software. Rather than specifying information to programs on the command line or using standard input, XML provides a self-documenting mechanism for specifying parameters and other information required by programs.

Most relational database products are now *XML enabled*. XML-enabled databases provide for the capability to transfer data between XML documents and the data structures of the database. This transfer capability typically relies on the specification of the schema of the XML document. Initially, a *Document Type Definition* (DTD) was used to describe the types contained within an XML document. More recently, the World Wide Web Consortium (W3C) has recommended XML Schema for the specification of the schema of an XML document. Some database products still use a DTD specification, while other database products use XML Schema. Therefore, both DTD and XML Schema will be explored in this chapter.

The goal of this chapter is to provide an introduction to the connection between XML and databases. The chapter begins with a brief overview of HTML to establish the foundation of XML. The chapter then presents the use of DTDs for describing the content of XML documents, providing a canonical table-based mapping of a relational database table stored as an XML document and described by a DTD. XML Schema is quite diverse and has myriad features, so a thorough exposition is beyond the scope of this book. However, XML Schema is covered in enough detail to illustrate the similar features for describing documents that are provided by DTDs. The chapter concludes with a motivating example that illustrates the exchange of data between XML-enabled databases.

6.1   HTML

HTML is used to create the multimedia hypertext documents that are displayed on Web browsers. HTML defines the structure and layout of a Web document by using a variety of *tags*. A tag is a label that describes how a Web browser should present a Web page. For example, Figure 6.1 presents some sample HTML code, and Figure 6.2 shows the

```
<HTML>
...
<BODY>
<CENTER>
<B>This is bold text. </B><BR>
<I>This text is in italics. </I><BR>
<A HREF="http://www.asu.edu">
This is a link to ASU's main Web page.
</A>
<BR><BR>
The following is in a table without a border:
<TABLE border="0">
<TR><TD>Row 1:Col 1</TD><TD>Row 1:Col 2</TD></TR>
<TR><TD>Row 2:Col 1</TD><TD>Row 2:Col 2</TD></TR>
</TABLE>
</CENTER>
</BODY>
</HTML>
```

Figure 6.1   Sample HTML

This is bold text.

This text is in italics.

This is a link to ASU's main Web page.

The following is in a table without a border:

Row 1:Col 1   Row 1:Col 2
Row 2:Col 1   Row 2:Col 2

Figure 6.2 Sample HTML Display

corresponding display. An HTML document is contained within an HTML opening and closing tag. A tag is a label enclosed in angle brackets (< and >). The closing tag for a label is formed by preceding the label with a slash character (/). The body of the HTML displayed in the Web browser is enclosed by the BODY opening and closing tag. Before the body of the page, other information about the Web page may be included, such as the title of the page that is displayed in the header of the browser window. Within the body, the opening tag <CENTER> indicates that the text appearing between the opening tag and its matched closing tag </CENTER> is centered within the Web page display. Similarly, the <B> tag displays the text between the opening and closing tags in a boldface font. The <BR> tag provides a line break, which starts a new line. Text is italicized when it appears between the opening tag <I> and its matching closing tag </I>.

Figure 6.1 also illustrates the use of links to other HTML documents within a Web page. The tag <A> begins a link specification. The HREF appearing as part of the opening tag is an attribute that describes the link. The value of the HREF attribute is enclosed in quotes and provides a URL specification. The text appearing after the angle bracket > of the opening tag until the matched closing tag </A> is underlined in the display. When the user clicks on the underlined text, the Web browser follows the URL given by the HREF attribute value.

Figure 6.1 also shows the use of a table in HTML. The border attribute specifies the width of the border around the table. In this case, the value "0" indicates that there is no border for the table. Each row of the table is enclosed in an opening tag <TR> and closing tag </TR>. Each cell of the table containing the table's data is scoped within the <TD> tag.

The example shown in Figure 6.1 and its corresponding display in Figure 6.2 provide only a glimpse of HTML to establish a foundation for XML. HTML is a rich language for the presentation of Web pages; however, its tags are fixed. XML is an extensible markup language that allows for the definition of new tags and the nesting of matching tags to an arbitrary depth. XML is also a semantic markup language that is a standard adopted by the W3C. Although originally designed for the flexible representation of documents, XML is now widely used to exchange data.

6.2 Overview of XML

Figure 6.3 is a simple motivational example of an XML document containing information about employees. The first tag is named employees, indicating that information for

```
<employees>
   <employee>
      <empid>123456789</empid>
      <lastname>Smith</lastname>
      <firstname>John</firstname>
      <title>Software Engineer</title>
      <salary>50000</salary>
   </employee>
   <!--Additional employees not shown for brevity-->
   ...
</employees>
```

Figure 6.3 XML Sample of Employee Data

multiple employees will appear within the opening and closing tag. The next opening tag is employee. The tags empid, lastname, firstname, title, and salary document the information that is recorded for each employee. Only one employee instance is shown in the figure; this is also documented with a comment in the XML code. An XML comment starts with `<!--` and concludes with `-->`.

As described earlier for HTML, tags are delimited by angle brackets (< and >). Unlike HTML, XML requires that every opening tag have an associated closing tag. The tags in XML are case sensitive and may *not* contain whitespace. Tags must start with a letter or underscore (_) and may contain letters, digits, periods (.), underscores (_), or hyphens(-). Since XML is a semantic markup language, it is strongly suggested that the tags describe its enclosed text.

The term *element* refers to an opening tag, its enclosed text, and its corresponding closing tag. For example,

```
<lastname>Smith</lastname>
```

represents an element in the example shown in Figure 6.3. The text appearing between the opening and closing tag of an element is called the *content* of the element.

Opening tags in an element may contain *attributes*. An attribute has a name and a value, which is enclosed in quotes:

```
<label attributeName="attributeValue">enclosed text</label>
```

For example, an employee's salary can be annotated with an attribute named effective, which indicates the effective date of the salary specified:

```
<salary effective="12Feb2001">50000</salary>
```

All XML elements must have a closing tag. If an element is empty, then XML allows an abbreviated closing tag, as in

```
<emptyElement attributeName="attributeValue" />
```

instead of

```
<emptyElement attributeName="attributeValue"></emptyElement>
```

An example given later in the chapter illustrates the use of an empty element that contains only an attribute value.

In addition to the syntax rules already specified for the definition of elements and attributes, a *well-formed XML document* must also contain a distinguished root element that contains the entire document, and all elements within the document must be properly nested. The distinguished root element has a unique opening and closing tag having the whole document as its enclosed text. In the example shown in Figure 6.3, `employees` represents the distinguished root element.

To illustrate the requirement of a well-formed XML document having the proper nesting of elements, consider, as a counterexample, the following HTML code, which displays text as bold and italicized:

```
<B><I>This text is bold and italics.</B></I>
```

Although the italicized opening tag occurs after the boldface opening tag, the closing tag for the boldface text appears before the closing tag for the italicized text. HTML will not complain about the improper nesting. However, a well-formed XML document requires the proper nesting of the elements:

```
<B><I>This text is bold and italics.</I></B>
```

This nesting structure for XML documents is hierarchical in nature. Typically, the outer element is called a *parent element*, and an element nested within it is called a *child element*.

XML also allows for the flexibility to mix textual data with child elements. For example,

```
<B>This text is bold only. <I>This text is bold and italics.</I></B>
```

illustrates mixing the textual data (This text is bold only.) with the (italicized) child element. This feature of XML is not typically used in a database context, where data are more structured.

A well-formed XML document contains an instance of data with self-describing tags that represent the meaning of the data. Similarly to describing a schema of a database, a DTD defines the type of information contained in an XML document. A *valid XML document* is a well-formed XML document that also follows a set of rules given by its corresponding DTD.

6.3 DTD

A DTD gives metadata information which is about the data contained in the XML document. A DTD is the initial approach to representing the metadata of an XML document. XML Schema is a more recent approach to describing the schema of an XML document that builds on the strengths of a DTD. XML Schema is discussed in the next section.

6.3.1 DTD Declarations

The DTD may appear either in the XML document before the opening root tag or in a separate file referenced in the XML document. The first case, known as an *internal declaration*, has the syntax

```
<!DOCTYPE rootElement [elementDeclarations]>
```

where `rootElement` is the name of the distinguished root element of the XML document and `elementDeclarations` represents the DTD for declaring the elements. The second case, called an *external declaration*, has the syntax

```
<!DOCTYPE rootElement SYSTEM "filename.dtd">
```

where `rootElement` is the name of the distinguished root element of the XML document and `filename.dtd` represents the name of the file that defines the DTD for the XML document.

Each element declaration consists of an element name and its content:

```
<!ELEMENT elementName contentSpecification>
```

The `contentSpecification` is either character data or the specification of nested elements. The content specification for character data is PCDATA, which represents parsed character strings. For example, the symbols <, >, ", ', and & are used in XML syntax. Therefore, to include these symbols in the XML data, the following strings are used to denote the symbols, which are prefixed by an ampersand (&) and suffixed by a semicolon: <, >, ", ', and &. The parsing of the XML data changes these strings into the associated symbol.

Nested elements represent more complex types of information. A sequence of elements, similar to a tuple in a table, is represented in a DTD by a comma-separated list enclosed in parentheses:

```
<!ELEMENT sequencedElements (element1, element2, element3)>
```

Each nested element (`element1`, `element2`, and `element3`) must appear exactly once in the order specified. However, a DTD also allows for the specification of the number of occurrences of nested elements, using the suffixes +, *, and ?. A + suffix indicates that the element occurs one or more times, a * suffix indicates that the element occurs zero or more times, and a ? suffix indicates that the element may appear at most once.

Consider the DTD specification of `occurrenceConstraintsExSeq`:

```
<!ELEMENT occurrenceConstraintsExSeq
   (element1+, element2*, element3?)>
```

The nested elements still must appear in order; however, `element1` must appear at least once, but may appear any additional number of times. The nested element `element2` may not appear or may appear any number of times, whereas `element3` is optional, but, if included, occurs once.

DTDs also provide for the specification of a choice of elements:

```
<!ELEMENT choiceOfElements (elementA | elementB | elementC)>
```

The element declaration for `choiceOfElements` denotes that only one of the nested elements (`elementA`, `elementB`, or `elementC`) can appear in a valid XML document.

Figure 6.4 gives the DTD for the XML document shown in Figure 6.3. The XML document must contain at least one occurrence of `employee`, and each `employee` element consists of the following sequence of elements: `empid`, `lastname`, `firstname`, `title`, and `salary`.

```
<!ELEMENT employees employee+>
<!ELEMENT employee (empid, lastname, firstname, title, salary)>
<!ELEMENT empid (#PCDATA)>
<!ELEMENT lastname (#PCDATA)>
<!ELEMENT firstname (#PCDATA)>
<!ELEMENT title (#PCDATA)>
<!ELEMENT salary (#PCDATA)>
```

Figure 6.4 DTD for Employee XML Document

The attributes allowable for elements are also defined as part of a DTD:

```
<!ATTLIST elementName attributeName attributeType defaultValue>
```

The type of an attribute can be character data (CDATA), an ID, or an enumerated value. The defaultValue is either a default value for the attribute enclosed in quotes or a specification for the requirements of the value of the attribute: #REQUIRED, #IMPLIED, or #FIXED. A value of a #REQUIRED attribute must be specified. If the attribute is #IMPLIED, then the attribute is optional. A #FIXED attribute means that the value of the attribute must be the value given in quotes following #FIXED.

For example, if the effective date is allowed as an attribute of an employee's salary, then the DTD contains the following attribute specification:

```
<!ATTLIST salary effective CDATA #IMPLIED>
```

This ATTLIST specification defines the attribute named effective for the salary element. The effective attribute is of type character data (CDATA), and its inclusion in the instance data is optional (#IMPLIED).

There is a distinction between the types CDATA and PCDATA. Although both the CDATA attribute type and the PCDATA element type represent character strings, the character data represented by CDATA are not parsed. The textual data are treated "as is." Therefore, the special characters, such as &, <, >, ", and ', can appear in the value of an attribute. The character strings that are element content are parsed unless the data are enclosed in a CDATA section, which starts with <![CDATA[and ends with]]>. As an example, consider the DTD specification of element anyElement having PCDATA as its content specification:

```
<!ELEMENT anyElement (#PCDATA)>
```

The following is sample XML data illustrating the use of a CDATA section for the content of anyElement:

```
<anyElement><![CDATA[This text won't be parsed.]]></anyElement>
```

To represent data from a database in XML, values from a relational table should be enclosed in a CDATA section in case the data contains special characters in XML. Further examples are provided in Section 6.3.2 in the context of DTDs and relational databases.

If an optional attribute can have a default value, then the default value itself follows the attributeType. Consider the example of using a rate attribute for salary that specifies whether the salary value is a yearly or an hourly rate. By default, it is assumed that the rate is a yearly specification:

```
<!ATTLIST salary rate (yearly | hourly) "yearly">
```

If the employee example is extended to include an attribute to determine whether the employee is active or not, then the attribute declaration

```
<!ATTLIST employee active (true | false) #REQUIRED>
```

requires a value for the `active` attribute and restricts the value of the attribute to be either `true` or `false`.

A `#FIXED` attribute specification indicates that the value of the attribute is fixed to the value specified. Consider extending the employee example to include a monetary format for the salary of an employee:

```
<!ATTLIST salary moneyFormat #FIXED "dollars">
```

For this fictitious company, all employee salaries are in dollars.

Another `attributeType` specification is ID. The value of an attribute of type ID must be unique for the declared element in the XML document. For example, each employee can be given an ID attribute value within the XML document:

```
<employee ID="e01">...</employee>
```

These attribute references can later be used to refer to the XML elements of interest. Now consider extending the employee example to include departments. A `department` element can include a list of employees by specifying the references to the employee ID, using the designated IDREFS attribute:

```
<department>...<hasEmployees IDREFS="e01 e02" /></department>
```

The value of IDREFS is given by ID values separated by whitespace enclosed in quotation marks. This use of references within the XML document also provides a sample use of an empty element, which is `hasEmployees` in this example.

It is worth mentioning when an element, as opposed to an attribute, is used. An element is typically a nested or structured specification of data and can have multiple occurrences. An attribute has a single value that is simple, since its value is given in quotes. As seen in the `effective` date of the `salary` of an employee, an attribute value tends to be metadata about the value of the element.

6.3.2 DTDs and Relational Databases

The XML employee data of Figure 6.3 and its corresponding DTD in Figure 6.4 illustrate the representation of a relational table in an XML document. The parent element for the table contains the child elements that represent each tuple of the table. The attributes of the table form a sequence of nested elements within each tuple element.

This representation of a relational table in XML forms the foundation of a table-based mapping approach to representing a relational database instance in XML, which is illustrated in the DTD of Figure 6.5 for a generic example. The element `database` forms the distinguished root element of the XML document. The database shown in the figure contains two tables: `table1` and `table2`. The element `table1` contains any number of tuples for `table1`, which is given by the `table1Tuple` element. The table `table1` has three attributes: `t1Attr1`, `t1Attr2`, and `t1Attr3`. Therefore, each element representing a tuple or row of `table1` contains three elements, named `t1Attr1`, `t1Attr2`, and `t1Attr3`.

```
<!ELEMENT database (table1 , table2)>
<!ELEMENT table1 (table1Tuple)*>
<!ELEMENT table1Tuple (t1Attr1, t1Attr2, t1Attr3)>
<!ELEMENT t1Attr1 (#PCDATA)>
<!ELEMENT t1Attr2 (#PCDATA)>
<!ELEMENT t1Attr3 (#PCDATA)>
... <!--table2 not shown for brevity-->
```

Figure 6.5 DTD for a Table-Based Mapping to an XML Document

```
<database>
    <table1>
        <table1Tuple>
            <t1Attr1><![CDATA[attr1Value]]></t1Attr1>
            <t1Attr2><![CDATA[attr2Value]]></t1Attr2>
            <t1Attr3><![CDATA[attr3Value]]></t1Attr3>
        </table1Tuple>
        ...
        <!--The rest of the tuples for table1 omitted.-->
    </table1>
    ...
    <!--The data for table2 omitted for brevity.-->
</database>
```

Figure 6.6 Sample Data for a Table-Based Mapping to XML

Figure 6.6 gives a sample database instance for the schema given in Figure 6.5. The database instance only shows one tuple of `table1`: (`attr1Value`, `attr2Value`, `attr3Value`). The rest of the instance is omitted for brevity of presentation. Note that the value of an attribute in the table is shown within a CDATA section. Since the values of attributes may contain characters that are special in XML, the use of a CDATA section in the XML data indicates that the enclosed character data should not be parsed but treated as is.

6.3.3 Checkpoint: DTD

A DTD provides metadata about the data contained in an XML document. DTDs allow for the declaration of elements with associated occurrence constraints. Elements may have attributes that consist of simple data, yet the DTD can specify whether the attribute's value is required, optional, or fixed and whether it has a default value. Table 6.1 summarizes the DTD constructs for declaring nested elements and specifying occurrence constraints.

TABLE 6.1 Abbreviated DTD Summary for Nested Elements and Occurrence Constraints

DTD Declaration	Description
(element1, element2, element3)	Sequence of elements
(elementA | elementB | elementC)	Choice of elements
element+	element occurs one or more times
element*	element occurs zero or more times
element?	element is optional (occurs at most once)
element	element appears exactly once

Although DTDs provide some information about the structure of an XML document, they lack the expressiveness that the database community expects for the specification of XML for data exchange. The W3C organization has introduced XML Schema as a language specifically designed for defining schemas of XML documents.

Exercises

1. There is no built-in syntax in a DTD for specifying an unordered collection of elements. Using the `choice` element and occurrence constraints, determine a DTD for defining an element named `unorderedCollectionOfElements` that represents an unordered collection of elements.

2. Using the canonical table-based mapping of relational data to an XML document shown in Figure 6.5, give a DTD for the SCHOOL DATABASE ENTERPRISE of Figure 3.2.

3. Give a *valid* XML document that corresponds to the DTD of the previous exercise.

6.4   XML Schema

XML Schema has several advantages over DTDs, while building on some of its strengths. Like DTDs, XML Schema has elements and attributes, but it also has the capability to define data types. XML Schema allows for the definition and use of both simple and complex types. Simple types contain only text, whereas complex types contain other elements or attributes. Elements can have simple or complex types, but attributes are always of a simple type, since they are textual.

Another advantage of XML Schema over DTDs is the ability of XML Schema to have both global and local declarations. In DTDs, all declarations are global—a restriction that may be problematic when it comes to dealing with databases. In a database schema, attribute names are unique within the scope of the table in which they are defined. Therefore, multiple tables can have an attribute with the same name. This scenario can be validated by using XML Schema, but not with DTDs, since DTD declarations are global and will not allow for more than one element of the same name.

XML Schema also uses *namespaces* to provide a collection of related element names. The name of a namespace must be unique. The design of a namespace name follows the format of a URL. For example, the namespace denoting the XML Schema standard is

`http://www.w3.org/2001/XMLSchema`

The URL is not meant to be dereferenceable but to be a unique name that doesn't change. The elements that are globally declared in a namespace are uniquely identifiable by a combination of the namespace and the element name. Thus, namespaces allow multiple XML documents to be used in one XML document, without name clashes on element names. Section 6.5, on data exchange, provides an example of the use of multiple namespaces.

Yet another advantage of XML Schema is that it is written in XML. The language used to create schema definitions for XML documents is called the XML Schema Definition Language (XSDL). The *.xsd* file extension denotes an XML document written in XSDL.

Figure 6.7 shows the outline of an XML Schema specification. An optional XML version declaration can appear before the beginning of the schema declaration. The schema is enclosed in the distinguished root element named `xsd:schema`. The `xsd:schema` element has an attribute to define the XML namespace or namespaces referenced in the schema, which in this example is the default namespace given by W3C. Any element or type prefixed by `xsd:` refers to this namespace. An `xsd:annotation` element allows for the inclusion of additional descriptions of schema components. The nested `xsd:documentation` element provides the text of a comment that is meant to be read by a person. Also, a nested `xsd:appinfo` element allows the inclusion of application-specific information that is meant to be recognized by an application. The rules for the definition of a schema will appear within the scope of the `xsd:schema` element.

XML Schema permits the declaration of elements and attributes to be of a specified data type to allow for the validation of the element content and attribute values. Data types can be simple or complex. A simple type is a type that contains only text. A complex type may contain child elements or attributes. The specification of a data type is referred to as a *definition*.

Declarations of elements and attributes and definitions of data types may be global or local. Global declarations or definitions must appear at the top level of the document as a child of the `xsd:schema` element. Global components must have unique names in the schema within the type of that component. For example, a schema *must not* contain two global elements of the same name, but a schema *may* contain a global element declaration and a global complex type definition that have the same name. Local declarations or definitions appear within the scope of the complex type in which they are being declared. Data type definitions that are locally defined cannot be used outside of the scope of the declaration in which they are defined. Local data type definitions need not be named. Unnamed data type definitions are referred to as *anonymous*.

6.4.1 Simple Types

XML Schema provides built-in simple types and allows the user to define custom simple types. A simple type is a type that contains only text. Some built-in simple types are `string`, `integer`, `decimal`, `float`, `boolean`, `date`, and `time`. The declaration of

```
<? xml version="1.0" ?>
<xsd:schema xmlns:xsd="http://www.w3.org/2001/XMLSchema">
<xsd:annotation>
   <xsd:documentation>
   The rules for validation will appear within the xsd:schema element.
   </xsd:documentation>
</xsd:annotation>
<!--Rules for schema definition go here-->
...
</xsd:schema>
```

Figure 6.7   XML Schema Outline

an element named `dateOfBirth`, of type `date`, is an example of the use of a simple type:

```
<xsd:element name="dateOfBirth" type="xsd:date" />
```

Custom simple types are defined with the `simpleType` element. Figure 6.8 shows an example of the definition of the `salaryRange` simple type. The `restriction` element indicates the `base` type on which the simple type is being built. The elements `min-Inclusive` and `maxInclusive` provide the value of the minimum and maximum allowable salaries. Note that *inclusive* means that the values specified are allowed, so `min-Inclusive` means greater than or equal to the value given. XSDL also allows for the elements `minExclusive` and `maxExclusive` to specify a greater-than or less-than relationship, respectively. It is not necessary to specify both a minimum and a maximum, unless the specification of both values is required by the semantics of the data.

The `restriction` element allows for the specification of various types of restrictions, which are also called *facets* in the literature. Figure 6.9 illustrates some of the additional

```
<xsd:simpleType name="salaryRange">
    <xsd:restriction base="xsd:integer">
        <xsd:minInclusive value="25000" />
        <xsd:maxInclusive value="100000" />
    </xsd:restriction>
</xsd:simpleType>
```

Figure 6.8   XSDL Example of a Custom Simple Type

```
<xsd:simpleType name="studentClassification">
    <xsd:restriction base="xsd:string">
        <xsd:enumeration value="Freshman" />
        <xsd:enumeration value="Sophomore" />
        <xsd:enumeration value="Junior" />
        <xsd:enumeration value="Senior" />
    </xsd:restriction>
</xsd:simpleType>

<xsd:simpleType name="deptType">
    <xsd:restriction base="xsd:string">
        <xsd:length value="3" />
    </xsd:restriction>
</xsd:simpleType>

<xsd:simpleType name="usaTelephoneNumberType">
    <xsd:restriction base="xsd:string">
        <xsd:pattern value="\d10" />
    </xsd:restriction>
</xsd:simpleType>

<xsd:simpleType name="gpaType">
    <xsd:restriction base="xsd:decimal">
        <xsd:precision value="3" />
        <xsd:scale value="2" />
    </xsd:restriction>
</xsd:simpleType>
```

Figure 6.9   Additional Examples of Restrictions in XSDL

types of restrictions. The enumeration element restricts the value of the type to be one of the enumerated values. The figure gives an example of the enumeration of undergraduate student classifications (studentClassification), from Freshman, indicating a first-year student, to Senior, indicating a fourth-year student. The length, minLength, and maxLength elements restrict the length of the type. The abbreviation for a department name (deptType) is restricted to be a string of length 3 in the figure. Alternatively, the minLength and maxLength elements can be used to restrict the value to a required minimum length or maximum length (or both). The value of the pattern element provides a regular expression to specify the restriction on a value of a string type. For example, the usaTelephoneNumberType in the figure is restricted to be a string value consisting of 10 digits. In the case of a decimal type, to specify the total number of digits and the number of digits appearing to the right of the decimal point, the precision and scale elements are respectively used. Figure 6.9 illustrates a gpaType, which restricts a decimal to have a total of 3 digits with 2 digits to the right of the decimal point.

6.4.2 Complex Types

An element that has attributes or that can contain other elements has a *complex type*. A complex type definition is enclosed within the content of the complexType element:

```
<xsd:complexType name="complexTypeName">
...
</xsd:complexType>
```

XML Schema allows for defining a complex type, using the elements sequence and choice. A sequence is similar to the comma (,) specification in DTDs, defining a sequence of elements in the given order. A choice corresponds to the usage of the vertical bar (|) in DTDs, providing a choice of one of the elements.

Defining a Complex Type with sequence

Figure 6.10 presents an example of the XSDL for defining the sequencedElements-Type. Recall the definition of the element sequencedElements in a DTD:

```
<!ELEMENT sequencedElements (element1, element2, element3)>
```

The declaration of sequencedElements in XSDL then uses the definition of the sequencedElementsType shown in Figure 6.10:

```
<xsd:element name="sequencedElements" type="sequencedElementsType" />
```

```
<xsd:complexType name="sequencedElementsType">
    <xsd:sequence>
        <xsd:element name="element1" type="xsd:string" />
        <xsd:element name="element2" type="xsd:string" />
        <xsd:element name="element3" type="xsd:string" />
    </xsd:sequence>
</xsd:complexType>
```

Figure 6.10 Example of a sequence Complex Type

This definition of the `sequencedElementsType` assumes that the type of each element is `string`. The group of elements declared within the `sequence` is called a *sequence group*.

A DTD uses a suffix (+, *, ?) on the element name to specify occurrence constraints. XSDL specifies these occurrence constraints via built-in attributes named `minOccurs` and `maxOccurs`. Table 6.2 summarizes the correspondence between the DTD suffix and the values of the `minOccurs` and `maxOccurs` attributes in XSDL. The attribute `minOccurs` has the built-in type `nonnegativeInteger`. The `maxOccurs` attribute value is either a `nonnegativeInteger` or "unbounded". As in a DTD, when the occurrence constraints are not explicitly specified, the `minOccurs` and `maxOccurs` attributes have a default value of 1.

Recall the DTD for `occurrenceConstraintsExSeq` from Section 6.3:

```
<!ELEMENT occurrenceConstraintsExSeq
   (element1+, element2*, element3?)>
```

Figure 6.11 gives a local definition of a complex type in XML Schema, which illustrates the occurrence constraints that correspond to `occurrenceConstraintsExSeq`.

Occurrence constraints on element declarations may be included on locally declared elements within complex type definitions, as shown in Figure 6.11. Occurrence constraints are not allowed on the declaration of global elements, which appear at the top level of the schema. Elements that are declared globally are referenced within an XML document. The references to the global elements may then specify occurrence constraints. Figure 6.12 gives a definition of a complex type similar to that shown in Figure 6.11. However, Figure 6.12 references the three globally declared elements `element1`, `element2`, and `element3`. Instead of specifying a `name` and `type` attribute for the element declaration, the value of the `ref` attribute specifies the name of the referenced global element. The global

TABLE 6.2   Occurrence Constraints in DTD versus XSDL

DTD Suffix	`minOccurs Value`	`maxOccurs Value`
+	1	unbounded
*	0	unbounded
?	0	1
no suffix	1	1

```
<xsd:complexType>
    <xsd:sequence>
        <xsd:element name="element1" type="xsd:string"
            minOccurs="1" maxOccurs="unbounded" />
        <xsd:element name="element2" type="xsd:string"
            minOccurs="0" maxOccurs="unbounded" />
        <xsd:element name="element3" type="xsd:string"
            minOccurs="0" maxOccurs="1" />
    </xsd:sequence>
</xsd:complexType>
```

Figure 6.11   XSDL Example of `sequence` Complex Type with Occurrence Constraints

```
<xsd:element name="element1" type="xsd:string" />
<xsd:element name="element2" type="xsd:string" />
<xsd:element name="element3" type="xsd:string" />
<xsd:complexType name="occurrenceConstraintsExSeqType">
    <xsd:sequence>
        <xsd:element ref="element1"
            minOccurs="1" maxOccurs="unbounded" />
        <xsd:element ref="element2"
            minOccurs="0" maxOccurs="unbounded" />
        <xsd:element ref="element3"
            minOccurs="0" maxOccurs="1" />
    </xsd:sequence>
</xsd:complexType>
```

Figure 6.12 XSDL Example of Sequence Complex Type with Element References

declaration of the `occurrenceConstraintsExSeq` element in XML Schema then uses the global type definition of `occurrenceConstraintsExSeqType` shown in Figure 6.12:

```
<xsd:element name="occurrenceConstraintsExSeq"
    type="occurrenceConstraintsExSeqType" />
```

Defining a Complex Type with choice

XSDL has a `choice` element that corresponds to the | usage in DTDs, providing a choice of one of the elements. Recall the definition of `choiceOfElements` in a DTD:

```
<!ELEMENT choiceOfElements (elementA | elementB | elementC)>
```

Figure 6.13 illustrates the definition of the `choiceOfElementsType` using XML Schema. The declaration of the `choiceOfElements` element then uses this type definition:

```
<xsd:element name="choiceOfElements" type="choiceOfElementsType" />
```

The group of elements declared within the `choice` is called a `choice` group.

In the context of structured data for a database, the `sequence` and `choice` groups represent the most common structures for defining complex types. XSDL also allows for `all` elements and references to *named groups* to appear in a complex type definition. The `all` element in XSDL allows the elements declared within its scope to appear in any order. In other words, an `all` element provides for an *unordered* collection of elements. Several conditions are placed on the use of the `all` element. A *named group* uses an explicit `group` element to name a grouping of individual element declarations. A reference to a named group acts as a textual substitution. Since this section focuses on the use of the XML Schema Definition Language for the representation of structured database content,

```
<xsd:complexType name="choiceOfElementsType">
    <xsd:choice>
        <xsd:element name="elementA" type="xsd:string" />
        <xsd:element name="elementB" type="xsd:string" />
        <xsd:element name="elementC" type="xsd:string" />
    </xsd:choice>
</xsd:complexType>
```

Figure 6.13 XSDL Example of Choice in a Complex Type

the details of the `all` and `group` elements for defining complex types are outside the scope of this discussion.

Deriving Complex Types from Existing Types

The complex types illustrated thus far are structured with the use of `sequence` and `choice` groups. XSDL also provides for deriving a complex type from an existing type. If the complex type are derived from a simple type, then the complex type has *simple content*. A complex type derived from another complex type has *complex content*.

A common example of a complex type derived from a simple type is the extension of a simple type to include an attribute. Figure 6.14 provides an example of a complex type definition for `SalaryRangeAndDate` having simple content. In this example, the simple `salaryRange` type is extended to include the `effective` attribute to record the associated date. The `simpleContent` element indicates that the content model for the complex type contains only textual data and no elements. The `extension` element indicates that the base simple type of the derivation is the previously declared `salaryRange` simple type. The `attribute` declaration extends the `salaryRange` type to include an attribute named `effective` of type `date`.

A DTD specifies whether an attribute value is required (REQUIRED) or optional (IMPLIED) or has a default or fixed (FIXED) value. In XSDL, an attribute declaration may contain additional attributes (beyond `name` and `type`) to specify constraints on its use and default or fixed values. The `use` attribute specifies whether the attribute is `"required"` or `"optional"`. If the `use` attribute is not specified, as in the example shown in Figure 6.14, then the use of the attribute is optional. There may also be `default` or `fixed` attributes for an attribute declaration, but not both. A `default` value provides a value for an attribute if the attribute is absent. Therefore, an attribute declaration that has a default value cannot be required. A `fixed` value indicates that the attribute must have the value specified. If the attribute is absent, then the `fixed` value is used, as in a default value. However, if the attribute is present, it must be the same as the `fixed` value; otherwise, the instance is invalid.

Table 6.3 provides examples of XSDL attribute declarations based on the corresponding DTD. The `effective` attribute for `salary` is `"optional"`. The `salary rate` attribute is one of the enumerated values `yearly` or `hourly`, which is assumed to be defined in the type `salaryRateType`. The `default` value for the `rate` attribute is `"yearly"`. The `active` attribute of `employee` is `"required"` and is a `boolean` type. The `moneyFormat` attribute for `salary` has a `fixed` value of `"dollars"`.

Figure 6.14 defined a complex type `salaryRangeAndDate` that extends the `salaryRange` with an `effective` date attribute. Now consider deriving a complex type from `salaryRangeAndDate` that extends the type to include the format of the currency

```
<xsd:complexType name="salaryRangeAndDate">
    <xsd:simpleContent>
        <xsd:extension base="salaryRange">
        <xsd:attribute name="effective" type="xsd:date" />
        </xsd:extension>
    </xsd:simpleContent>
</xsd:complexType>
```

Figure 6.14 XSDL Example of Complex Type with Simple Content

TABLE 6.3 DTD and XSDL Sample Attribute Declaration Constraints

DTD	`<!ATTLIST salary effective CDATA #IMPLIED>`
XSDL	`<xsd:attribute name="effective" type="xsd:date"` `    use="optional" />`
DTD	`<!ATTLIST salary rate (yearly | hourly) "yearly">`
XSDL	`<xsd:attribute name="rate" type="salaryRateType"` `    default="yearly" />`
DTD	`<!ATTLIST employee active (true | false) #REQUIRED>`
XSDL	`<xsd:attribute name="active" type="xsd:boolean"` `    use="required" />`
DTD	`<!ATTLIST salary moneyFormat #FIXED "dollars">`
XSDL	`<xsd:attribute name="moneyFormat" type="xsd:string"` `    fixed="dollars" />`

of the salary. Figure 6.15 illustrates extending the existing `salaryRangeAndDate` type with a `moneyFormat` attribute having type `moneyFormatType`, which is assumed to be an enumeration of one of the different monetary formats, such as dollars, francs, or pounds.

Empty elements are elements that contain neither elements nor text but possibly contain attributes. An earlier example illustrating the use of IDREFs in DTDs also provided an example of an empty element, since the values of the IDREFs attribute supplied the values of the IDs of the employees working in the department. There are several ways to define a type for an empty element that only contains an attribute in XSDL. Figure 6.16 shows two methods. The first definition is the long version, which extends the built-in wild-card type, called `anyType`, with the attribute declaration. The second definition is the abbreviated version, which indicates that the complex type contains only an attribute.

6.4.3 XML Schema and Relational Databases

Figure 6.17 gives the XSDL for the table-based mapping of relational tables to XML data. The global `database` element has a local type given by the `complexType` element within its content. The type of the `database` element is a sequence of references to the tables in the database. The reference to element `table1` is a reference to the

```
<xsd:complexType name="salaryRangeDateFormat">
    <xsd:complexContent>
        <xsd:extension base="salaryRangeAndDate">
        <xsd:attribute name="moneyFormat" type="moneyFormatType" />
        </xsd:extension>
    </xsd:complexContent>
</xsd:complexType>
```

Figure 6.15 XSDL Example of Complex Type with Complex Content

```
<xsd:complexType name="emptyElementTypeLongVersion">
    <xsd:complexContent>
        <xsd:extension base="xsd:anyType">
        <xsd:attribute name="attrName" type="xsd:string" />
        </xsd:extension>
    </xsd:complexContent>
</xsd:complexType>

<xsd:complexType name="emptyElementTypeAbbreviated">
    <xsd:attribute name="attrName" type="xsd:string" />
</xsd:complexType>
```

Figure 6.16   XSDL Examples of Empty Element Type Definitions

```
<xsd:schema xmlns:xsd="http://www.w3.org/2001/XMLSchema">
<xsd:element name="database">
    <xsd:complexType>
        <xsd:sequence>
            <xsd:element ref="table1" />
            <xsd:element ref="table2" />
        </xsd:sequence>
    </xsd:complexType>
</xsd:element>
<xsd:element name="t1Attr1" type="xsd:string" />
<xsd:element name="t1Attr2" type="xsd:string" />
<xsd:element name="t1Attr3" type="xsd:string" />
<xsd:element name="table1">
    <xsd:complexType>
        <xsd:sequence minOccurs="0" maxOccurs="unbounded">
            <xsd:element ref="table1Tuple" />
        </xsd:sequence>
    </xsd:complexType>
</xsd:element>
<xsd:element name="table1Tuple">
    <xsd:complexType>
        <xsd:sequence>
            <xsd:element ref="t1Attr1" />
            <xsd:element ref="t1Attr2" />
            <xsd:element ref="t1Attr3" />
        </xsd:sequence>
    </xsd:complexType>
</xsd:element>
...
</xsd:schema>
```

Figure 6.17   XSDL for Table-Based Mapping

global element declaration for table1, which appears later in the XML document. The declaration for table2 is not shown, for brevity of presentation. The table1 element has a local complex type consisting of a sequence of only one element, which is a reference to the table1Tuple element. The occurrence constraints indicate that there can be an unbounded number of occurrences of table1Tuple. Each table1Tuple element consists of a sequence of references to the attributes appearing in table1 (t1Attr1, t1Attr2, t1Attr3). Note that in this example, all elements that correspond to the table names, the attribute names, and the tuples of the tables are declared globally and referenced with appropriate occurrence constraints within the complex type definitions.

6.4.4 Checkpoint: XML Schema

XML Schema is a powerful language for expressing the schema of XML documents, with the focus of this section being on the use of the XML Schema Definition Language to represent structured database content.

XML Schema builds on the strengths of DTDs by declaring elements and attributes to be of specific data types. XML Schema allows for the definition and use of both simple and complex types. Table 6.4 summarizes some of the restrictions available for the definition of customized simple types in XSDL. A summary of the definition of complex types is given in Table 6.5.

XML Schema also provides a strong foundation for the exchange of data between XML-enabled databases, discussed in the next section.

Exercises

1. Assume a global element declaration for usPostalAddress, which includes a person's name, street address, city, state, and zip code. Define a complex type for a person's contact information that extends the usPostalAddress with a person's email address, home phone number, and work phone number.

2. Using the canonical table-based mapping of relational data to an XML document, give an XML Schema Definition for the SCHOOL DATABASE ENTERPRISE of Figure 3.2.

3. Is the *valid* XML document of Exercise 3 in Checkpoint 6.3.2 still valid with respect to the XML Schema specification in the previous exercise? Explain your answer.

6.5 Data Exchange

XML has become a de facto industry standard for data exchange. Most relational database products are now XML enabled, providing the capability to transfer data between XML documents and the data structures of a database. Although there are numerous details regarding the technology for data exchange, the goal of this section is to motivate the use of XML for interchanging data between XML-enabled databases. Specifically, this section describes one way to exchange data between Microsoft Access and Oracle relational databases.

Earlier in the chapter, Figure 6.3 provided an XML document for the representation of employee data and Figure 6.4 gave its corresponding DTD. Figure 6.18 gives part of the XML Schema specification for an employee table defined in Microsoft Access with the attributes renamed to eID, eLast, eFirst, eTitle, and eSalary. This XSDL illustrates additional features. For example, the schema element uses an additional namespace xmlns:od for Microsoft's office data. The distinct root element is named dataroot,

TABLE 6.4 Abbreviated XSDL Simple Type Definition

Element	Description
`<xsd:simpleType>`	Custom simple type definition.
`<xsd:restriction base="`*baseType*`">`	Restriction of a simple *baseType*.
`<xsd:minInclusive value="`*minValue*`" />`	Restricts numeric base type to be greater than or equal to *minValue*.
`<xsd:maxInclusive value="`*maxValue*`" />`	Restricts numeric base type to be less than or equal to *maxValue*.
`<xsd:minExclusive value="`*minValue*`" />`	Restricts numeric base type to be greater than *minValue*.
`<xsd:maxExclusive value="`*maxValue*`" />`	Restricts numeric base type to be less than *maxValue*.
`<xsd:enumeration value="`*enumValue*`" />`	Restricts value to be one of the enumerated values given by *enumValue*.
`<xsd:length value="`*lenValue*`" />`	Restricts string to be at most *lenValue* in length.
`<xsd:minLength value="`*minValue*`" />`	Restricts string to be at least *minValue* in length.
`<xsd:maxLength value="`*maxValue*`" />`	Restricts string to be at least *maxValue* in length.
`<xsd:precision value="`*precValue*`" />`	Restricts the number of digits in a decimal to be *precValue*.
`<xsd:scale value="`*scaleValue*`" />`	Restricts the number of digits to the right of the decimal point to be *scaleValue*.
`<xsd:pattern value="`*patternValue*`" />`	Restricts value to follow the specified *patternValue*.

which has an unbounded number of references to the `employee` element. The `employee` element has an `annotation` which includes an `appinfo` element that uses elements in the `od` namespace. For example, the `eID` attribute of the `employee` table is the primary key for the table and thus has a unique index. The second `index` element in the `appinfo` content is a secondary index on the `eTitle` attribute of the `employee` table, which is a nonunique index on the title of the employee. The `employee` element is defined as a complex sequence type of the corresponding elements for the attributes of the `employee` table. For brevity, only the `eID` specification is shown. The `eID` element is a simple type,

TABLE 6.5 Abbreviated XSDL Complex Type Definition

Element	Description
`<xsd:complexType>`	Custom complex type definition.
`<xsd:sequence>`	A sequence of elements in the given order.
`<xsd:choice>`	A choice of one of the elements.
`<xsd:simpleContent>`	A complex type derived from a simple type, such as extending a simple type to include an attribute.
`<xsd:complexContent>`	A complex type derived from a complex type, such as extending a complex type to include another attribute or element.

which is a restriction of a string to be of a maximum length of 3 characters. Figure 6.19 shows valid XML data for the `employee` table, based on the XSD given in Figure 6.18.

Oracle is another well-known database product that is XML enabled. Oracle's default format for XML data is quite simple, having a distinguished root named ROWSET, with each tuple shown within a ROW element. For each ROW element, an attribute named NUM assigns each row a unique number. As with Access, the attributes in the row of the table form nested elements. Figure 6.20 gives the Oracle XML data corresponding to the Access XML data for the `employee` table shown in Figure 6.19.

There are similarities between the Access and Oracle XML documents representing relational tables. Each must have a distinguished root element to be a valid XML document. Access uses the element name `dataroot`, whereas Oracle uses the element name ROWSET. Both have an element representing a tuple of the table. Access uses the table name as the element name to represent a tuple. In this example, the tuple is given by an `employee` element. Oracle uses the ROW element with a NUM attribute to uniquely identify a tuple. Both use the column names of the table to provide the data of the tuple itself.

6.5.1 Access to Oracle

Access generates the XML data file for a table (and its corresponding `xsd` file) by selecting the XML data format from an export menu. From the `File` menu, choose `Export`, and then select the XML file type. To load the XML document generated by Access into Oracle, code must be written to call the appropriate routines to insert the XML data into a newly defined table.

Oracle provides a `DBMS_XMLSave` package to load data from an XML document into a database table. Figure 6.21 shows the definition of a procedure in Oracle for inserting an XML document given by the first parameter, `xmlDoc` (defined as a Character Large Object (CLOB)), into the table given by the second parameter, `tableName`. The third parameter, `rowTag`, specifies the name of the element tag that encloses each row or tuple of the table. The local variable `insCtx` stores the handle to the new XML context associated with the `tableName`. The method `setRowTag` changes the ROW default tag to the `rowTag` passed in as a parameter. Since XML is case sensitive and database table and attribute names typically are not case sensitive, the `setIgnoreCase` method indicates that the matching of

```
<?xml version="1.0" encoding="UTF-8"?>
<xsd:schema xmlns:xsd="http://www.w3.org/2001/XMLSchema"
    xmlns:od="urn:schemas-microsoft-com:officedata">
<xsd:element name="dataroot">
    <xsd:complexType>
        <xsd:choice maxOccurs="unbounded">
            <xsd:element ref="employee" />
        </xsd:choice>
    </xsd:complexType>
</xsd:element>
<xsd:element name="employee">
    <xsd:annotation>
        <xsd:appinfo>
            <od:index index-name="PrimaryKey" index-key="eID "
                primary="yes" unique="yes" clustered="no" />
            <od:index index-name="eTitle" index-key="eTitle "
                primary="no" unique="no" clustered="no" />
        </xsd:appinfo>
    </xsd:annotation>
    <xsd:complexType>
        <xsd:sequence>
            <xsd:element name="eID" od:jetType="text"
                od:sqlSType="nvarchar" od:nonNullable="yes">
                <xsd:simpleType>
                    <xsd:restriction base="xsd:string">
                        <xsd:maxLength value="3" />
                    </xsd:restriction>
                </xsd:simpleType>
            </xsd:element>
                ...
        </xsd:sequence>
    </xsd:complexType>
</xsd:element>
...
</xsd:schema>
```

Figure 6.18 Access XSD for the `employee` Table

XML elements to database attributes should be case insensitive. The `insertXML` method inserts the XML document (`xmlDoc`) into the table given by the `insCtx` context, returning the number of rows inserted. The method `closeContext` closes the context.

Note that the SQL DDL to define the table given by the `tableName` parameter must be executed before calling the procedure. For the `Employee` example, the procedure call `saveXML(employeeXML, 'Employees', 'employee')` results in inserting the XML document given by the `employeeXML` CLOB variable into the `'Employees'` table, given that the `rowTag` is `'employee'`.

6.5.2   Oracle to Access

The process for exchanging data from Oracle to Access is quite similar to that for exchanging data from Access to Oracle. The XML data must be generated by Oracle in the format expected by Access. The process involves writing code to call the appropriate routines to generate the XML document that corresponds to a table. The insertion of the XML

```
<dataroot>
    <employee>
        <eID>456</eID>
        <eLast>Last456</eLast>
        <eFirst>First456</eFirst>
        <eTitle>Software Engineer</eTitle>
        <eSalary>45456</eSalary>
    </employee>
    <employee>
        <eID>789</eID>
        <eLast>Last789</eLast>
        <eFirst>First789</eFirst>
        <eTitle>Database Administrator</eTitle>
        <eSalary>78789</eSalary>
    </employee>
    ...
    <employee>
        <eID>999</eID>
        <eLast>Last999</eLast>
        <eFirst>First999</eFirst>
        <eTitle>Manager</eTitle>
        <eSalary>100999</eSalary>
    </employee>
</dataroot>
```

Figure 6.19 Access XML Data for the employee Table

```
<ROWSET>
    <ROW NUM="1">
        <eID>456</eID>
        <eLast>Last456</eLast>
        <eFirst>First456</eFirst>
        <eTitle>Software Engineer</eTitle>
        <eSalary>45456</eSalary>
    </ROW>
    <ROW NUM="2">
        <eID>789</eID>
        <eLast>Last789</eLast>
        <eFirst>First789</eFirst>
        <eTitle>Database Administrator</eTitle>
        <eSalary>78789</eSalary>
    </ROW>
    ...
    <ROW NUM="19">
        <eID>999</eID>
        <eLast>Last999</eLast>
        <eFirst>First999</eFirst>
        <eTitle>Manager</eTitle>
        <eSalary>100999</eSalary>
    </ROW>
</ROWSET>
```

Figure 6.20 Oracle XML Data for the employee Table

```
CREATE OR REPLACE PROCEDURE saveXML
   (xmlDoc IN CLOB,
   tableName IN VARCHAR2,
   rowTag IN VARCHAR2) IS

insCtx DBMS_XMLSave.ctxType;
rows NUMBER;

BEGIN
insCtx := DBMS_XMLSave.newContext(tableName);
DBMS_XMLSave.setRowTag(insCtx, rowTag);
DBMS_XMLSave.setIgnoreCase(insCtx, 1);
rows := DBMS_XMLSave.insertXML(insCtx, xmlDoc);
DBMS_XMLSave.closeContext(insCtx);
END;
```

Figure 6.21   Oracle Procedure for Inserting XML Data

data in Access is straightforward. Access supports the import of external XML data from an item on a drop-down menu. From the File menu, choose Get External Data, and then Import the XML document generated by Oracle.

Oracle provides a DBMS_XMLGen package to generate an XML document from the data in a table. Figure 6.22 illustrates a procedure generateXML for generating an XML document for a tableName, using the rowsetTag to enclose the table and the rowTag to enclose each row of the table. The corresponding XML document is written to the given fileName. A context handle ctx is created by using the newContext method, which retrieves all rows of the table. The methods setRowSetTag and setRowTag change the respective tags to the ones passed in as parameters. The getXML method generates the XML document for the context specified, returning the XML document as a CLOB. The call to the printCLOBtoFile procedure prints out the XML document generated to the given fileName.

For the Employee example, assuming that there is an Employees table in Oracle, the procedure call generateXML('Employees', 'dataroot', 'employee', 'employee-Access.xml') results in the creation of an XML document, named employeeAccess.xml,

```
CREATE OR REPLACE PROCEDURE generateXML
   (tableName IN VARCHAR2,
   rowsetTag IN VARCHAR2,
   rowTag IN VARCHAR2,
   fileName IN VARCHAR2) IS
myxml CLOB;
ctx DBMS_XMLGEN.ctxhandle;

BEGIN
ctx := DBMS_XMLGEN.newContext('SELECT * FROM ' || tableName);
DBMS_XMLGEN.setRowsetTag(ctx,rowsetTag);
DBMS_XMLGEN.setRowTag(ctx,rowTag);
myxml := DBMS_XMLGEN.getXML(ctx);
printCLOBtoFile(myXML, fileName);
END;
```

Figure 6.22   Oracle Procedure to Generate XML Data

for the data of the `Employees` table, where the distinguished root is named `dataroot` and each row of the table is represented by an `employee` element. The `employeeAccess.xml` file can then be imported into Access.

6.6   Checkpoint

XML is a universal language for representing data and its underlying semantics. XML is a flexible markup language with user-defined tags to define the meaning of the contextual data. Both DTDs and the more recent XML Schema specification provide a description of valid data in an XML document. XML Schema is more expressive than DTDs, since XML Schema uses namespaces and data types to specify the valid contents of an XML document. XML Schema is more complex and verbose compared with the succinctness of a DTD. XML facilitates the exchange of data between various commercial database products.

Exercises

1. If you have access to a commercial relational database system, explore the XML capabilities of that database product.

2. Based on your exploration of the XML features of a commercial relational database product in Exercise 1, export a table into an XML document. Examine the resulting XML.

3. Based on your exploration of the XML features of a commercial relational database product in Exercise 1, create a small XML document that you can import into a relational table.

6.7   Bibliographic References

There are numerous resources on XML. The W3C's Web site provides a wealth of information and links related to XML (`http://www.w3.org/XML/`). Although HTML was used as a motivation for XML, XML is derived from the Standard Generalized Markup Language (`www.w3.org/MarkUp/SGML/`). There are numerous books available on XML-related information, from quick guides on XML [Castro 2001] to definitive reference books on XML Schema [Walmsley 2002]. The book by Abiteboul et al., [2000] provides an initial look at the relationship between databases and XML. The Web site http://www.rpbourret.com/xml/XMLAndDatabases.htm provides a good overview of XML and databases. The DB2XML tool (`http://www.informatik.fhwiesbaden.de/~turau/DB2XML/index.html`) generates an XML representation of a relational database using a JDBC connection. DB2XML uses a DTD based on the table-based mapping for the representation of data from relational tables in XML. The Dtd2Schema tool (`http://www.syntext.com`) automatically converts a DTD to an XML Schema. The W3C also has a DTD and XSD representation of XML

Schema (`http://www.w3.org/2001/XMLSchema`). Chaudhri et al. [2003] offer a recent collection of papers on the research and practice of XML data management.

The relationship between XML and databases will continue to grow. Future releases of commercial database products promise increasing support for XML and related technology. The W3C is working on XQuery (`http://www.w3.org/XML/Query`), which provides flexible query capabilities over XML documents. The SQL:2003 standard added the SQL/XML specification [Eisenberg and Melton 2002]. The XML-related specification includes the import and storage of XML data in a relational database, the manipulation of XML within the database, and the export of XML.

There is also an Extensible Stylesheet Language (XSL) (`http://www.w3.org/Style /XSL/`) family designed to transform and present XML data, so that the data content and display can be separated. XSL consists of an XSL Transformation (XSLT) language for transforming XML and an XSL Formatting Objects (XSL-FO) language for formatting objects. Although the language initially was designed for the flexible display of XML data to Web pages, XSL is also used by software engineers for the generation of code (e.g., Java code) guided by data expressed in XML format. XSL also provides another mechanism for transforming XML documents to the required format for import into a database product.

The motivational `Employee` example used in this chapter is based on the EMPLOYEE TRAINING ENTERPRISE from Dietrich [2001].

Chapter 7

Object-Oriented Databases and the ODMG Standard

Synopsis

The Object Data Management Group (ODMG) standard for object databases provides a foundation for the discussion of data definition and manipulation in object-oriented databases (which use an object-oriented programming language to provide inherent support for objects) and object-relational databases (which extend the relational model to include support for object technology). After presenting the fundamental concepts of object-oriented databases, this chapter covers the Object Definition Language (ODL) of the ODMG standard, the mapping of the EER and UML conceptual models to ODL, and the ODMG Object Query Language (OQL). Object-relational databases are discussed in Chapter 8 in the context of the object-relational features of the SQL standard.

Assumed Knowledge

- Fundamentals of Object-Oriented Programming Languages

- Enhanced Entity Relationship (EER) Diagrams (Chapter 1)

- Unified Modeling Language (UML) Conceptual Class Diagrams (Chapter 2)

- The SQL Standard: Advanced Relational Features (Chapter 3)

Implementation Examples on Web

- Object-Oriented Implementation of the HOLLYWOOD ENTERPRISE

Case Study

- Object-Oriented Design of the SCHOOL DATABASE ENTERPRISE (Chapter 9)

This chapter begins with a historical view of object-oriented databases and then gives an overview of the fundamental concepts of *Object-Oriented Database Systems (OODBs)*. After establishing the characteristics of OODB technology, the chapter presents the Object Data Management Group (ODMG) standard, developed by the OODB community as a means of establishing a common object interface specification to promote portability among commercial OODB products. The ODMG data model is based on the data model of the Object Management Group standard, which provides object-oriented interface capabilities for interoperability across applications. A database designer uses the Object Definition Language (ODL) of the ODMG standard to specify the object types in the application according to the ODMG object model. After covering the object model and the object definition language, the chapter provides details on mapping the EER and UML object-oriented conceptual data models to ODL. Once the schema is defined in ODL, the Object Query Language (OQL) of the ODMG standard provides a declarative language for querying the database.

7.1   A Historical View of Object-Oriented Databases

For many years, relational database systems (RDBs) were well suited to a wide range of business applications that effectively represented the enterprise of interest using a collection of tables. As interest in database technology began to spread, relational database systems were used for a variety of new applications, including areas such as engineering design, geographic information systems, and telecommunications systems. A common characteristic of these new applications involved the use of large amounts of complex data, a feature that is challenging to represent in the atomic-valued requirement of the relational model.

Although Chapter 4 illustrates how the enterprises represented by the EER and UML object-oriented conceptual data models can be mapped to the relational data model to represent the data and constraints of the underlying application, the discussion in that chapter did not examine whether the approaches to representing objects in a relational data model are efficient. The view of an object in such a model requires the computation of joins over the various tables that may describe the object's properties, including the inherited ones. This join computation may require accessing multiple tables that may not be physically stored near each other on disk. In an OODB, by contrast, the properties of an object are typically clustered together on disk, so that when an object is retrieved, all of its properties are accessible in memory. Another efficiency concern regarding RDBs versus OODBs is based on the navigation of associations. In an RDB, associations are by value, requiring a join on the value given by the association. In an OODB, associations are inherently represented by object references, which are an integral component of the underlying database system. Therefore, navigation through associations between objects may be more efficient in OODBs than simulated navigation using joins in RDBs. Consequently, forcing complex data into the atomic-valued requirement of the relational model may result in inefficient query execution, with numerous join conditions required to reconstruct complex objects.

Furthermore, these new applications often required the representation of nontraditional data forms, such as spatial, multimedia, or voice data. The relational data model, which restricted column types to be atomic values such as strings, integers, real numbers, and

Boolean types, did not provide the type of extensibility needed to fully capture the data semantics of these new application domains. OODBs were developed in response to a need for managing data that did not fit well in the traditional table-oriented view of the relational model.

The development of OODBs in the mid-1980s was also influenced at the time by the growing interest in *Object-Oriented Programming Languages (OOPLs)*. These languages, such as Simula and C++, had emerged on the programming language scene to provide a new approach to software development that emphasized the use of objects, with encapsulation of object structure *and* behavior through the use of abstract data types. With similar interests in modeling complex, persistent data as objects within the database community, the merger of object-based persistent data with OOPLs provided the promise of a new database paradigm for the efficient representation of large, complex data sets, together with the extensibility offered by the programming language capability of user-defined abstract data types. A major advantage of the object-based data–language merger of the OODB paradigm, however, was that it resolved the *impedance mismatch* problem, thus providing *seamless integration* of the database with the programming language. As described in Chapter 3, the impedance mismatch problem refers to the differences that have traditionally existed between the set-oriented, declarative database approach to relational data access and the one-record-at-a-time, imperative programming language approach to data access. These different styles of data access, coupled with differences in data types between relational database systems and application programming languages, cause data translation and conversion problems for data-intensive applications. OODBs do not suffer from the impedance mismatch problem, because the computationally complete programming language *is* the database language. Furthermore, the database and programming language data types are aligned into a consistent view of objects as instances of abstract data types.

In response to the development of OODBs, the relational database community has developed object-relational databases (ORDBs), which extend the relational data model, with support for many of the similar object-oriented concepts described in this chapter. The details of ORDBs are discussed in Chapter 8 in the context of the object-relational features of the SQL standard. These features were first introduced in the SQL:1999 version of the standard. ORDBs blur the distinction between object-oriented and relational databases. In fact, the term *object databases* has been used to refer to either an OODB or an ORDB.

7.2 Fundamental Concepts

The goal of an OODB is to provide seamless integration for the persistence of objects in an OOPL, while supporting the myriad of features expected of a database system. Some of these expected database features include the efficient management of persistent data; transactions, concurrency, and recovery control; and an ad hoc query language. The challenge for an OODB is to provide these database features in the context of the complexities introduced by object orientation.

7.2.1   Object Orientation

An *object* is an abstract concept, generally representing an entity of interest in the enterprise to be modeled by a database application. An object has a *state* and a *behavior*. The state of an object describes the internal structure of the object—that is, the descriptive properties of the object. Viewing a person as an object, the state of the object might contain descriptive information such as an identifier, a name, and an address. The behavior of an object is the set of methods used to create, access, and manipulate the object. A person object, for example, may have methods to create the object, to modify the object's state, and to delete the object. The object may also have methods to relate the object to other objects, such as enrolling a person in a course or assigning a person to the instructor of a course. A method has a *signature* that describes the name of the method and the names and types of the method parameters. An object has an *interface* that describes the state of the object, as well as the signature of its methods. Objects having the same interface are described by a *class*, which essentially defines the type of the object, where each object is viewed as an *instance* of the class. A method is a specific implementation of a method signature.

Given this fundamental definition of an object, the following object-oriented concepts are typically associated with the object-oriented data model:

- complex objects

- object identity

- encapsulation

- extensibility

- class hierarchies and inheritance

- overriding, overloading, and late binding

The ability to define *complex objects* from simpler ones is an important property of object orientation. Complex objects are defined by means of constructors, such as a tuple constructor that combines simple objects to create a high-level form of an object. Using an engineering design example, one can view an airplane as a higher level object that is constructed from lower level objects, such as the airplane's body, wings, tail, and engine. Each of these objects can, in turn, be complex objects constructed from other simple or complex objects. Another example of a constructor is a collection constructor, which defines sets, bags, or lists. Sets are unordered collections of elements without duplication, bags are unordered collections that may contain duplicate elements, and lists are a sequenced or ordered collection of elements. A plane, for example, has two wing objects, which can be represented as a set. If the seats inside of the plane are viewed as objects, then a list can be used to represent the ordered sequence of seats. Complex objects are not part of the pure relational data model. RDBs restrict the value of attributes to simple, atomic values. OODBs provide inherent support for the construction of complex objects.

Objects also have *object identity* through an internally assigned *object identifier* (*oid*). Unlike keys in the relational model, an oid is *immutable*, which means that once an object is created, the oid remains invariant during the lifetime of the object. In contrast, the state of the object is *mutable*, which means that the values of the properties of an object can change. The database system uses the oid for references between objects. Values of properties within the state of the object are not used to uniquely identify the object in the database. Therefore, changing the value of a property of an object does not change the object's identity. This approach is in contrast to that characterizing the relational data model, which uses the values of the attributes that form a candidate key of the table to uniquely identify a tuple in the table. If the values of the attributes that form a candidate key change in the relational data model, then every value-oriented reference to the tuple must be updated.

The term *encapsulation* refers to the ability to create a class as an abstract data type, which has an interface and an implementation. The interface defines the behavior of the abstract data type at a conceptual level. The implementation defines how this abstract behavior is realized with the use of the programming language. Utilizing the concept of encapsulation, the implementation of a class can change without affecting the interface that the class provides to the rest of the application. Encapsulation therefore supports an important software engineering concept of separating class specification from class implementation. OODBs support encapsulation through the specification of user-defined types. Furthermore, in an OODB, user-defined types are orthogonal to persistence. As a result, user-defined types can be used to define transient or persistent data.

The ability of an OODB to support encapsulation also contributes to the *extensibility* of the OODB. With extensibility, there is no distinction between the usage of system-defined types and user-defined types. In other words, users can create new types that correspond to the semantics of the application and then use these new types in the same manner as they use system-defined types. Extensibility is an appealing feature of nontraditional database applications that require the use of types other than the base types provided by the database management system. RDBs originally provided a system-defined table as an unordered collection of tuples of simple types, where operations on tables are theoretically captured by the relational algebra operators and pragmatically realized by SQL. OODBs provide a more flexible approach to extensibility through the use of user-defined types via the OOPL. Since the development of OODBs, relational databases have also been extended with the capability of defining new types. These issues are addressed in the context of object-relational database technology in Chapter 8.

Another capability of object orientation is the power to express *class hierarchies* and the *inheritance* of state and behavior. The earlier chapters on the EER and UML object-oriented conceptual data models discussed the details of how those models support inheritance. Chapter 4 illustrated how the object-oriented conceptual data models can be mapped to a relational schema using tables, views, and constraints to creatively capture the semantics of an object-oriented enterprise. OODBs, however, inherently support class hierarchies and inheritance as an integral component of the data definition language.

Overriding, *overloading*, and *late binding* are additional characteristics of object orientation. In defining the behavior of class hierarchies, a default behavior for a method name can be specified at the superclass level and redefined with a specialized behavior for the subclass. This redefinition is known as *overriding* because the redefinition at the subclass level overrides the default behavior at the superclass level. The term *overloading* refers to a concept that allows a single class or multiple classes to have methods with the same name. The methods are distinguished by the number and types of the parameters.

Overloading is used together with the concept of *late binding*, which means that the translation of an operation name to its appropriate method implementation must be resolved at run time, based on the type of an object. OODBs support overriding, overloading, and late binding in accordance with the semantics of the underlying OOPL.

7.2.2   A Closer Look at Object Identity

Since object identity represents a feature fundamentally different from the concept of keys in the relational model, it is useful to examine object identity in further detail. To illustrate object identity, Figure 7.1 provides a UML diagram of a small UNIVERSITY ENTERPRISE, with classes for Course, Student, Faculty, and Department. The associations among these classes capture information about the courses that students take, the advisor–advisee relationship between students and faculty, and the chair relationship between departments and faculty.

Figure 7.2 illustrates the instances of three Student objects, two Faculty objects, one Department object, and three Course objects over the UNIVERSITY ENTERPRISE.

Course	0..*			1..*	Student	0..*		1..1	Faculty	1..1	0..1	Department
cName	coursesTaken	studentsInCourse			sName	advisees	advisor		fName	chair	chairOf	dName

Figure 7.1   UML Diagram of a UNIVERSITY ENTERPRISE

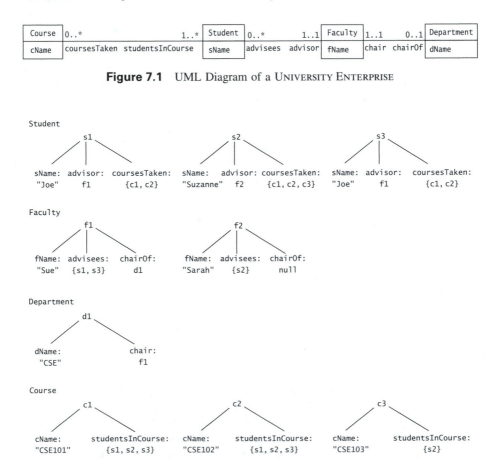

Figure 7.2   Sample Object Instances for the UNIVERSITY ENTERPRISE

Recall that an object is composed of an immutable oid and a mutable object state. The state of an object can be viewed as a tuple of property values, denoted as:

[property1: property1Value, ..., propertyN: propertyNValue]

where [...] is a tuple constructor. In the figure, this (oid, [object state]) pair is represented in graphical form. The root of the graph for each object gives its oid. The edges link an object to the property values of its tuple-oriented state representation, giving the name and value of the property. For example, a Student object has an oid and the properties sName, advisor, and coursesTaken. The values of the properties can be

- literals, such as a string or number;

- object references, given by an oid;

- sets of literals or objects, enclosed in curly braces ({ }), where the braces represent the set constructor; or

- tuples of literals or objects.

In this example, the s1 instance of Student has the name "Joe" and has an advisor given by the f1 object reference to an instance of Faculty. The object s1 has also taken a set of courses, as shown by the set containing oids for the c1 and c2 Course objects. The object references provide a basis for navigation from one object to its related objects.

Although object identity simplifies updating the value of the properties of an object, an added complexity arises in comparing, assigning, or copying objects. In comparing two object references, it is important to distinguish between a comparison based on *identity* and one based on *equality*. Two object references are identical if the references point to the same object. Let S represent a reference to the Student object with oid s1, and let D represent a reference to the Department object with oid d1. Then the advisor of S and the chair of D are identical, since the values of the properties point to the same Faculty object with oid f1.

In determining whether two object references are equal, there are two conceptualizations of equality: *shallow equality* and *deep equality*. Two object references are *shallow equal* if the values of the immediate properties are identical. For example, references to the distinct objects given by s1 and s3 are shallow equal. Note that in the test for shallow equality, literals (i.e., values that do not have object identifiers) are identical *and* equal. Two object references o1 and o2 are *deep equal* under the following conditions:

- If o1 and o2 are literals, then o1 and o2 are deep equal if their values are equal.

- If o1 and o2 are set objects, then o1 and o2 are deep equal if they have the same cardinality and the elements of each set are pairwise deep equal.

- If o1 and o2 are tuple objects, then o1 and o2 are deep equal if their values for each property are deep equal.

The intuition behind deep equality is to define a concept of equality based on the leaves of the objects, where the internal nodes of the objects may not be identical. On the basis of the foregoing definitions of identity and shallow versus deep equality, identical object references must be shallow equal and object references that are shallow equal must be deep equal. Therefore, by transitivity, identical objects must also be deep equal. Two deep equal objects, however, may not be identical.

7.3 The ODMG Standard

Unlike the relational data model, which was introduced theoretically before the implementation of commercial relational database products, the object-oriented data model evolved by adding the capability of persistence to objects in an object-oriented programming language. Several object-oriented database products emerged before the development of the ODMG standard. The standard provides common ground for describing an object model, the specification of a schema over the object model, and a query language. The standard also specifies language bindings for C++, Smalltalk, and Java. Language bindings are libraries of classes and functions that implement the concepts for the definition and manipulation of objects based on the standard in the given OOPL.

The modeling primitives of the ODMG standard are objects and literals. Objects have object identifiers. Literals, by contrast, do not have object identifiers. Objects and literals are characterized by their types, which define their states and behaviors. *State* refers to the values of the properties and *behavior* refers to the defined operations.

The standard also includes two object specification languages. The Object Definition Language (ODL) specifies a database schema over the object types allowed by the underlying object model. The Object Interchange Format (OIF) specifies a language for storing and loading the state of an OODB to and from files for interoperability.

The Object Query Language (OQL) is an ad hoc declarative query language used to retrieve data from an OODB. OQL is similar in structure to SQL, the industry-standard query language for relational databases, having the familiar `select-from-where` syntax. Queries are specified over a schema expressed in the ODL.

The rest of this chapter focuses on the ODMG Object Definition Language, the mapping of object-oriented conceptual data models to a specification in ODL, and the use of the ODMG Object Query Language for expressing queries over an ODL schema of an OODB.

7.4 The ODMG Object Definition Language

The Object Definition Language (ODL) defines an object-oriented schema that is consistent with the underlying principles of the ODMG object model. Figure 7.3 gives an ODL syntax summary for the definition of a class. In the figure, the class `className` has an extent `extentName` and a key `keyName`. The declaration of an extent for a class specifies that the database system automatically maintains a set of all instances of that class. The instances can be referenced by `extentName`. The `keyName` references the set of properties that can uniquely identify instances of the class. A composite key is specified by enclosing the list of properties that form the key in parentheses:

```
key (compositeKeypart1, compositeKeypart2)
```

```
class className
(          extent          extentName
           key             keyName )
{          attribute       attributeType attributeName;
           relationship    relationshipType relationshipName
                           inverse inverseSpecification;
           methodSignatures;
}
```

Figure 7.3 ODL Syntax Summary

Multiple candidate keys in a list are separated by commas:

`keys key1, key2`

A key declaration is optional, but a key can be declared only in the context of an extent declaration.

The state of an object is defined by the value of the object's properties. The term *property* refers to either an *attribute* or a *relationship* of a class. Both attributes and relationships have a name and a type. An attribute describes a characteristic of an object, whereas a relationship represents a binary association between two classes. In Figure 7.3, `className` has an attribute `attributeName` of type `attributeType` and a relationship `relationshipName` of type `relationshipType`. The `relationshipType` is either the type of the class given by the association or a collection of the associated type when the cardinality or multiplicity of the association is greater than one. In the ODMG object model, a collection can be a set, a bag, or a list. Since an OODB system is responsible for automatically maintaining the integrity of a relationship, the declaration of a relationship must include the *inverse* specification for the relationship. The `inverseSpecification` is a scoped name, giving the name of the role of the association as a relationship in the associated class. The behavior of the class is given by the signatures of the methods defined on the class.

Since inheritance is an important feature provided by OODBs, the ODL provides inherent support for the specification of inheritance. There are two forms of inheritance supported by ODL: inheritance of both state and behavior and inheritance of behavior only. A class may inherit both the state and behavior of another class, as specified by the optional `extends` clause:

```
class subclass extends superclass
( ... )
{ properties and behavior specific to the subclass are defined here
}
```

In this example, the `subclass` inherits both the state and behavior of the `superclass`, allowing for the specification of additional properties and behavior for the `subclass`. The ODL also provides support for the inheritance of behavior only. Since an interface describes the abstract behavior of a type, a type can inherit behavior only by using the `":"` symbol, which is similar to the `implements` clause in Java:

```
interface interfaceName
{       methodSignatures; };
class className: interfaceName ( ... ) { ... };
```

Both forms of inheritance can be used in combination to achieve a form of multiple inheritance:

```
class subclassName extends superclassName: interfaceName ( ... ) { ... };
```

Here subclassName inherits the state and behavior of superclassName and inherits the behavior of interfaceName. Detailed examples of ODL are provided throughout the next section, which illustrates how to map object-oriented conceptual models to the ODL.

7.5 Mapping Object-Oriented Conceptual Models to ODL

Chapter 4 presented a detailed approach to mapping the EER and UML object-oriented conceptual models to the relational data model. This section uses the side-by-side illustrations from that chapter to map similar concepts from the EER and UML diagrams into an object-oriented schema expressed in the ODL. The fundamental concepts of mapping classes, attributes, and associations are presented first in the context of the ABSTRACT ENTERPRISE. The mapping of class hierarchies and categories is discussed using the HOLLYWOOD ENTERPRISE as an example.

7.5.1 Classes, Attributes, and Associations

Recall class A of Figure 4.1, which has simple attributes (keyOfA, attrOfA), a composite attribute (compositeOfA), and a derived attribute (derivedAttr). In ODL, class A is mapped to a class having an extent extentOfA, which uniquely identifies instances of the class by using the key keyOfA. The simple attributes keyOfA and attrOfA are declared as type string for simplicity. Since ODL provides inherent support for complex types, the composite attribute of A can be directly represented. A type CompositeStruct consisting of the attributes (attrA1, attrA2, and attrA3) is first defined, and the attribute compositeOfA is declared to be of type CompositeStruct. The derived attribute is defined by means of a get method. The signatures of the methods associated with the behavior of the class for creating new instances, destroying instances, and providing standard access are also part of the class definition. For brevity, the method signatures are not included in the following example:

```
struct CompositeStruct
{       string attrA1;
        string attrA2;
        string attrA3;
};
class A
(       extent extentOfA,
        key keyOfA)
{       attribute string keyOfA;
        attribute string attrOfA;
        attribute CompositeStruct compositeOfA;
        ...
        // provide get method signature for derivedAttr
        // method signatures for behavior
}
```

Class C of Figure 4.2 illustrates a multivalued attribute named `multiValuedAttr`. In the relational data model, a multivalued attribute must be mapped to its own table that includes the key attribute of the class. Since an object-oriented data model supports collections, `multiValuedAttr` can be represented directly as an attribute of C having a collection as its type. Although the `set` collection type is used in this example, the choice of the appropriate collection type (`set`, `bag`, or `list`) is ultimately based on the semantics of the enterprise:

```
class C ( ... )
{            ...
             attribute set<String> multiValuedAttr; };
```

Binary associations without attributes are mapped to a relationship in the ODL. Such a relationship has a name, a type, and an inverse specification. As an example, consider the 1:1 bc association between the classes B and C illustrated in Figure 4.5. In class B, define a relationship named bTOc of type C having as its inverse the relationship named cTOb in class C and specified as C::cTOb. In class C, the relationship cTOb is of type B with inverse B::bTOc:

```
class B (...)
{            ...
             relationship C bTOc inverse C::cTOb; };
class C (...)
{            ...
             relationship B cTOb inverse B::bTOc; };
```

The specification of a relationship requires the definition of its inverse, since the database is responsible for maintaining the integrity of the relationship. For example, if the instance of the bTOc relationship for an object b_i is assigned the object c_j, then the database system automatically updates the instance of the relationship cTOb of c_j to the object b_i.

The cardinality ratio constraints of the association are made inherent in the specification of the object-oriented schema by defining the type of the relationship and its inverse. For the bc association in Figure 4.5, the type of each association is a single object of the appropriate class. One type of constraint that is not defined implicitly in the schema is the total participation of class B in the bc association. The specification of this constraint is straightforward in the relational data model by using the `not null` attribute constraint. In an object-oriented database, such a constraint must be handled as part of the behavior of the object. For example, the constructor method for class B must ensure that the value of the bTOc relationship is not null.

The preceding example illustrated the mapping to ODL for a 1:1 association. A similar template applies to a binary association without attributes having 1:N or M:N cardinality ratios. The only difference is that the type of the *many* side of the association is a collection. The appropriate choice for the type of the collection as `set`, `bag`, or `list` depends on the semantics of the enterprise.

Since the ABSTRACT ENTERPRISE does not have 1:N or M:N binary associations without attributes, the illustration of these cardinality ratios requires the introduction of associations that are not part of the original enterprise. Consider, for example, a fictitious

M:N association between the classes B and C. The binary association is mapped to a
relationship in ODL, where an instance of B is related to potentially many instances of C
and an instance of C is related to potentially many instances of B:

```
class B (...)
{       ...
        relationship set<C> bTOMANYc inverse C::cTOMANYb; };
class C (...)
{       ...
        relationship set<B> cTOMANYb inverse B::bTOMANYc; };
```

As another example, consider a fictitious 1:N association between B and C, where an
instance of B is related to potentially many instances of C, but an instance of C is related
to at most one instance of B:

```
class B (...)
{       ...
        relationship set<C> bTOMANYc inverse C::cTOONEb; };
class C (...)
{       ...
        relationship B cTOONEb inverse B::bTOMANYc; };
```

When binary associations have attributes, an association class must be introduced
to represent the attributes of the association. The association class also includes two
relationships: one for each class participating in the binary association. Consider the M:N
ab association between classes A and B that has a descriptive attribute `attrOfAB`, as
shown in Figure 4.3. Figure 7.4 gives the UML diagram for the corresponding reified
association. An association class is defined as the class named AB having the attribute
`attrOfAB` and two relationships: `abTOa` and `abTOb`. The relationship `abTOa` is of type
A, indicating the instance of class A that is participating in the relationship instance.
Similarly, the relationship `abTOb` is of type B, indicating the instance of class B that
is participating in the relationship instance. The definitions for the classes involved in
the association include relationships to the new association class. Class A contains the
relationship `aTOab` having as its type a set of AB objects, since an object of type A is
related to potentially many Bs through the AB association class. Similarly, class B contains
the relationship `bTOab` having as its type a set of AB objects, since an object of type B is
related to potentially many As through the AB association class.

```
class AB
(       extent extentOfAB)
{       attribute string attrOfAB;
        relationship A abTOa inverse A::aTOab;
        relationship B abTOb inverse B::bTOab;
};
class A (...)
{       ...
        relationship set<AB> aTOab inverse AB::abTOa; };

class B (...)
{       ...
        relationship set<AB> bTOab inverse AB::abTOb; };
```

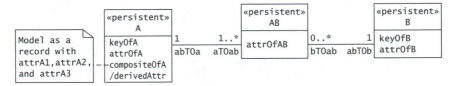

Figure 7.4 Reified M:N Association for the ABSTRACT ENTERPRISE

The mapping of recursive associations is similar to the mapping of nonrecursive associations, except that the recursive association relates the same class to itself. In Figure 4.7, the class B has a recursive association bb. One straightforward approach to mapping a recursive association is to use the role names of the association as the names of the relationships in ODL. For example, the `parent` role of the bb association is of type B having the `child` role as its inverse relationship. The `child` role is a collection type, representing the children of the parent. Again, by defining a relationship, the database system is responsible for automatically maintaining the integrity of the relationship. For example, when the `parent` relationship instance is assigned a value, the database system automatically adds the associated object to the `child` relationship:

```
class B
(       extent extentOfB
        key keyOfB)
{
        ...
        relationship B parent inverse B::child;
        relationship set<B> child inverse B::parent;
};
```

The mapping of N-ary associations is similar to the mapping of binary associations having descriptive attributes. An association class is defined to represent the N-ary association, and there are N relationships defined, one for each class involved in the association. Consider, for example, the ternary relationship given in Figure 4.8. In this relationship, Finance is the association class, with relationships `financedBank`, `financedCar`, and `financedPerson` that respectively refer to the Bank, Car, and Person involved in the transaction. In the inverse direction, Bank, Car, and Person define relationships that point back to Finance. The cardinality of each inverse relationship indicates the number of times an object of the class can participate in a Finance association. The relationships in Bank and Person, for example, are set valued, indicating that a bank can finance many cars and a person can buy many cars. The relationship in Car is single valued, indicating that a car can be sold only once:

```
class Finance
(       extent extentOfFinance)
{       attribute real loanAmount;
        relationship Bank financedBank inverse Bank::carsFinanced;
        relationship Car financedCar inverse Car::financedBy;
        relationship Person financedPerson
            inverse Person::carsFinanced;
};
class Bank (...)
{
        ...
        relationship set<Finance> carsFinanced
```

```
                 inverse Finance::financedBank; };
class Car (...)
{        ...
         relationship Finance financedBy
             inverse Finance::financedCar; };

class Person (...)
{        ...
         relationship set<Finance> carsFinanced
             inverse Finance::financedPerson; };
```

The UML conceptual class diagrams have the ability to represent unidirectional associations through navigability. Unidirectional associations store the association in one direction. Since a relationship in ODL requires an inverse specification, relationships are inherently bidirectional. Unidirectional associations are defined in ODL through the use of an attribute whose value is a class type. For example, the unidirectional association bc shown in Figure 4.10 is defined as an attribute in class B having the type C. It is possible to derive the inverse direction of the unidirectional association by providing a method in C to derive the B values to which it is related:

```
class B ( ...)
{        ...
         attribute C bc;
};
```

A weak class in an EER diagram is typically related to its identifying owner by a 1:N relationship. In Figure 4.11, the Weak class is related to its identifying owner class A by its identifying relationship dependsOn. The candidate key of a weak class is formed by the combination of the primary key of its identifying owner and its own partial key, which uniquely identifies the weak object in the context of the identifying owner. In the UML diagram of Figure 4.11, dependsOn represents a qualified association based on the partialKey. One way to map this type of an association is to define a relationship that links the weak class to its identifying owner:

```
class A
(        extent extentOfA
         key keyOfA)
{        attribute string keyOfA;
         relationship set<Weak> linkToWeak inverse Weak::linkToOwner;
         ...
};
class Weak
(        extent extentOfWeak
         key (keyOfA, partialKey))
{        attribute string partialKey;
         attribute string keyOfA;
         relationship A linkToOwner inverse A::linkToWeak;
         ...
};
```

The relationship linkToWeak defined in class A represents the collection of Weak objects associated with an instance of class A. The inverse relationship defined as link-ToOwner in the Weak class links the Weak instance to its identifying owner instance, which is of type A having the attribute keyOfA as its candidate key. One may also choose to maintain the extent of the Weak class, which requires storing the value of the key of the identifying owner (keyOfA) to use in combination with the partialKey.

Constraints on Classes, Attributes, and Associations

In mapping the object-oriented conceptual data models to the relational data model, there are a number of constraints that need to be captured at the implementation level. For the relational data model, these constraints for classes, attributes, and associations include the specification of candidate keys, referential integrity, participation, and multiplicity constraints.

The mapping to the relational model uses the primary key and uniqueness constraints in SQL's data definition language to specify candidate keys. In ODL, a key clause is used to specify the uniqueness of candidate keys. The referential integrity constraint in the relational data model uses the specification of foreign keys to make sure that the value of a nonnull attribute refers to the value of a primary key in its referencing table. Referential integrity is inherent in the ODL by the specification of the type of a property. The type specification in ODL also inherently supports simple cardinality constraints. For example, the type of a property is a class type when the property is related to one object of that type or a collection of a class type when the property is related to more than one object of that type.

For more complicated participation and multiplicity constraints, the constraints must be implemented as part of the behavior of the object. A total participation constraint requires that the behavior for constructing an object and modifying the property verify that the value of the property is not null. This verification is written in the underlying OOPL for the OODB, rather than as a separate constraint specification language as in the relational model. Similarly, verifying specific multiplicity constraints (other than the simple 1:1 or 1:N cardinality constraints that are inherent in the specification of relationships) requires the constraint to be checked in the behavior of the object.

7.5.2 Checkpoint: ODL Mapping of Classes, Attributes, and Associations

Table 7.1 summarizes the mapping of classes, attributes, and associations to ODL, using the names C, C1, and C2 to represent generic classes. In the table, the first column indicates the component being mapped to the object model. The third column, named **ODL Definition**, gives the ODL that is added to the definition of the class, which is indicated in the second column, to realize the component in the object model. As indicated in the table, ODL inherently supports the specification of class, attributes, and associations. The specification of class hierarchies in ODL is described in the next section.

Exercises

1. Map the ECLECTIC ONLINE SHOPPING ENTERPRISE in Figure 1.1 to an ODL schema. For each constraint associated with the schema, discuss whether the constraint is inherent in the ODL schema specification or whether it must be captured in the behavior of the objects.

TABLE 7.1 Summary of ODL Mapping Heuristics for Classes, Attributes, and Associations

Component	Class	ODL Definition
class C	C	`class C (extent extentOfC)`
single-valued or composite attribute s of C	C	`attribute typeOfS s;`
multivalued attribute m of C	C	`attribute set<typeOfElementInM> m;`
binary association: no	C1	`relationship C2 c1TOc2 inverse C2::c2TOc1;`
attributes (1:1 shown)	C2	`relationship C1 c2TOc1 inverse C1::c1TOc2;`
binary association ac	C1	`relationship set<AC> c1TOac inverse AC::acTOc1;`
with attributes	C2	`relationship set<AC> c2TOac inverse AC::acTOc2;`
(e.g., attrOfAC):	AC	`attribute typeOfAttrOfAC attrOfAC;`
Use an association class		`relationship C1 acTOc1 inverse C1::c1TOac;`
(M:N shown)		`relationship C2 acTOc2 inverse C2::c2TOac;`
recursive association cc	C	`relationship C parent inverse C::child;`
(1:N shown)		`relationship set<C> child inverse C::parent;`

2. Generate an ODL schema for the GET FIT HEALTH CLUB ENTERPRISE, which is described in Exercise 2 in Checkpoint 1.1.3. Compare the ODL schema with the relational schema. Identify advantages and disadvantages of the ODL schema versus the relational schema.

3. Map the MEDICAL PRACTICE ENTERPRISE to an ODL schema as described in Exercise 3 in Checkpoint 1.1.3. Verify that all of the constraints of the enterprise are captured in the resulting ODL schema, and compare the ODL schema with the corresponding relational schema.

4. Generate an ODL schema for the MUSIC AGENCY ENTERPRISE described in Exercise 4 in Checkpoint 1.1.3. Verify that all of the constraints of the enterprise are captured in the resulting ODL schema, and compare the ODL schema with the corresponding relational schema.

7.5.3 Class Hierarchies

Object-oriented schemas provide inherent support for the specification of class hierarchies. In ODL, the inheritance of state and behavior is supported by the extends clause. Consider, for example, the Person class hierarchy from the Hollywood Enterprise, which represented a partial specialization of Person into its disjoint subclasses MovieProfessional and Celebrity:

```
class Person
( ... ) { ... };

class MovieProfessional extends Person
( ... )
{ // Specific properties and methods for MovieProfessional
... };

class Celebrity extends Person
( ... )
{ // Specific properties and methods for Celebrity
... };
```

The EER and UML conceptual data models both provide support for the specification of specialization constraints: disjoint versus overlapping specialization and total or mandatory participation in the class specialization. An OODB uses its underlying OOPL as the basis of its semantics for specialization constraints. Most OOPLs do not provide for an overlapping specialization of subclasses. Therefore, by default, a specialization in an OODB is disjoint. If an overlapping specialization is required for the application, then the programmer can be creative in simulating the inheritance by using an explicit reference to the superclass and calling its methods. The total specialization constraint is also based on the semantics of the underlying OOPL. For a total specialization, the superclass can be specified as an abstract class if permitted by the programming language. Otherwise, the total specialization constraint must be built into the behavior of the objects.

For the mapping of shared subclasses, most OOPLs do not directly support multiple inheritance of both state and behavior. ODL does not support the specification of shared subclasses. Multiple inheritance can be simulated in a class definition by using the extends clause to inherit state and behavior from one class and by using the interface feature to inherit only behavior from another class. This is a common programming practice in OOPLs.

As an example, recall the Business interface of Figure 2.27 and its corresponding ODL specification as follows:

```
interface Business
{ ...
        string getTaxPayerId(...);
        void setTaxPayerId(...);
        integer calcTotalIncome(...);
};
class Person
( ... ) { ... };

class Company: Business
```

```
( ... ) { ... };

class SelfEmployedPerson extends Person: Business
( ... ) { ... };
```

In this example, the `Business` interface describes the behavior of a business with method signatures to get and set the `TaxPayerId` property and to calculate total income. The example also defines a `Person` and a `Company`, where a `Company` implements the `Business` interface. A `SelfEmployedPerson` class is defined to inherit the state and behavior of `Person`, using the `extends` clause, and to inherit the behavior of `Business`, thus allowing the `SelfEmployedPerson` to provide an implementation of the `Business` interface.

7.5.4 Categories

A category in the EER or the xor constraint in UML can be represented by introducing a class for the category. Properties are introduced in the category class to represent the association to its related superclasses. For example, consider the partial `Sponsor` category from the HOLLYWOOD ENTERPRISE, where a `Sponsor` is either a `Person` or a `Company`. A unidirectional association, modeled as an attribute in ODL, is added to the category class for each class participating in the category. The `Sponsor` class has two attributes: `personSponsor` and `companySponsor`. Only one of the unidirectional attributes can have a value, indicating the type of the `Sponsor` category as either a `Person` or a `Company`. The other unidirectional attribute must always be null, since a `Sponsor` cannot be both a `Person` and a `Company`. This category constraint must be implemented within the behavior of the (`Sponsor`) category class:

```
class Person
(          extent Persons
           key ...)
{          ...};
class Company
(          extent Companies
           key ...)
{ ... };
class Sponsor
(          extent Sponsors)
{          attribute Person personSponsor;
           attribute Company companySponsor;
           ...
};
```

When the category is partial, the unidirectional association is preferable. It is still possible to find out whether a person or company is a sponsor and to find out the projects that the person or company sponsors by navigating the unidirectional associations from the `Sponsor` class. If the category is total, requiring that each superclass participate in the category, then the category associations can be implemented via bidirectional relationships. The relationship provides an explicit access path to the category class. The behavior of the superclasses must enforce the total categorization constraint by verifying that the relationship value to the category class is not null. Again, the category class must enforce the exclusive-or constraint of the category.

7.5.5 Checkpoint: Mapping to ODL

An object-oriented database schema provides inherent support for most of the constraints specified in the object-oriented conceptual data models. The constraints that are not captured in ODL must be implemented as part of the behavior of the object. Figure 7.5 gives the ODL mapping of the HOLLYWOOD ENTERPRISE. Figure 7.6 provides the UML diagram that corresponds to the ODL specification of Figure 7.5. Since ODL does not inherently support overlapping subclasses, the specialization of Celebrity into the MovieStar and Model subclasses is now disjoint. The Paid association class of Figure 7.6 is represented as a reified association, which corresponds to its ODL specification. Since the Sponsor category is not total, the associations relating a Sponsor to its corresponding superclass are unidirectional.

Exercises

1. Generate an ODL schema for the ECLECTIC ONLINE SHOPPING ENTERPRISE that was revised in Exercise 1 in Checkpoint 1.2.5 to use class hierarchies. Compare the resulting ODL schema with the ODL schema generated in Exercise 1 in Checkpoint 7.5.2 which mapped the ER of the ECLECTIC ONLINE SHOPPING ENTERPRISE that did not use class hierarchies.

2. Map the FICTITIOUS BANK ENTERPRISE, which is described in Exercise 2 in Checkpoint 1.2.5 to an ODL schema. Are all of the constraints of the enterprise captured in the resulting ODL schema? Compare the ODL schema with the corresponding relational schema from Exercise 2 in Checkpoint 4.7.

3. Generate an ODL schema for the HORSE RACING ENTERPRISE as described in Exercise 1 in Checkpoint 1.4. Verify that all of the constraints of the enterprise are captured in the resulting schema, and compare the ODL schema with the corresponding relational schema from Exercise 3 of Checkpoint 4.7.

7.6 The ODMG Object Query Language

The Object Query Language (OQL) of the ODMG standard is based on the SQL industry-standard query language for relational databases. In SQL, the basic select-from-where clause selects a list of attributes from the specified tables where a condition holds. The from clause specifies the tables that are relevant to answering the query, allowing for table aliases or variables to range over tuples of a table. The where clause describes the conditions that must hold on the data in the tables to be selected as a result of the query. The select clause gives a list of attributes from the relevant tables that are to appear in the query result.

OQL also has the familiar format of the select-from-where clause. Since OQL is based on an object model, the from clause specifies the collections of objects that are relevant to answering the query and uses variables to range over the relevant object collections. Recall that the ODL provides for the definition of an extent and that the name of an extent denotes a collection of objects of the same type. Variables in the from clause

```
class Person
(    extent people
     key pId)
{
  attribute string pId;
  attribute string name;
  attribute string gender;
  attribute string phone;
  attribute string address;
  attribute string isMarriedTo;
...};

class MovieProfessional extends Person
(    extent movieProfessionals)
{
  attribute string company;
...};

class Celebrity extends Person
(    extent celebrities)
{
  attribute date birthDate;
  relationship Agent celebrityAgent
                inverse Agent::agentFor;
...};

class MovieStar extends Celebrity
(    extent movieStarts)
{
  attribute string movieType;
  relationship set<FilmProject> actsIn
                inverse FilmProject::actors;
...};

class Model extends Celebrity
(    extent models)
{
  attribute string preferences;
  relationship set<Paid> modelsInProjects
                inverse Paid::modelOfProject;
...};

class Critic extends MovieProfessional
(    extent critics)
{
  attribute string popularity
...};

class Agent extends MovieProfessional
(    extent agents)
{
  attribute float agentFee;
  relationship set<Celebrity> agentFor
    inverse Celebrity::celebrityAgent;
...};
```

Figure 7.5 ODL Schema for the HOLLYWOOD ENTERPRISE

```
class Project
(     extent projects
      key projectID)
{
  attribute string projectID;
  attribute string location;
  attribute float  cost;
  attribute string type;
...};

class FilmProject extends Project
(     extent filmProjects)
{
  attribute string title;
  relationship set <MovieStar> actors
              inverse MovieStar::actsIn;
...};

class ModelingProject extends Project
(     extent modelingProjects)
{
  attribute string description;
  relationship set<Paid> paidModels
              inverse Paid::paidByProject;
  relationship Sponsor sponsoredBy
              inverse Sponsor::projectsSponsored;
...};

class Paid
(     extent paidModelsInProjects)
{
  attribute float salary;
  relationship Model modelOfProject
              inverse Model::modelsInProjects;
  relationship ModelingProject paidByProject
              inverse ModelingProject::paidModels;
...};

class Company
(     extent companies
      key cId)
{
  attribute string cId;
  attribute string cName;
...};

class Sponsor
(     extent sponsors)
{
  attribute Person personSponsor;
  attribute Company companySponsor;
  relationship set<ModelingProject> projectsSponsored
              inverse ModelingProject::sponsoredBy;
...};
```

Figure 7.5 (*continued*)

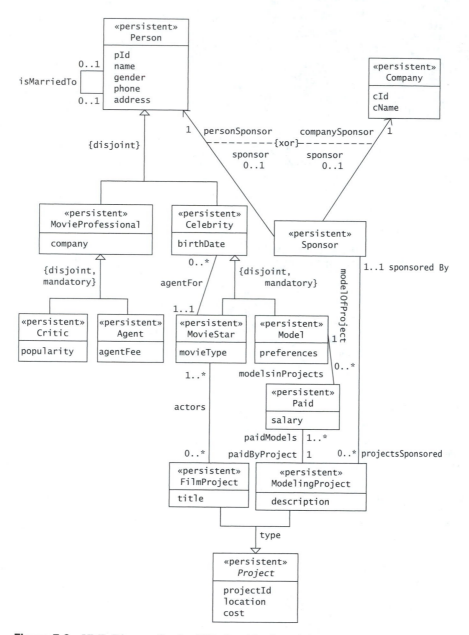

Figure 7.6 UML Diagram for the ODL Specification of the HOLLYWOOD ENTERPRISE

typically range over extents or the multivalued properties of an object. The `where` clause similarly describes the properties that must hold for the data to be in the result of the query. The `select` clause in OQL also defines the structure of the result of the query, but OQL's `select` clause is more expressive than its relational counterpart, which will be illustrated through examples later in the chapter.

To summarize, an OQL query has the following format:

```
select   defines the data to be returned and its structure
from     specifies collections relevant to answering the query and
         identifiers to iterate over those collections
where    specifies conditions for selecting objects;
```

Consider a simple query over the HOLLYWOOD ENTERPRISE schema given in Figure 7.5 that finds the titles of the movies filmed in "Phoenix":

```
select   f.title
from     f in filmProjects
where    f.location = "Phoenix";
```

The properties of an object are accessed by using the familiar dot notation from object-oriented programming languages. In the `from` clause, the variable identifier f ranges over the objects in the `filmProjects` extent. The `where` clause finds the `filmProject` objects whose location is `"Phoenix"`. The `select` clause returns the title of the selected film projects. Note that the `from` clause could have used the SQL-like syntax wherein the identifier appears after the expression over which the variable ranges (e.g., `filmProjects f`). The exposition in this book follows the syntactical convention of `identifier in expression`.

7.6.1 Path Expressions

Path expressions allow navigation from one object to another. OQL uses either the dot (.) notation or the arrow ($\rightarrow$) notation to indicate a path expression. For example, assume that the variable C is defined over the `Celebrity` class. Then the following path expressions return the name of the agent's spouse for the celebrity given by C:

- C.celebrityAgent.isMarriedTo.name

- C$\rightarrow$celebrityAgent$\rightarrow$isMarriedTo$\rightarrow$name

The property `celebrityAgent` denotes the `Agent` of the celebrity. Since an `Agent` is a `Person`, the `isMarriedTo` property denotes the `Person` married to the agent. The `name` property gives the name of the spouse. Rather than employ multiple notations, this book follows the convention of using dot notation for path expressions.

In the preceding example, the properties in the path expressions were single-valued attributes. OQL does not allow path expressions to traverse over multivalued attributes and relationships. The query must be expressed so that all variables over multivalued properties are explicitly defined in the `from` clause.

As an example, consider a query to retrieve the names of movie stars that appear in film projects located in "Phoenix":

```
select   a.name
from     f in filmProjects,
         a in f.actors
where    f.location = "Phoenix";
```

The variable identifier a is introduced in the `from` clause to range over the `actors` multivalued property of a `filmProject` that is located in "Phoenix". The `actors` property is a set of `MovieStar` objects that act in the film project. Since a `MovieStar` is a `Person`, the `select` clause returns the `name` of the actor.

7.6.2 OQL Expressions and Query Results

In the examples of OQL presented so far, the `select` clause looks quite similar to that of SQL. Query results in SQL are a collection of tuples or structures that are formed by listing the desired attributes. If the keyword `distinct` is used, the collection is a *set* of tuples. Otherwise, the collection is a *multiset* or *bag* of tuples, allowing duplicate elements. However, the results of query expressions in OQL are more expressive than those in SQL.

Expressions in OQL yield atoms, structures, collections, and literals as results. The type of a result can be inferred from the query expression. The result type of the previous example that retrieves the names of movie stars appearing in film projects located in "Phoenix" is *bag < String >*.

The select clause in OQL can return a collection of structured results. Consider the query that retrieves the name of the actor and the actor's agent for each actor in the film project named "Days of Thunder:"

```
select  struct( movieStarName: a.name,
                agentName: a.celebrityAgent.name)
from    f in filmProjects, a in f.actors
where   f.title = "Days of Thunder";
```

For each field of the structure, the label is specified along with the source of the field. In this case, the label for the name of the movie star is `movieStarName`, and the label for the name of the actor's agent is `agentName`. The result type of the query is *bag < struct(movieStarName : String, agentName : String) >*.

Consider another query that returns a collection of `Sponsor` objects along with the set of the sponsored modeling projects:

```
select  struct( sponsorObject: s, projectsOf: s.projectsSponsored )
from    s in sponsors;
```

The result type of the query is *bag < struct(sponsorObject : Sponsor, projectsOf : set < ModelingProject >) >*.

Queries do not always have to use the `select-from-where` clause. A database extent (e.g., `filmProjects`) is a valid OQL query expression. Other examples of valid OQL queries that do not use the `select-from-where` syntax include path expressions involving a named persistent object as a database entry point.

Define Statement

The `define` statement gives a persistent name to a query expression. The define statement is similar to a view in SQL. For example, the object `phxFilms` is defined as the collection of film projects located in "Phoenix":

```
define  phxFilms as
select  f
from    f in filmProjects
where   f.location = "Phoenix";
```

This query is similar to the query that returned the titles of the film projects located in "Phoenix," but, instead, returns the corresponding `FilmProject` objects. The type of phxFilms is *bag < FilmProject >*.

The `define` statement can also be used to identify a named persistent object. In the next example, the name `daysOfThunder` is defined as the film project whose title is "Days of Thunder".

```
define  daysOfThunder as
element (select    f
        from       f in filmProjects
        where      f.title = "Days of Thunder");
```

The subquery returns a bag of `FilmProject` objects. The `element` operator returns a singleton of type `FilmProject`. Note that an error results if there is more than one object in the operand to the `element` operator. In this case, an error occurs if there is more than one film project having the name "Days of Thunder".

Defined expressions can then be used to return other values. For example, `daysOf-Thunder.cost` is a valid OQL query expression.

Methods in Queries

OQL allows methods to be used in queries in the same way that attributes are used. As an example, assume that the `Celebrity` class has an `age` method that calculates the age of a celebrity by using his or her birth date. The following query finds the names of celebrities under the age of 30:

```
select  c.name
from    c in celebrities
where   c.age < 30;
```

The query result type is *bag < String >*.

Embedded Queries

OQL is a well-typed language. Queries can be embedded in the `select` and `from` clauses, provided that the type system is respected. Following is an example that embeds a query in the `from` clause, where the variable phx iterates over the embedded query that returns the `FilmProject` objects located in "Phoenix":

```
select  struct(title: phx.title, cost: phx.cost )
from    phx in (select f
                from f in filmProjects
                where f.location = "Phoenix")
where   phx.cost > 10,000,000;
```

This query retrieves the title and the cost of film projects located in "Phoenix" that cost more than $10 million. The query result type is *bag < struct(title : String, cost : Float) >*.

Queries can also be embedded in the `select` clause. Here is a query that returns the title of each film and the set of movie stars acting in that film:

```
select  struct(filmTitle: f.title,
               filmActors: (select distinct a
                            from a in f.actors))
from    f in filmProjects;
```

The query result type is *bag < struct(filmTitle : String, filmActors : set < MovieStar >) >*.

7.6.3   Set Membership and Quantification

OQL also supports queries involving set membership, as well as existential and universal quantification. The type of these queries is a Boolean value: TRUE or FALSE.

Queries testing membership in a set use the syntax

```
e in c
```

which returns TRUE if the element e is in the collection c. As an example, the following query determines whether daysOfThunder is in phxFilms:

```
daysOfThunder in phxFilms;
```

The syntax for existential quantification is

```
exists i in c: exp
```

which returns TRUE if at least one element of the collection c satisfies the exp expression, where the variable i iterates over elements in the collection. For example, the following query determines whether there any film projects located in "Phoenix":

```
exists f in filmProjects: f.location = "Phoenix";
```

Another example of a query involving existential quantification that identifies those models which have at least one modeling project located in "Phoenix" is

```
select   modelName: m.name
from     m in models
where    exists p in m.modelsInProjects:
         p.paidByProject.location = "Phoenix";
```

The query returns the name of a model if there exists a modeling project for that model which is located in "Phoenix".

The syntax for universal quantification is

```
for all i in c: exp
```

which returns TRUE if all elements in the collection c satisfy the exp expression. For example, the following query tests whether all film projects cost more than $10 million:

```
for all f in filmProjects: f.cost > 10,000,000;
```

The following query lists all of the movie stars whose film projects cost more than $20,000,000, illustrating the use of the universal quantifier in the where clause of a query:

```
select   m.name
from     m in movieStars
where    for all fp in m.actsIn: fp.cost > 20,000,000;
```

The following more complex example uses both existential and universal quantification to find the names of companies where all modeling projects of the company include at least one male model:

```
select   s.companySponsor.cName
from     s in sponsors
where    s.companySponsor <> null and
         for all mp in s.projectsSponsored:
         (exists p in mp.paidModels: p.modelOfProject.gender = "M");
```

7.6.4   Ordering

OQL provides the familiar `order` by clause, with the keywords `asc` and `desc` used to specify ascending and descending order, respectively. The following query provides a list, in descending order, of the costs of film projects located in "Phoenix", along with the title of the film:

```
select     struct(phxTitle: fp.title, phxCost: fp.cost)
from       fp in filmProjects
where      fp.location = "Phoenix"
order by   fp.cost desc;
```

When ordering is used, the collection is considered a list, which is a sequenced collection. The result type of the sample query is *list* < *struct(phxTitle* : *String, phxCost* : *Float)* >.

The `order` by clause can also be used in embedded queries to generate a list. The following query provides an alphabetical order of movie stars for each film project filmed in "Phoenix":

```
select     struct(phxTitle: fp.title,
                   phxMovieStars: (select   ms.name
                                   from      ms in fp.actors
                                   order by ms.name)
from       fp in filmProjects
where      fp.location = "Phoenix"
order by   fp.title asc;
```

The query result type is *list* < *struct(phxTitle* : *String, phxMovieStars* : *list* < *String* >) >.

7.6.5   Using Collections

Collections are an important feature of OODBs. OQL provides explicit operators for extracting elements from a collection and for manipulating collections. Earlier in the chapter, when the persistent named object `daysOfThunder` was defined, the `element` operator illustrated the extraction of an element from a collection that consisted of a singleton. A singleton collection is common when the query is selecting an object on the basis of the value of the key. Note that an error results if there is more than one object in the operand of the `element` operator.

OQL also provides explicit notation for extracting the `first`, `last`, and indexed elements from an indexed collection, such as a list. For example, by ordering a collection of model name and salary pairs for modeling projects located in Phoenix in ascending order on salary, the `last` operator returns the model and salary for the highest-paid model. This query assumes that there is only one model having the highest salary:

```
last ( select    struct(modelName: m.name, modelSalary: p.salary)
       from      m in models, p in m.modelsInProjects
       where     p.paidByProject.located = "Phoenix"
       order by  modelSalary asc);
```

By reordering the query in descending order on salary, an indexed expression returns the top 10 paid models for a Phoenix modeling project. Note that the index of the first element is 0, so the indexed expression [0:9] returns the first 10 elements:

```
(select   struct(modelName: m.name, modelSalary: p.salary)
 from     m in models, p in m.modelsInProjects
 where    p.paidByProject.location = "Phoenix"
 order by modelSalary desc) [0:9];
```

The result type of the query is *list* < *struct*(*modelName* : *String, modelSalary* : *Float*) >.

7.6.6 Aggregation and Grouping

OQL provides aggregate operators (`min`, `max`, `count`, `sum`, `avg`) over a collection of the appropriate type. The operators `min`, `max`, `sum`, and `avg` must have an operand collection of numerical elements, where `count` counts the number of elements of any type in the operand collection. As an example of using `count`, find the number of film projects in which a movie star has acted:

```
select    struct ( name: m.name,
                    filmCount: count(m.actsIn))
from      m in movieStars
order by  name asc;
```

The property `actsIn` for a `MovieStar` is a collection—in this case a set—of `FilmProject` objects in which the movie star has acted.

The following query finds the total salary of a model for all of the modeling projects in which he or she models:

```
select    struct ( name: m.name,
                    salaryTotal: sum(select p.salary
                                     from p in m.modelsInProjects))
from      m in models
order by  name asc;
```

Since OQL is well typed, the use of aggregation over a collection is more intuitive than aggregation in SQL, which requires understanding the implicit operation of the aggregation in conjunction with the `group by` clause. SQL also requires that any non-aggregate attribute in the `select` clause appear in the `group by` clause. The `group by` clause in OQL, although similar to the corresponding clause in SQL, provides an explicit reference to the collection of objects within each group or partition.

The result type of a grouping specification is always of the type

set < *struct*(`groupingFields`, `partition` : *bag* < *struct*(`fromIterators`) >) >

where

- `groupingFields` consists of the fields and their types in the `group by` clause,

- `partition` is a distinguished field representing the result of the grouping, and

- `fromIterators` consists of the variables and their types used in the `from` clause to iterate over collections.

The following query returns a count and a set of the models that an agent represents by grouping the models on the basis of the names of the agent:

```
select    struct(agentName: m.celebrityAgent.name,
                 modelCount: count(partition),
                 modelNames: (select p.m.name from p in partition))
from      m in models
group by  agentName: m.celebrityAgent.name;
```

The result type of the grouping specification is

$set < struct(agentName : String, partition : bag < struct(m : Model) >) >$

For each group given by the agentName, there is a distinguished field called partition that gives the values of the iterator variables appearing in the from clause using a structure. To find the number of models that the agent represents, the aggregate operator count counts the number of models in the partition. To retrieve the names of the models from the group, the select clause uses an embedded query to iterate over the elements in the partition. Since the partition always returns a structure consisting of the variables in the from clause, dot notation (p.m.name) is used to access a field from within the group. The result type of a group by query is always a set, since there is exactly one partition for each value of the grouping fields. The result type of the sample query is

$set < struct(agentName : String, modelCount : Integer,$
$modelNames : bag < String >) >$

Just as in SQL, a having clause filters the partitioned sets. To return only the agents that represent more than three models, append the following having clause to the previous query specification:

```
having count(partition) > 3
```

7.6.7 Checkpoint: OQL

Although OQL looks similar to the SQL industry standard, it is important to think out of the relational box when answering queries in OQL. Consider the query to retrieve the name and preferences of models who work on modeling projects located in "Phoenix". As in SQL, there are several ways to correctly answer this query in OQL. One solution is to start from the models extent and determine whether the model models in projects that are located in "Phoenix":

```
select   struct(modelName: m.name,
                modelPreferences: m.preferences)
from     m in models, p in m.modelsInProjects
where    p.paidByProject.location = "Phoenix";
```

Another solution is to start from modeling projects that are located in "Phoenix" and find the corresponding models:

```
select   struct(modelName: p.modelOfProject.name,
                modelPreferences: p.modelOfProject.preferences)
from     mp in modelingProjects, p in mp.paidModels
where    mp.location = "Phoenix";
```

Both of these solutions represent an object-oriented approach that navigates through the associations between objects.

Exercises

1. Answer the following queries in OQL over the HOLLYWOOD ENTERPRISE ODL schema given in Figure 7.5. The expected return type of the query is specified following the query statement:

   (a) Find the names of movie stars who are married to models.

       bag < String >

   (b) Find the movie stars who have appeared in more than two films located in "Phoenix".

       bag < MovieStar >

   (c) Find the description of modeling projects sponsored by each sponsor.

       set < struct(sponsorName : String, sponsoredProjects : bag < String >) >

   (d) Which models have modeled in at least one project in their hometown?

       set < struct(modelName : String, modelingProjectLocation : String) >

   (e) Which female models were paid more than $10,000 for all their modeling projects?
       Return the model's name and average paid salary.

       bag < struct(modelName : String, avgSalaryPaid : Float) >

   (f) Which agents charge the highest fee?

       element < struct(highestFee : Float, agentNames : set < String >) >

7.7 Checkpoint

Object-oriented databases are an alternative data model to that provided by the traditional relational data model. An object-oriented data model more closely represents the enterprises expressed in an object-oriented conceptual data model, such as an EER or a UML diagram. The Object Data Standard provides a standard data definition language and an ad hoc query language that form a foundation for the discussion and portability of object-oriented databases.

Exercises

1. Answer the following queries in OQL over the ODL schema for the ECLECTIC ONLINE SHOPPING ENTERPRISE, resulting from Exercise 1 in Checkpoint 7.5.5 (the desired result type of the query is given following the query specification):

(a) Find the item and category information for items that are low on stock (less than 10).

bag < struct(itemName : String, categoryDesc : String, itemQty : Long, itemColor : String, itemSize : Long, itemPrice : Float) >

(b) Find the name, email, and phone number of customers in "Arizona" who have placed more than five orders.

bag < struct(custName : String, custPNumber : String, custEmail : String) >

(c) Which category description has the most item types available in that category? The result type assumes that there is only one category that contains the most item types.

element < String >

(d) Are there any categories in which every item costs more than $20?

set < struct(categoryId : String, categoryDesc : String) >

(e) Which customers have placed an order totaling over $1,000?

set < struct(custName : String) >

(f) For each category, find the total number of items in that category and return the items in that category, including the item name and price.

set < struct(categoryId : String, categoryDescription : String, totalItemsInCategory : Integer, catItems : bag < struct(itemName : String, itemPrice : Float) >)

2. Answer the following queries in OQL over the ODL schema for the GET FIT HEALTH CLUB ENTERPRISE, resulting from Exercise 2 in Checkpoint 7.5.2 (the desired result type of the query is given following the query specification):

(a) Which members have registered for at least one "Yoga" class?

bag < struct(lastName : String, firstName : String) >

(b) Which instructors teach only the "Pilates" classes?

bag < struct(insLName : String, insFName : String) >

(c) Find the number of classes and the names of the classes taught by each instructor.

set < struct(insLName : String, insFName : String, classCount : Long, classNameList : bag < String >) >

(d) For each account that joined this year, list the account number, the date joined, the number of members on the account, and the names of the members associated with that account.

set < *struct(clubAcctNum : String, joinedDate : Date,*
  memberCount : Integer, memberNames : bag < String >) >

3. Using the ODL schema for the MEDICAL PRACTICE ENTERPRISE resulting from Exercise 3 in Checkpoint 7.5.2, answer the following queries in OQL (the desired result type is given following the query specification):

(a) Which patients have been diagnosed with "High blood pressure"? Return the dates that the patient has been diagnosed with "High blood pressure". Order the results alphabetically by last name and first name.

list < *struct(lastName : String, firstName : String, bag < Date >) >*

(b) What is the sum of the charges for visits for each patient for the current year? Order the results alphabetically by last name and first name.

list < *struct(lastName : String, firstName : String,*
  totalVisitChargesForYear : Float) >

(c) Find the minimum, average, and maximum balances for accounts that have only one patient.

element(struct(minbalance : Float, avgBalance : Float,
  maxBalance : Float)

(d) Which accounts are associated with patients who have made more than two visits in the year 2005? Order the results in descending order on account balance.

list < *struct(accountID : String, accountBalance : Float) >*

(e) Which patients have not visited a doctor in the practice in 2005? Order the results alphabetically by last name and first name.

list < *struct(lastName : String, firstName : String) >*

(f) Which patients have visited all doctors associated with the practice? Order the results in ascending order by the patient identifier.

list < *struct(patientID : String, lastName : String, firstName : String) >*

4. Using the ODL schema for the MUSIC AGENCY ENTERPRISE resulting from Exercise 4 in Checkpoint 7.5.2, answer the following queries in OQL (the desired result type is given following the query specification):

(a) Which CD titles have more than 12 songs?

bag < *String* >

(b) For each recording label, find the number of CD titles published and return the set of titles.

set < struct (recordingLabelName : String, cdCount : Long,
cdTitles : set < String >) >

(c) Which artists born after 1975 are composers?

bag < struct (artistFirstName : String, artistLastName : String) >

(d) Which CD titles were top CDs in the year 1975?

set < String >

(e) Which musical groups have at least three top CD titles? Return the number of top CDs and their titles.

set < struct (groupName : String, cdCount : Long,
cdTitle : set < String >) >

(f) Which artist has composed the most songs?

element < struct (artistLastName : String, artistFirstName : String) >

(g) For each recording label, find the total number of CDs sold by that company.

bag < struct (labelName : String, amountSold : Long) >

5. Using the ODL schema for the FICTITIOUS BANK ENTERPRISE resulting from Exercise 2 in Checkpoint 7.5.5, answer the following queries in OQL (the desired result type is given following the query specification):

(a) Which customers have accounts in more than one branch?

bag < struct (customerName : String, set < branchCode : String >) >

(b) Find the names of customers that have a savings and a checking account at the same branch.

bag < String >

(c) Find the number of accounts by branch.

set < struct (branchCode : String, numberOfAccounts : Float) >

(d) Which customers do not have a combined balance of all accounts totaling at least $10,000?

set < struct (customerName : String, combinedBalance : Float,
customerAccounts : set < acctNumber : String >) >

(e) For each branch, find the savings account that has the highest balance.

set < struct (branchCode : String, accountNumber : String,
highestSavingsBalance : Float) >

6. Answer the following queries in OQL over the ODL schema for the HORSE RACING ENTERPRISE, resulting from Exercise 3 in Checkpoint 7.5.5 (the desired result type of the query is given following the query specification):

(a) For those owners who own more than 50% in the share of a horse, find the owners and their horses.

bag < struct(ownerName : String, horseName : String) >

(b) Which jockeys have participated in at least one race on a given date?

bag < struct(jockeyName : String) >

(c) Which horses have won more than one race?

set < struct(horseName : String, wonRaces : bag < Race >) >

(d) Which horses have never placed better than third in any race?

bag < horseName : String >

(e) List the trainers and the female horses they trained that cost more than $10,000.

set < struct(trainerName : String, horseNames : bag < String >) >

(f) For each track, find the schedule of races for a given date.

set < struct(trackName : String, raceSchedules : bag < RaceSchedule >) >

(g) What is the name of the horse that has participated in the most races?

element < String >

7.8 Bibliographic References

Initially, characterizing OODB technology was complicated by the fact that many commercial OODB products were developed before the existence of any common, formal definition of an OODB model. This situation is contrary to that of RDB technology, in which commercial development followed a clear, formal definition of the relational data model. The *Object-Oriented Database System Manifesto* [Atkinson et al., 1990] is generally considered to be the most definitive summary of OODB characteristics, with numerous other research papers providing more formal definitions of object-oriented data models. The research paper by Koshafian and Copeland [1989] gives a formal definition of object identity. The Object Data Standard [Cattell et al., 2000] was developed to provide a common ground for describing an object model, the specification of a schema over the object model, and a query language. Several recent books include a collection of papers describing the use of object-oriented databases in practice [Loomis and Chaudhri, 1997] and [Chaudhri and Zicari, 2000].

Chapter 8

The SQL Standard: Object-Relational Features

Synopsis

Chapter 3 presented several advanced features of the SQL standard. This chapter continues that coverage with a presentation of the object-relational features of the standard. After presenting the use of constructed types such as row types and arrays, the chapter focuses on the use of User-Defined Types (UDTs). UDTs provide extensibility to the SQL predefined types, where the behavior of the type is defined through the use of methods. UDTs also provide the basis for the creation of typed tables. Typed tables are the relational equivalent of classes in the object-oriented data model, where typed tables can be formed into hierarchies and instances of typed tables have object identifiers. References to objects can then be used to create relationships between typed tables. This chapter elaborates on the use of these object-relational features, also providing guidelines for mapping EER and UML conceptual designs to object-relational designs via the SQL standard.

Assumed Knowledge

- Enhanced Entity Relationship (EER) Diagrams (Chapter 1)
- Unified Modeling Language (UML) Conceptual Class Diagrams (Chapter 2)
- The SQL Standard: Advanced Relational Features (Chapter 3)
- Mapping Object-Oriented Conceptual Models to the Relational Data Model (Chapter 4)
- Object-Oriented Databases and the ODMG Standard (Chapter 7)

Case Study

- Object-Relational Design of the SCHOOL DATABASE ENTERPRISE (Chapter 9)

Since the introduction of the first commercial relational database products in the early 1980s, relational database technology has become a multibillion-dollar business. During this growth period, the practical use of relational technology for more complex, non-business-oriented applications was challenged in the wake of the object-oriented database movement. Users began to experiment with relational databases in applications that required data types above and beyond the simple built-in data types provided by most commercial systems. These nontraditional applications typically involved large amounts of data, such as video, audio, and spatial data, or complex, hierarchically structured data, such as designs of engineering artifacts. Researchers subsequently began to investigate ways to incorporate object-oriented concepts, such as those covered in Chapter 7, into relational database systems, creating object-relational database technology. Whereas object-oriented database technology provides a *revolutionary* approach that requires the construction of new object storage and server facilities, object-relational database technology provides an *evolutionary* approach to the use of objects in databases by building on established relational database research results. Today, the SQL standard captures many of these original concepts as object extensions to the relational standard, with companies such as Oracle, IBM, and Sybase providing object-relational products (also known as *universal servers*).

This chapter presents the object features that have been incorporated into the SQL standard. A fundamental concept supporting object extensions to the relational model is that of *extensibility* through the use of *user-defined types* (*UDTs*). UDTs allow application developers to go beyond the built-in data types of the relational model, defining more complex, structured data types that are appropriate to the application at hand. UDTs in the SQL standard fully support the object-oriented concept of encapsulation, wherein users can define methods for manipulating the instances of a UDT. UDTs can also be formed into inheritance hierarchies, supporting the inheritance of attributes and methods, as well as the object-oriented concepts of polymorphism and overriding of method implementations. A UDT can then be used in the same way as any other built-in data type: for defining the types of columns in tables, for defining parameters, or for defining variables in SQL routines.

Although UDTs can be used strictly as a means for creating more complex column, variable, or parameter *values*, they also provide the basis for the creation of *objects*. In this regard, UDTs can be used together with a new form of table known as a *typed table*. When a typed table is formed on the basis of a UDT, the rows of the table become objects, with object identifiers that are referred to as *references*. References can then be used to create object-based associations between typed tables, in the same way that object relationships are formed between classes in an object-oriented database. Coupling the use of object references with the array data type of the SQL standard also supports the creation of multivalued object associations, providing an intuitive way to model 1:N and M:N associations between objects. In addition, typed tables can be formed into an inheritance hierarchy that corresponds to the hierarchy of the UDTs on which they are based, thus supporting object inheritance.

This chapter begins with a discussion of the SQL built-in *constructed types* (i.e., row types and arrays) for the construction of more complex values. Although the built-in constructed types are not part of the object features of the standard, they support mapping object-oriented conceptual models to object-relational representations. The remainder of the chapter then addresses constructed types in the form of UDTs, illustrating how UDTs and typed tables can be used to take an object-oriented approach to the design of relational databases. The chapter concludes by defining techniques for mapping EER and UML models to the object-relational features of the SQL standard. Since the motivational background and fundamental object-oriented concepts for object-relational technology are the same as those for object-oriented database technology, readers of this chapter are encouraged to read Chapter 7 first before embarking on an examination of object-relational features.

8.1 Built-In Constructed Types

SQL has traditionally supported atomic types for the definition of columns, variables, and parameters. A list of these atomic types is given in Table 3.1 from Chapter 3. Table 3.1 also identifies a category of data type known as *constructed types*, consisting of *user-defined types* (*UDTs*), a *reference type*, a *row type*, and a *collection type*. Constructed types are data types that are capable of holding more than one value. Of the four constructed types listed in the table, row types and collection types are built-in data types, while UDTs and reference types provide a user-defined approach to extending the built-in types that are available in relational database systems.

This section presents an overview of the built-in row and collection types, used later in the chapter to support the mapping of object-oriented conceptual models to object-relational implementations. Since UDTs and reference types are the main topic of this chapter, each of these constructed types is covered in more detail in separate sections.

8.1.1 Row Types

In relational database terminology, a *row* is a nonempty collection of values, where the type of each value corresponds to a column definition within a table. A traditional relational table is composed of rows with the distinguishing characteristic that each column value in each row must be atomic, which is the basic definition of first normal form (1NF). The SQL standard relaxes the 1NF requirement with the introduction of the row type, which allows a row to be stored as a column value inside of another row. A row type is therefore similar to record structures in programming languages and a `struct` in ODL.

Using the SCHOOL DATABASE ENTERPRISE in Figure 2.16, suppose the location of a campus club consists of a street name, a building name, and a room number. These three values could be represented as three separate columns in a table. With a row type, however, the location of a club can be conceptually viewed as one column with a nonatomic value. Each element of the column is referred to as a *field*. In the following example, `location` is identified as a row type with the keyword row, followed by field name and type pairs enclosed in parentheses and separated by commas:

```
create table campusClub
(cId        varchar(10),
 name       varchar(50) not null,
 location   row (street varchar(30), bldg varchar(5), room varchar(5)),
 advisor    varchar(11) references faculty(pId),
 primary key (cId));
```

The row constructor is used to assign values to the fields of a row. The values in the row constructor can either be a list of values or the result of a query. In either case, the types of the values must conform to the field types in the row type definition. The following example illustrates inserting a club into the campusClub table, where the club is located in Room 222 of the Brickyard Building on Mill Avenue. The location of the club is represented as one column in the table, but the location is a nonatomic value composed of three separate character string values:

```
insert into campusClub values
('CC123',
 'Campus Computer Club',
 row('Mill Avenue', 'Brickyard Building', 'Rm 222'),
 'FA123');
```

The values of a row type can be retrieved by using dot notation to access the individual fields that are part of the column. The following query will return the street, building, and room number for the location of the specified club:

```
select c.location.street, c.location.bldg, c.location.room
from campusClub c
where c.name = 'Campus Computer Club';
```

8.1.2 Arrays as Collections

The collection type provides an additional way to represent nonatomic values in a relational schema. Theoretically, a collection can be a data structure such as an array, a set, a list, or a bag, but the current version of the SQL standard supports only the array type.

A column in a table can be specified as an array by following the column type with the array keyword. The maximum number of elements in an array is enclosed in square brackets. The first position in an array is accessed with an index value of one.

Again citing the campusClub table as an example, a members array can be used to directly store the identifiers of the club members inside of each row of the campusClub table:

```
create table campusClub
(cId       varchar(10),
 name      varchar(50) not null,
 location  row (street varchar(30), bldg varchar(5), room varchar(5)),
 advisor   varchar(9)  references faculty(pId),
 members   varchar(11) array[50] references student(pId),
 primary key (cId));
```

The array constructor is used to reserve space for an array and can also be used to assign values to the array elements. The following insert statement illustrates how to initialize the members array to an empty value, using the array constructor with no elements:

```
insert into campusClub values
('CC123',
 'Campus Computer Club',
```

```
row('Mill Avenue', 'Brickyard Building', 'Rm 222'),
'FA123',
array[]);
```

The specific identifiers of club members can then be added to the array by using the array constructor in an update statement. The following statement assigns values to the first three positions in the members array:

```
update campusClub
set    members = array['ST111', 'ST222', 'ST333']
where  name = 'Campus Computer Club';
```

Assignments can also be made to individual positions in an array by using a specific index value:

```
update campusClub
set    members[4] = 'ST444'
where  name = 'Campus Computer Club';
```

An index is used to access a specific position of an array. The following query returns the identifier of the second element of the members array for the specified club:

```
select members[2]
from   campusClub
where  name = 'Campus Computer Club';
```

The cardinality function can be used to get the size of an array. For example, cardinality(c.members) returns the current size of the members array (assuming that c is a cursor to a row in the campusClub table). The cardinality function can be used to support iteration through array contents within SQL routines. (See Chapter 3 for coverage of control structures in SQL routines.)

The cardinality of an array is adjustable, ranging from an empty array to the maximum size specified in the array definition. Given the four values that were assigned to the array in the previous examples, the current cardinality of the array is four. Suppose an additional update statement sets position six to the value "ST666". Then the cardinality of the array becomes six, with position five set to null.

In general, arrays are useful for representing multivalued attributes. Arrays can also be used to directly model the *many* side of a 1:N or M:N association, as in the use of relationships in ODL. In the remainder of this chapter, arrays will be used to illustrate a more object-oriented approach to the representation of multivalued relationships in an object-relational schema.

8.1.3 Checkpoint: Built-In Constructed Types

Row types and arrays extend the pure relational model with capabilities for representing nonatomic values in table columns. Row types are useful for representing composite values, where each component of the row type is of a possibly different data type.

Arrays can be used to represent an indexed collection of values with a homogeneous data type.

Exercises

1. Create a `person` table that uses row types and arrays to satisfy the following requirements: Every person has an identifier and a name, where the name is composed of a first name, a middle initial, and a last name. Every person also has an address, composed of a street, city, state, and zip. Each person can have multiple phone numbers, such as a work number, a home number, and a cellphone number. Each person can also have multiple college degrees, such as B.S., M.S., Ph.D. M.D., and D.D.S.

2. Write an SQL procedure that illustrates how to populate rows in the `person` table of Exercise 1 with assignments to the name and address fields. Set the phone and college degrees arrays to empty values.

3. Write an SQL procedure that illustrates how to add values to the phone array of a row in the `person` table of Exercise 1. The procedure should accept the person identifier and a phone value and add the phone value to the next available space in the array. You will need to use the `cardinality` function together with control structures for SQL routines from Chapter 3 to complete this exercise. Write a similar procedure for the college degrees array.

8.2   User-Defined Types

The term *user-defined type* (*UDT*) is the SQL standard terminology for *abstract data type*. Most readers should already be familiar with the concept of abstract data types, according to which users define new types having some form of internal structure, together with methods that represent the behavior of the type. The internal representation of the type is *encapsulated* by the behavior of the type, meaning that the internal implementation of the type is hidden from the outside world and can even change without affecting the manner in which a user interfaces with the type. UDTs in the SQL standard are somewhat different from the strict definition of an abstract data type, since all internal attributes of a UDT and their associated methods are public and cannot be marked as protected or private, as they can in languages such as Java or C++. The use of public attributes and methods allows the internal structure of an instance of the type to be queried through a language such as SQL. The primary advantage of a UDT is that it allows database developers to define new application-oriented types, above and beyond built-in atomic and constructed types, that can be used in the definition of relational tables. UDTs also provide the basis for the creation of objects in the relational world.

This section describes the two basic types of UDTs in the SQL standard: the *distinct type* and the *structured type*. The syntax for defining a UDT with the `create type` statement is presented in Figure 8.1. The details of the syntax will be addressed in the subsections that follow.

```
create type <user_defined_type_body>

<user_defined_type_body> ::= <user_defined_type_name>
    [under <user_defined_type_name>]
    [as <representation>]
    [[not] instantiable]
    [not] final
    [ref is system generated | ref using <predefined type> |
        ref from <attribute_name> [{,attribute_name}...]]
    [<method_specification_list>]

<representation> ::= <predefined_type> | <member_list>

<member_list> ::=
    (<attribute_definition> [{,<attribute_definition>}...])

<attribute_definition> ::=
    <attribute_name> {<data_type> | <collection_type>}
    [<reference_scope_check>] [default <default_value>]

<data_type> ::= <predefined_type> | <reference_type>

<collection_type> ::= <data_type> array [unsigned_integer]
                      /* [ ] part of syntax*/

<method_specification_list> ::=
    <method_specification> [{,<method_specification>}...]

<method_specification> ::=
    <partial_method_specification> | <overriding_method_specification>

<overriding_method_specification> ::=
    overriding <partial_method_specification>

<partial_method_specification> ::=
    [constructor] method <method_name> <SQL_parameter_declarations>
    returns <data_type>
```

Figure 8.1 SQL Syntax for Creating User-Defined Types

8.2.1 Distinct Types

A distinct type provides a way of attaching special meaning to an existing atomic type. Once a distinct type is defined, it cannot be freely mixed with the atomic type on which it is based. The distinct type essentially defines a new form of the atomic type.

As an example, suppose you need a table that maintains the age and weight of each person in a database. You could always define columns for personAge and personWeight that are of type integer. You could then add the age and weight of the person, since both values are of the same type, even though the addition of the age and weight values is not meaningful.

To prevent meaningless calculations with values that are of the same type, but conceptually have different semantics, distinct types can be defined via the create type statement in Figure 8.1. In the example that follows, age and weight are defined as two distinct types, both based on the integer atomic type, with the use of the as clause of the `create type` statement.

```
create type age as integer final;
create type weight as integer final;

create table person
(personId      varchar(3),
 personAge     age,
 personWeight  weight,
 primary key (personId));
```

The keyword `final` is required syntax for distinct types in the current version of the SQL standard and simply means that a subtype of the distinct type cannot be defined. The distinct types in the example are then used to define the `personAge` and `personWeight` columns, respectively.

Once defined, `age` and `weight` values cannot be compared. In fact, `age` and `weight` values cannot be mixed with the regular `integer` type, since `age`, `weight`, and `integer` are conceptually different types.

As an example of using distinct types, the following query retrieves the `personId` values of each person having an age less than the age of the person with a `personId` of "123":

```
select p1.personId
from    person p1, person p2
where   p2.personId = '123' and p1.personAge < p2.personAge;
```

The following query is invalid, because it mixes the use of `age`, `weight`, and `integer` values:

```
select personId
from    person
where   (personAge * 2) < personWeight;
```

Mixing the use of distinct types with the atomic types on which they are based is allowed, but requires the deliberate use of the `cast` function. The invalid query in the preceding code can be revised as follows to cast all values to the `integer` type, thus transforming the condition in the `where` clause into a valid condition:

```
select personId
from    person
where   cast (personAge as integer) * 2 < cast (personWeight as
            integer);
```

Methods can also be defined on distinct types to create specialized operations for manipulating and comparing such types. Rather than elaborate on the use of methods with distinct types, the next section discusses the use of methods in the context of structured types.

8.2.2 Structured Types

Whereas a distinct type creates a new type from one specific atomic type, a structured type is a UDT that is composed of several internal components, each of which can be of a different type. An instance of a structured type is a value, but since a structured type can contain several components, the value is composite.

As a simple example of a structured type definition, recall the earlier example of defining a campus club location as a row type. Instead of using a row type, a structured type can be used. In the example that follows, `locationUdt` is defined as a structured type:

```
create type locationUdt as
(street varchar(30),
 bldg   varchar(5),
 room   varchar(5))
 not final;
```

The representation of the type in the `as` clause defines the type to contain the `street`, `bldg`, and `room` components. These components are the *attributes* of the structured type, where the type of each attribute can be a built-in atomic or a constructed type, as well as any user-defined type. The keywords `not final` are referred to as the *finality* clause of the type definition. In a structured type definition, the finality clause must always be `not final` (a current restriction of the SQL standard), indicating that it is possible to define subtypes of the type. Type hierarchies will be discussed in more detail later in the chapter.

The following example uses `locationUdt` to define the type of the `location` column in the `campusClub` table:

```
create table campusClub
(cId           varchar(10),
 name          varchar(50) not null,
 location      locationUdt,
 advisor       varchar(11) references faculty(pId),
 members       varchar(11) array[50] references student(pId),
 primary key (cId));
```

Built-In Methods

In Chapter 3, the discussion of SQL-invoked routines mentioned that there were three types of stored procedures: functions, procedures, and methods. Methods are associated specifically with structured types. In particular, methods are functions that are tightly bound to the definition of the structured type. Structured types therefore support encapsulation, where the type is manipulated only through the methods that are defined on it. In the SQL standard, methods cannot be defined as procedures. Specific implementations of structured types, however, such as that found in Oracle, allow methods to be defined as functions or procedures. (See the Oracle object-relational case study in Chapter 9.)

There are three types of built-in methods for structured types: a *constructor function*, *observer functions*, and *mutator functions*. These methods are automatically provided as part of the type definition. The constructor function has the same name as the type and is used for creating instances of the type. The constructor function must always be invoked by using the `new` expression. Observer functions are used for retrieving the attribute values of a structured type. There is an observer function for every attribute of the type, where the function has the same name as the attribute. In a similar manner, mutator functions are used to modify the attribute values of a structured type. For every attribute of the type, there is a mutator function having the same name as the attribute. Observer functions and mutator functions are always invoked by using dot notation (`variable.functionName`) instead of traditional functional notation (`functionName(parameters)`), which is used only for functions that are not methods.

The next example illustrates a sequence of code from an SQL routine that uses the constructor function and mutator functions to create an instance of `locationUdt`:

```
begin
    declare loc locationUdt;
    /* invoking the constructor function */
    set loc = new locationUdt();
    /* invoking the mutator functions */
    set loc.street  = 'Mill Avenue';
    set loc.bldg = 'Brickyard Building';
    set loc.room = 'RM 222';
    insert into campusClub values
    ('CC123',
     'Campus Computer Club',
     loc, /* initializing location */
     'FA123',
     array[]);
end;
```

The code defines the variable `loc` to be of type `locationUdt`. The variable is then initialized with a new instance by using `new locationUdt()` to invoke the constructor function. This system-defined constructor function has no parameters. The new instance of the type has all of its attribute values set either to `null` or to a default value that can be specified in the type definition. In our current use of structured types, it is important to understand that the new instance is a *value* and not an *object*. Using structured types together with typed tables to create objects will be addressed in more detail later in the chapter.

For each attribute of the instance, mutator functions are invoked to assign values to that attribute. For example, `loc.street` invokes the mutator function for `street` to assign the value "Mill Avenue" to the attribute. There are actually two parameters to any mutator function. The first parameter is implicit and is the instance of the type. In this example, the implicit parameter is the instance stored in the `loc` variable. The second parameter is explicit and is the value assigned to the attribute ("Mill Avenue" for the `street` mutator function). The value returned by a mutator function is a new instance of the type with the modified attribute value. The `loc` variable is then used in the `insert` statement to assign the location value to the `location` column of a row in the `campusClub` table.

The query that follows illustrates the use of observer functions to retrieve the attribute values of the structured type. For example, `c.location.street` invokes the `street` observer function to access the value of the `street` attribute. Similar to mutator functions, the instance of the type is an implicit parameter of the function. Mutator functions, however, have no explicit parameters. The value returned by the mutator function is the value of the attribute that it accesses.

```
select name, c.location.street, c.location.bldg, c.location.room
from    campusClub c
where   name = 'Campus Computer Club';
```

Because of potential naming ambiguities in SQL, structured types and observer functions can be accessed only through the use of alias names in queries (e.g., `c` in the previous query). As a result, a reference such as `location.street` or `campus-Club.location.street` is not allowed.

User-Defined Methods

In addition to built-in methods, users can define their own methods on structured types, which is one of the main advantages of UDTs. The syntax for the `create type` statement in Figure 8.1 indicates an option for a method specification list, wherein the user defines the *signature* of each method, indicating the name of the method, together with the names and types of its parameters. The implementation of the method is defined separately from the type specification with the use of the `create method` statement. Since a method is a function, the syntax for the `create method` statement is similar to the syntax for the `create function` statement in Figure 3.8.

The next example illustrates the definition of the `sum` method on the `threeNumbers` structured type. The signature indicates that this particular method has no explicit parameters defined. The method also returns a value of type `integer`. Every method, however, has one implicit parameter, which is the instance of the type on which the method is defined. The value of the implicit parameter is accessed in the method implementation by using the `self` keyword. The code is as follows:

```
create type threeNumbers as
(one integer,
 two integer,
 three integer)
 not final
 method sum() returns integer;

create method sum() returns integer for threeNumbers
begin
      return self.one + self.two + self.three;
end
```

Users can override the constructor function of a structured type. Since the system-defined constructor function does not allow parameters, overriding the constructor function creates a different version of the function that can be used to set the values of specific attributes at the time an instance of the type is created.

The next example illustrates overriding the constructor function of the `locationUdt` type. As indicated in the syntax of Figure 8.1, the keyword `overriding` must be specified to indicate that the method is overriding an existing function:

```
create type locationUdt as(
(street       varchar(30),
 bldg         varchar(5),
 room         varchar(5))
 not final
 overriding constructor method /* a new constructor with parameters */
    locationUdt(street varchar(30), bldg varchar(5), room varchar(5))
    returns locationUdt;

create method locationUdt(st varchar(30), bl varchar(5), rm varchar(5))
    returns locationUdt for locationUdt
begin
    set self.street = st;
```

```
      set self.bldg = bl;
      set self.room = rm;
      return self;
end;
```

Since the method to be overridden is also a constructor function, the `constructor` keyword must be specified. The name of the method in the above example must be the same as the name of the system-defined constructor function (i.e., `locationUdt`). The method specification includes the definition of parameters and their types. The method implementation demonstrates the manner in which the parameters are used to assign values to an instance of the type via the mutator functions. Notice that the method returns `self` as a value, which is the modified instance of `locationUdt`.

The user-defined constructor function can then be used to construct a new instance of `locationUdt` and to set the values of its attributes at the same time:

```
declare loc locationUdt;
set loc =
  new locationUdt('Mill Avenue', 'Brickyard Building','Rm 222');
```

8.2.3   Checkpoint: User-Defined Types

User-defined types allow database programmers to extend the built-in SQL data types to define new types that are appropriate for a specific application. Distinct types provide a way to rename a built-in type for the purpose of attaching special meaning to the type. Structured types allow the definition of a composite type, supporting the specification of methods that are tightly bound to the type for purposes of manipulation and access. Structured types automatically provide a constructor method, as well as accessor and mutator methods, for each component of the structured type.

Exercises

1. Revise the `person` table in Exercise 1 in Checkpoint 8.1.3 to use structured types for names and addresses.

2. Revise the SQL procedure in Exercise 2 in Checkpoint 8.1.3 to illustrate how to populate rows in the `person` table with names and addresses represented as structured types.

8.3   Typed Tables

As described in the previous section, an instance of a UDT in the SQL standard is a value. To create the notion of an object as in object-oriented database technology, a UDT must be used together with a *typed table*. A typed table is a new form of table in the SQL standard that is always associated with a specific structured type. A typed table has a column for every attribute of the structured type on which it is based. In addition, a typed table has a *self-referencing column* that contains a unique object identifier, known as a *reference*, for each row in the table. Other than the self-referencing column and the attributes of the structured type, additional columns cannot be added to the table definition.

When a structured type is used to define a typed table, an instance of the type is viewed as an object, with the self-referencing column providing the object identifier. Unlike object identifiers in object-oriented database technology, an object identifier is unique only within a specific typed table. As a result, it is possible to have two typed tables with rows that have identical self-referencing values.

As an example of using typed tables, suppose you would like to implement the Department class of the SCHOOL DATABASE ENTERPRISE in Figure 2.16 as a typed table. It is first necessary to define a departmentUdt structured type:

```
create type departmentUdt as
(code          varchar(3),
 name          varchar(40))
 instantiable not final ref is system generated;
```

The departmentUdt type defines the code and name attributes. A new syntactic feature from Figure 8.1 introduced in the type definition is the instantiable clause, which indicates that a constructor function exists for the type and that it is possible for the user to directly create instances of the type. If a type is specified as not instantiable, then there is no constructor function for the type. The use of not instantiable makes sense only in the context of a type that has a subtype, where instances of the type are created at the subtype level only. Type hierarchies are addressed in more detail in the next section. A structured type that is used together with a typed table, as in the example of this section, must always be specified as instantiable.

Another new feature introduced in the type definition is the ref clause. This clause allows the user to specify the means for generating the value for the object reference. As indicated in Figure 8.1, there are three options for the ref clause. If the reference is system generated, then the database system is responsible for generating a unique object reference for instances of the type. The ref using clause indicates that the reference is user generated. The user must then provide a unique reference for each instance of the type, where the value of the reference is the type indicated in the ref using clause. If the ref from clause is used, then the user must specify the list of attributes from the structured type that will be used to derive a unique object reference. For user generated and derived references, it is the user's responsibility to ensure the uniqueness of the reference. The examples in this book use system generated references, since they are the most natural approach to take for the use of objects.

After a UDT is defined, a typed table is created that corresponds to the structure of the UDT. The syntax for creating typed tables is shown in Figure 8.2. As an example, consider the definition of the department typed table:

```
create table department of departmentUdt
(primary key (code),
 ref is departmentID system generated);
```

The of clause indicates the structured type on which the typed table is based. As a result, the table automatically acquires columns that correspond to the attributes of the structured type. The typed table definition supports the same table and column constraints that are associated with traditional table definitions. For example, in the department table definition, the code attribute of departmentUdt is defined as a primary key. Other constraints, such as unique or not null, can also be specified, using either the column or table constraint format. Only the attributes with constraints are listed in the typed table definition.

According to the syntax in Figure 8.2, a typed table definition must also repeat a reference generation specification that is consistent with the reference generation specification of the structured type: system generated, user generated, or derived. In addition, the ref is specification must assign a name to the self-referencing column. This name (departmentID) can be used to manipulate the self-referencing column in the case of user-defined references. The self-referencing column is also used to access the self-referencing value. Accessing the self-referencing column will be addressed in more detail in Section 8.6.

Rows are inserted into a typed table by using an insert statement in the same manner as for any relational table. Consider the following insert statements for department:

```
insert into department
  values ('cse', 'Computer Science and Engineering');
insert into department
  values ('ece', 'Electrical and Computer Engineering');
insert into department
  values ('mae', 'Mechanical and Aerospace Engineering');
```

The resulting rows of the table are as shown in Table 8.1, where the values for the self-referencing column are system generated. If the reference is user defined, the insert statement must include the value for the self-referencing column. If the reference is derived from attributes of the type, the primary key constraint or the unique and not null constraints can be used in the table definition to ensure a unique reference value for the appropriate attributes.

```
create table <table name> of <user_defined_type_name>
  [under <supertable_name>] [<table_element_list>]

<table_element_list> ::= (<table_element> [{ ,<table_element>}...])

<table_element> ::= <table_constraint> |
  <self_referencing_column_specification> | <column_options>

<self_referencing_column_specification> ::=
  ref is <self_referencing_column_name> <reference_generation>

<reference_generation> ::= system generated | user generated | derived

<column_options> ::= <column_name> with options <column_option_list>

<column_option_list> ::=
  [scope <table_name>[<reference_scope_check>]]
  [default <default_value>] [<column_constraint>...]
```

Figure 8.2 SQL Syntax for Creating Typed Tables

TABLE 8.1 Rows in the department Typed Table

(self-referencing column) departmentID	code	name
10287534556	cse	Computer Science and Engineering
27259489035	ece	Electrical and Computer Engineering
90324854948	mae	Mechanical and Aerospace Engineering

8.4 Type and Table Hierarchies

Structured types and typed tables can be formed into hierarchies to directly represent the class hierarchies of conceptual models such as the EER model and UML class diagrams. Structured types are first formed into a hierarchy with the use of the under clause, as specified in the syntax for the create type statement in Figure 8.1. This clause allows the specification of the supertype of the type being defined. Creating a supertype/subtype relationship between structured types fully supports the inheritance of attributes and methods of the supertype at the subtype level. Typed tables are then created to correspond to the type hierarchy, also using an under clause, as specified in Figure 8.2 for the syntax of typed table specifications. In addition, inheritance is supported among the object instances of typed tables.

As an example of creating type and table hierarchies, the SCHOOL DATABASE ENTERPRISE in Figure 2.16 provides a Person superclass with the Student and Faculty subclasses. Chapter 4 illustrated several techniques for mapping such a hierarchy to traditional relational tables. Typed tables, however, can be used in object-relational technology to directly represent the hierarchy, to provide object identifiers for the data associated with the hierarchy, and to directly support the inheritance of attributes and methods. Structured type definitions are first created for the Person, Student, and Faculty classes from Figure 2.16:

```
create type personUdt as
(pId            varchar(11),
 firstName      varchar(20),
 lastName       varchar(20),
 dob            date)
 instantiable not final ref is system generated;

create type facultyUdt under personUdt as
(rank         varchar(10))
 instantiable
 not final;

create type studentUdt under personUdt as
(status varchar(10))
 instantiable
 not final;
```

To form the hierarchy, facultyUdt is defined as a subtype of personUdt with the under personUdt clause. In a similar manner, studentUdt is defined as under personUdt, indicating that studentUdt is a subtype of personUdt. Recall that structured types must always be defined as not final in the current version of the SQL standard. Furthermore, since these types are intended to be used with typed tables, the instantiable clause is required.

As a result of the supertype/subtype relationship between personUdt and facultyUdt, an instance of facultyUdt will inherit the pId, firstName, lastName, and dob attributes, as well as the mutator and accessor functions associated with each attribute. An instance of facultyUdt will therefore have five attributes: the four inherited attributes and the rank attribute that is directly defined at the facultyUdt level. If the personUdt type had any additional user-defined methods, these methods would also be inherited by facultyUdt. The same inheritance situation exists for the supertype/subtype relationship that exists between personUdt and studentUdt.

With the person type hierarchy defined, typed tables can be created that directly correspond to the type hierarchy. The example that follows illustrates the manner in which the person, faculty, and student typed tables are defined:

```
create table person of personUdt
(primary key (pId),
 ref is personID system generated);

create table faculty of facultyUdt under person;
create table student of studentUdt under person;
```

The under specification of the subtables must be consistent with the under specification of the corresponding types. For example, facultyUdt was defined to be under person-Udt. Since the person table is associated with the personUdt type and the faculty table is associated with the facultyUdt type, faculty must be defined to be under person. The same constraints hold for the definition of the student table.

There are several rules associated with the definition of type and table hierarchies. In each case, only single inheritance is supported. As a result, every subtype and corresponding subtable must have only one maximal supertype and supertable. A primary key can be defined only for a maximal supertable. In the person table hierarchy, pId is identified as a primary key only within the person table. The primary key is inherited by all of the subtables. Subtables can indirectly define additional candidate keys through the use of the not null and unique constraints.

A self-referencing column can be defined only at the supertype and supertable level. Referring again to the personUdt type hierarchy and the person table hierarchy, the ref is clause is used only in the personUdt type definition and the person table definition. The self-referencing column is inherited by all subtables of person.

An additional rule is associated with the definition of constraints in typed tables. Column and table constraints can be defined only on *originally-defined attributes* and not on inherited attributes. Originally-defined attributes are the attributes introduced in the structured type on which the table is based. For example, rank is an originally-defined attribute of the faculty table. As a result, the table definition could be modified to place a not null constraint on rank, but not on an inherited attribute such as lastName.

Although this section has introduced type hierarchies in parallel with the use of table hierarchies, it is important to understand that type hierarchies can be used independently of table hierarchies. In that case, use of the type hierarchy supports valued-based inheritance rather than object-based inheritance. Furthermore, the `not instantiable` clause can be used only in type hierarchies that are not associated with typed tables. For example, a user can define a supertype A as `not instantiable` and then define B and C as `instantiable` subtypes of A. Since A is `not instantiable`, users cannot directly create instances of A, but can directly create instances of B and C that inherit the attributes and methods of A.

All types associated with a typed table hierarchy *must* be defined as `instantiable` to support the use of `insert` statements on typed tables. As a result, abstract supertables and the total specialization constraint cannot be inherently enforced.

8.5 A Closer Look at Table Hierarchies

The advantage of table hierarchies is that they support the same form of object-based inheritance as is found in class hierarchies in object-oriented database systems. As a result, object-relational applications can directly model class hierarchies from conceptual models, where the rows of typed tables are actual objects with object identifiers. This section demonstrates the manipulation of rows into a table hierarchy, the inheritance behavior of rows in a table hierarchy, and the manner in which such rows are queried and manipulated in SQL.

8.5.1 Inserting Rows into a Table Hierarchy

Inserting a row into a table hierarchy is similar to the creation of objects in a class hierarchy of an object-oriented database. Each row has a most specific table that defines the type of the row. This type corresponds to the type of the table into which the row is directly inserted. Inserting a row into a table makes the row visible in all supertables of the table. The row is not visible, however, in any of the subtables of the table. Once inserted, a row cannot migrate to other tables in the hierarchy. The most specific type or table of a row can be changed only by deleting the row and reinserting it into a different table. If the self-referencing column is system generated, then deleting the row and reinserting it into a different table will result in the row having a different reference value. The contents of subtables are therefore always disjoint and cannot represent overlapping constraints.

To illustrate the behavior of rows in a typed table, consider the following `insert` statements over the `Person` hierarchy from the SCHOOL DATABASE ENTERPRISE assuming that the `Person` specialization is not total:

```
insert into person
  values ('PP111', 'Joe', 'Smith', '2/18/82');
insert into person
  values ('PP222', 'Alice', 'Black', '2/15/80');
insert into student
  values ('ST333', 'Sue', 'Jones', '8/23/87','freshman');
insert into student
  values ('ST444', 'Joe', 'White', '5/16/86','sophomore');
insert into faculty
  values ('FA555', 'Alice', 'Cooper', '9/2/51','professor');
```

Notice that, since the `student` and `faculty` tables inherit attributes from the `person` table, the `insert` statements for these tables include values for the inherited attributes.

The value for the self-referencing column is automatically generated as a result of the `insert` statements.

A graphical view of the resulting rows is shown in Figure 8.3. This graphical view does *not* necessarily reflect the manner in which the tables are actually implemented. For example, the figure illustrates each row, together with its inherited attributes, existing in one table only. An alternative view could show student objects as rows split between the `student` table and the `person` table, with values for originally-defined attributes in the `student` table and values for inherited attributes in the `person` table. Several other representations also exist, similar to the mapping options for hierarchies described in Chapter 4. The graphical view in Figure 8.3, however, is the simplest view for explaining the semantics of the hierarchy in response to `insert`, `select`, `delete`, and `update` statements.

8.5.2   Querying a Table Hierarchy

Table hierarchies support the ISA constraint introduced in Chapter 1, meaning that an instance of a subtable is an instance of its supertable. As a result, consider the following query over the `person` table:

```
select firstName, lastName
from    person;
```

The query will produce the following names as output: `Joe Smith, Alice Black, Sue Jones, Joe White, Alice Cooper`.

The query essentially performs the union of the `person` table with all of the common attributes from rows of the subtables and returns all direct instances of the `person` table as well as all instances of its subtables. In contrast, consider the following query over the `faculty` table:

```
select firstName, lastName
from    faculty;
```

The only name returned from the query is `Alice Cooper`. Unless otherwise specified, a query over any typed table will return the direct instances of the table, as well as instances of its subtables. A similar query over the `student` table will return `Sue Jones` and `Joe White`.

To retrieve only the direct instances of a table, the `only` option can be used in the `from` clause to constrain the query results. The following query will return only `Joe Smith` and `Alice Black` in the query result:

```
select firstName, lastName
from only (person);
```

8.5.3   Deleting Rows from a Table Hierarchy

Consider the case of a `delete` statement expressed over the root of a table hierarchy. The following statement over the `person` table will delete any row from the table hierarchy with the first name of "Alice", even if the most specific type of the row is a `student` or a `faculty`:

```
delete from person where firstName = 'Alice';
```

(self-referencing column) personID	pId	firstName	lastName	dob
39872367901	PP111	Joe	Smith	2/18/82
50986752134	PP222	Alice	Black	2/15/80

(self-referencing column) personID	pId	firstName	lastName	dob	rank
76400123578	FA555	Alice	Cooper	9/2/51	professor

(self-referencing column) personID	pId	firstName	lastName	dob	status
10227899023	ST333	Sue	Jones	8/18/82	freshman
9055403216	ST444	Joe	White	5/16/80	sophomore

Person
pId
firstName
lastName
dob

Faculty
rank

Student
status

Figure 8.3 Rows in the person Table Hierarchy

Note that this behavior is as expected, according to the ISA constraint for class hierarchies, since a `student` ISA `person` and a `faculty` ISA `person`. In particular, the statement will delete the rows for Alice Black and Alice Cooper.

Deleting a tuple from a subtable also implicitly deletes the tuple from its supertables. For example, since a `student` ISA `person`, the deletion of Sue Jones from the `student` table will also result in Sue Jones no longer being visible from the `person` table (because the tuple no longer exists in the `student` table):

```
delete from student where firstName = 'Sue' and lastName = 'Jones';
```

As a result of the preceding `delete` statement, a query to return all rows of the `person` table will not include Sue Jones, since the row for Sue Jones has been removed from the table hierarchy. Recall that each row has a most specific type. Once the row is removed, it is considered to be removed from the entire table hierarchy.

It is possible to restrict the rows that are deleted by using the `only` option. The following statement will delete rows with a first name of "Joe" from `person` only if the person does not have a most specific type of `student` or `faculty`:

```
delete from only (person) where firstName = 'Joe';
```

As a result of the statement, the row for Joe Smith is the only row deleted. The row for Joe White remains in the table hierarchy.

8.5.4 Updating Rows in a Table Hierarchy

The `update` statement operates in a manner similar to the way the `delete` statement operates. For example, the following statement will change the first name of each row in the `person` table and in any subtables of `person`.

```
update person
set    firstName = 'Suzy'
where  firstName = 'Sue';
```

As a result, the name of Sue Jones in the `student` table will be changed, even though the query is expressed over the `person` table.

To restrict an update operation to rows that do not appear in any subtables, the `only` option is used. The following query will change the first name of Joe Smith in the `person` table and not the first name of Joe White in the `student` table:

```
update only (person)
set    firstName = 'Joey'
where  firstName = 'Joe';
```

It is important to note that the condition in the `where` clause of an `update` statement also applies to all rows that are in supertables of the table identified in the `update` statement. If the `set` clause refers to attributes that do not appear in the supertable, then the `set` clause is ignored.

8.5.5 Checkpoint: Typed Table Hierarchies

Together with typed tables, structured types can be used to provide the object-relational equivalent of classes in the object-oriented data model. Instances of typed tables have object identifiers that are known as references, which can be system generated, user generated, or derived from attributes of the table. The under clause in structured types and their corresponding table definitions can be used to form tables into hierarchies that support the inheritance of state and behavior. Multiple inheritance is not supported in the formation of table hierarchies. Queries can be expressed over table hierarchies to return all of the objects in a table, including objects in the table's subtables. Queries can also be restricted to return only the direct instances of a table. As with object-oriented data models, overlapping subclasses, abstract classes, total specialization, and attribute-defined subclasses from conceptual models are not directly supported by table hierarchies in the SQL standard. Programmers must find creative ways to enforce such constraints over table hierarchies.

Exercises

1. Using the SQL standard to represent the Project hierarchy from the HOLLY-WOOD ENTERPRISE in Figure 7.6 (the version with a disjoint Celebrity hierarchy), develop a typed table hierarchy. For this exercise, ignore all class associations other than ISA relationships. Can all constraints of the hierarchy be directly represented in the table hierarchy? If not, how are the constraints enforced?

2. Using the SQL standard to represent the Person hierarchy from the HOLLYWOOD ENTERPRISE in Figure 7.6, develop a typed table hierarchy. For this exercise, ignore all class associations other than ISA relationships.

   Using the table hierarchy that you developed, write insert statements to populate the table with the following data (only the person names are indicated; you can make up values for the other attributes):

   (a) person table: John Smith, Sue Jones, Jan Wisniewski

   (b) critic table: Andy Andrews, Edward Joseph

   (c) agent table: Christine Chandler, Buzz Baker, Jake Jacobs

   (d) movieStar table: Jillian Elizabeth, Tess Tessier, Bruce Darling

   (e) model table: Karen Joyce, William Albert, Lucky O'Malley, Lance Luke

   Show the full contents of each table in the hierarchy, assuming the conceptual view of table contents as in Figure 8.3. Then develop solutions to the following queries and show the output for each query:

   (f) Return information about all person objects.

   (g) Return information about all celebrity objects.

   (h) Return information about all movieProfessional objects.

   (i) Return information about all model objects.

(j) Return information about all `person` objects that are not also `movieProfessional` or `celebrity` objects.

(k) Return information about all `celebrity` objects that are not also `movieStar` or `model` objects.

Assume that Lance Luke, Tess Tessier, Buzz Baker, Edward Joseph, and Jan Wisniewski are deleted from the database. Show the revised results of executing the queries.

3. Explain how to enforce the total specialization constraint for `MovieProfessional` and `Celebrity` in Exercise 2.

4. Using the SQL standard to represent the `Person` hierarchy from the HORSE RACING DATABASE in Exercise 1 in Checkpoint 1.4, develop a typed table hierarchy. A modified description of this hierarchy is as follows:

> Information about people involved in the horse-racing business should be maintained. An identifier, name, address, and phone number should be maintained on every person. If a person is a horse trainer, the salary of the trainer should be indicated. If a person is a jockey, the weight of the jockey must be recorded, along with the date of the last recorded weight. It is possible for a person to be a trainer and a jockey. Name and contact information can also be maintained on people other than trainers and jockeys.

Can all of the requirements of the preceding description be implemented as a typed table hierarchy in the SQL standard? Why or why not? If not, can you develop a solution that resolves any of the conflicts between the requirements and the rules for the use of typed tables?

5. Consider the `Person` hierarchy from the ER diagram in Figure 1.12, where `homeCountry` and `gender` define two different specializations of `Person`. What challenges does this design cause for an object-relational representation that uses a table hierarchy? Does a pure relational representation using the mapping techniques from Chapter 4 offer a better solution? Explain your answer.

8.6   Reference Types

Previous sections in this chapter have mentioned the use of the self-referencing column. Recall that the self-referencing column is the internal object identifier, or reference, to a row. This reference is a data type known as a `reference type`, or `ref`. The syntax for defining `ref` types is shown in Figure 8.4. A `ref` type is a valid SQL data type and can therefore be used to define the type of a column in a table, an attribute in a structured type definition, a variable, or a parameter. When used as an attribute of a structured type in combination with the use of typed tables, reference types can model object associations between typed tables that are based on object identity rather than on

```
<reference type> ::=
   ref (<referenced_type>) [<scope_clause>] [array [unsigned_integer]]
   [<reference_scope_check>] /* [] part of syntax*/

<scope_clause> ::= scope <table_name>

<referenced_type>::= <user_defined_type_name>

<reference_scope_check> ::=
   references are [not] checked [on delete <action>]
```

Figure 8.4 Syntax for Defining Reference Types

foreign keys. Reference types therefore provide a way of modeling object relationships as in the object-oriented data model.

To illustrate the use of reference types, consider again the SCHOOL DATABASE ENTERPRISE in Figure 2.16. There is a 1:N relationship between CampusClub and Faculty, where a club has one advisor and a faculty member can advise many clubs. There is also an M:N relationship between CampusClub and Student, indicating that students are members of many clubs and clubs have many student members. The campusClubUdt type can be redefined to use reference types as a means for defining relationships with faculty and student objects:

```
create type campusClubUdt as
(cId       varchar(10),
 name      varchar(50) not null,
 location locationUdt,
 phone     varchar(12),
 advisor   ref(facultyUdt),
 members   ref(studentUdt) array[50])
 instantiable not final ref is system generated;

create table campusClub of campusClubUdt
(primary key (cId),
 ref is campusClubID system generated);
```

The revised campusClubUdt illustrates the use of two different ref types, one to model a single-valued relationship and another to model a multivalued relationship. The type of advisor is defined to be ref(facultyUdt). This type definition indicates that the value to be stored in the advisor attribute is the value of a self-referencing column from a typed table that is associated with the facultyUdt type, thus storing an object reference to a row instead of a value-oriented foreign key as in traditional relational tables. The name of the self-referencing column of the faculty table (personID) can be used to assign a ref value to a column defined as a ref type:

```
update campusClub
set advisor = (select personID
                 from person
                 where firstName = 'Alice' and lastName = 'Cooper')
where name = 'Campus Computer Club';
```

The `members` attribute in `campusClubUdt` is defined to be an array of references to student objects, defined as `ref(studentUdt) array[50]`, thus allowing typed tables to directly model multivalued object references. Arrays of references are generally manipulated and queried through the use of SQL routines. Mapping issues for generating object-relational schemas from conceptual models will be addressed in more detail in Section 8.7.

8.6.1 Scopes and Reference Checking

Since a structured type can be used as the basis for creating several typed tables, a `scope` clause can be used in the specification of a `ref` type to restrict reference values to those from a specific typed table. The syntax for the `scope` clause is shown in Figure 8.4.

If the `scope` clause is omitted, then the reference value stored in the attribute can be a row from any table having the specified type. If the `scope` clause is specified, then a reference scope check can also be specified. Specifying that `references are checked` indicates that dangling references (i.e., invalid reference values) are not allowed. By default, references are not checked. The `on delete` clause of the reference scope check syntax allows the user to specify the same referential actions as used with the specification of referential integrity for foreign keys. In the following example, the `advisor` attribute is redefined to indicate that object references must be from the `faculty` table and that references are checked for validity. The `on delete` clause indicates that deletion of a referenced `faculty` object will cause the `advisor` attribute to be set to `null`:

```
advisor ref(facultyUdt) scope faculty
        references are checked on delete set null;
```

Notice that the syntax in Figure 8.2 also supports the specification of table scopes and reference checks during the creation of typed tables. The syntax is the same as that used in the specification of structured types.

8.6.2 Querying Reference Types

When querying tables that contain columns with reference values, users are generally not interested in seeing the reference value. The reference value is typically a system-generated value that is useful for establishing object relationships but has little meaning from the users' point of view. Instead, the reference value is most often used to perform an *implicit join* as a means of accessing some attribute of the row that is being referenced.

The SQL standard supports the dereference operator, denoted as a right arrow ($\rightarrow$), to traverse through object references. The query that follows returns the name of the advisor of the "Campus Computer Club". The query is expressed over the `campusClub` table, but the value returned is from the `faculty` table. The dereference operator is used to implicitly join the `campusClub` and `faculty` tables on the basis of the reference value. The dereference operator provides a more concise, object-oriented way of traversing from one object to another than the use of explicit join conditions over relational tables.

```
select  advisor → fName
from    campusClub
where   name = 'Campus Computer Club';
```

The SQL standard also provides a deref() function that can be used to return the entire structured type associated with a reference value. The following query will return all instances of the facultyUdt type for advisors of campus clubs that are located in the Brickyard Building:

```
select deref (advisor)
from   campusClub c
where  c.location.bldg = 'Brickyard Building';
```

The result of the query is a table with one column of type facultyUdt. This resulting table can then be queried to access any of the attributes of the advisors.

The use of reference types is an important feature for mapping object-oriented conceptual designs to an object-relational representation. The next section provides more specific examples of the use of reference types in the mapping process.

8.7 Mapping to the SQL Standard Object-Relational Features

Chapter 4 addresses techniques for mapping EER and UML conceptual models to the relational data model, while Chapter 7 addresses techniques for using the same EER and UML conceptual designs to generate an object-oriented database schema. This section revisits the side-by-side EER and UML illustrations from Chapter 4 in the context of mapping to object-relational database designs. The fundamental concepts of mapping classes, attributes, and associations are presented in the context of the ABSTRACT ENTERPRISE from Figure 1.2 (ER version) and from Figure 2.23 (UML version). All of these concepts will be combined with mapping techniques for class hierarchies to present the complete object-relational representation of the SCHOOL DATABASE ENTERPRISE from Figure 2.16. The HOLLYWOOD ENTERPRISE in Figure 1.16 (EER version) and in Figure 2.28 (UML version) will also be used to illustrate mapping techniques for categories. Keep in mind that the mapping techniques presented in this chapter can be mixed with the relational mapping techniques described in Chapter 4. The emphasis in this chapter, however, is strictly on the use of the object-relational features of the SQL standard.

8.7.1 Classes, Attributes, and Associations

The general approach to mapping EER and UML conceptual diagrams to object-relational features is to translate each class in the conceptual design to a structured type with a corresponding typed table and to represent associations between classes by using reference types. Reference types can be combined with arrays to implement multivalued associations. Arrays and methods can also be used to implement multivalued attributes and derived attributes, respectively. The subsections that follow elaborate on the details of the mapping process.

Simple and Derived Attributes

Recall class A of Figure 4.1, which has simple attributes (keyOfA, attrOfA), a composite attribute (compositeOfA), and a derived attribute (derivedAttr). By means of the object-relational features of the SQL standard, class A is mapped to a typed table a with a corresponding structured type aUdt:

```
create type aUdt as
(keyOfA        varchar(3),
 attrOfA       varchar(3),
 compositeOfA row(attrA1 varchar(3), attrA2 varchar(3), attrA3
          varchar(3)))
 instantiable not final ref is system generated
 method derivedAttr() returns varchar(3);

create table a of aUdt
(primary key(keyOfA),
 ref is aID system generated);
```

The simple attributes keyOfA and attrOfA are defined in the structured type as varchar, for simplicity. Since the SQL standard provides inherent support for complex types, the composite attribute of a can be directly represented as either a row type or a structured type. For simplicity, a row type is used in this example. Structured types are useful for representing composite attributes when the attribute must be used in multiple table or type definitions or when there is a need for defining parameters or variables that correspond to the composite value. Structured types are also useful for representing composite values that require specific method definitions for manipulation of the value.

The derived attribute derivedAttr is defined as a method within the aUdt structured type. Recall that a constructor function, as well as observer and mutator functions, will also be generated for keyOfA, attrOfA, and compositeOfA. Constraints associated with the attributes of the class are expressed in the typed table definition. The definition of table a identifies keyOfA as the primary key of the typed table, in addition to the use of a system-generated internal object identifier aID. Even with the use of object identifiers, primary keys are still useful from an application-oriented point of view.

Multivalued Attributes

Class C of Figure 4.2 illustrates a multivalued attribute, named multiValuedAttr. In a pure relational representation, a multivalued attribute must be mapped to its own table, including the key attribute of the class. Since the SQL standard supports arrays as a collection type, multiValuedAttr can be directly represented as an attribute of the structured type cUdt for the typed table c, where the attribute is defined as an array of a specific data type (varchar in this case):

```
create type cUdt as
(keyOfC        varchar(3),
 attrOfC       varchar(3),
 multiValuedAttr varchar(3) array[10])
 instantiable not final ref is system generated;

create table c of cUdt ...
```

Bidirectional Associations without Attributes

In ODL as described in Chapter 7, bidirectional associations without attributes are mapped to a relationship with an inverse specification for both classes involved in the association. The object-relational features of the SQL standard do not support inverse specifications as in ODL, but reference types can be used on each side of the association to achieve an object-oriented approach to the representation of bidirectional associations. As an example, consider the 1:1 bc association between the classes B and C as illustrated in Figure 4.5. Define a typed table b having a structured type bUdt with an attribute named bTOc of type ref (cUdt). Also, define a typed table c having a structured type cUdt with an attribute cTOb of type ref (bUdt):

```
create type bUdt as
(...
 bTOc ref(cUdt) scope c references are checked on delete no action,
 ...)
 instantiable not final ref is system generated;

create type cUdt as
(...
 cTOb ref(bUdt) scope b references are checked on delete set null,
 ...)
 instantiable not final ref is system generated;

create table b of bUdt ... bTOc with options not null ...
create table c of cUdt ...
```

Note that this definition is a circular reference, which technically requires the use of an alter type statement to add the definition of bToC to the bUdt type after the cUdt type is defined. For conceptual presentation of the type definitions in this example and in other circular definitions in the remainder of this chapter, the alter type statement is omitted.

Unlike the object-oriented data model, which provides automatic support for inverse relationships, the user is responsible for maintaining the inverse relationship that exists between b and c. For example, if the attribute bTOc for a row b_i in b is assigned the object reference for the row c_j in c, then the application must be designed to update the attribute cTOb of the row c_j to the object reference for the row b_i. The inverse relationship can be maintained through the use of triggers or stored procedures. The Oracle case study in Chapter 9 provides specific implementation examples of maintaining inverse relationships between associations that are represented by reference types.

The cardinality ratio constraints of the association are inherent in the specification of the association by defining the reference type on each side of the association. For the bc association in Figure 4.5, the type of each association is a single object reference of the specified structured type. The total participation of class B in the bc association is defined by using the not null constraint in the typed table definition for b. (Note the different syntax for defining column constraints in typed tables, as specified in Figure 8.2.) In the object-oriented database mapping of Chapter 7, this constraint must be handled as part of the behavior of the object and is not directly supported by the database. The object-relational representation therefore provides more direct database support for the enforcement of attribute constraints.

Each reference in the bc association is constrained to store object references from a specific typed table using the scope clause. Even though object-relational implementations do not automatically maintain inverse relationships in bidirectional associations, the references are checked clause can be used to enforce referential integrity. As a result, the bTOc and cTOb attributes will never contain reference values for rows that do not exist in the referenced tables. If the clause is omitted or if the specification is `references are not checked`, then the attribute values may contain dangling reference values. In addition, an `on delete` action can be specified. For the bTOc attribute, the delete action is `no action`, since rows of b have required participation in the association. As a result, a row in c cannot be deleted if it is related to a row in b, because deleting a row in c may violate the total participation constraint of b. In the opposite direction, the action is `set null`, indicating that if a row in b is deleted, then the cTOb attribute can be set to null, thus reflecting the partial participation of c in the association.

The mapping approach described for a 1:1 association also applies to a bidirectional association without attributes having 1:N or M:N cardinality ratios. The only difference is that the type on the *many* side of the association is an array of reference types. To illustrate the mapping, consider a fictitious M:N association between the classes B and C (not represented in the ABSTRACT ENTERPRISE). The bidirectional association is mapped to an object-relational schema by using two separate arrays of reference types, where a row in b is related to potentially many object references to rows of c and a row of c is related to potentially many object references to rows of b:

```
create type bUdt as
(...
 bTOMANYc ref(cUdt) scope c array[10]
   references are checked on delete cascade, ...)
 instantiable not final ref is system generated;

create type cUdt as
(...
 cTOMANYb ref(bUdt) scope b array[10]
   references are checked on delete set null, ...)
 instantiable not final ref is system generated;

create table b of bUdt ...
create table c of cUdt ...
```

The following example illustrates the mapping for a fictitious 1:N association between B and C, where a row of b is related to potentially many object references to rows of c, but a row of c is related to at most one object reference to a row of b:

```
create type bUdt as
(...
 bTOMANYc ref(cUdt) scope c array[10]
   references are checked on delete cascade, ...)
 instantiable not final ref is system generated;
create type cUdt as
(...
 cTOb ref(bUdt) scope b
   references are checked in delete set null, ...)
 instantiable not final ref is system generated;

create table b of bUdt ...
create table c of cUdt ...
```

Bidirectional Associations with Attributes

When binary associations have attributes, an association typed table must be introduced to represent the attributes of the association. The association table includes two attributes with reference types—one for the structured type of each typed table participating in the binary association. Consider the M:N association ab between classes A and B that has a descriptive attribute `attrOfAB`, as shown in Figure 4.3. Figure 7.4 gives the UML diagram for the corresponding reified association. An association table is defined as a typed table named ab, with a structured type abUdt having the attribute `attrOfAB` and two reference type attributes: abTOa and abTOb. The reference type of abTOa is `ref(aUdt)`, having `scope` a, indicating the row of typed table a that is participating in the relationship instance. Similarly, the reference type of abTOb is `ref(bUdt)`, having `scope` b, indicating the row of typed table b that is participating in the relationship instance. The definitions for the structured types involved in the association include attributes with reference types to the structured type of the association table:

```
create type aUdt as
(...
 aTOab ref(abUdt) scope ab array[10]
   references are checked on delete set null, ...)
 instantiable not final ref is system generated;

create type bUdt as
(...
 bTOab ref(abUdt) scope ab array[10]
   references are checked on delete set null, ...)
 instantiable not final ref is system generated;

create type abUdt as
(...
 attrOfAB varchar(3),
 abTOa ref(aUdt) scope a references are checked on delete cascade,
 abTOb ref(bUdt) scope b references are checked on delete cascade, ...)
 instantiable not final ref is system generated;

create table a of aUdt ...
create table b of bUdt ...
create table ab of abUdt ...
```

The structured type aUdt contains the attribute aTOab having as its type `ref(abUdt)` `array[10]`, since an object of type aUdt is related to potentially many objects of type bUdt through the abUdt structured type of the ab association table. (The number 10 in the array definition is arbitrary and can be set to a number appropriate for the specific association.) Similarly, the structured type bUdt contains the attribute bTOab having as its type `ref(abUdt)` `array[10]`, since an object of type bUdt is related to potentially many objects of type aUdt through the abUdt structured type of the ab association table. Because the participation of a in the association is required, the application will need to ensure that there is always at least one value in the aTOab array.

Recursive Associations

The mapping of recursive associations is similar to the mapping of nonrecursive associations, except that the recursive association relates the typed table to itself, using a recursive reference to the structured type of the typed table. In Figure 4.7, the class B has a recursive association bb. A straightforward approach to mapping a recursive association is to use the role names of the association as the names of the reference attributes in the structured type. For example, the `parent` role of the bb association is of type `ref(bUdt)`, having the `child` attribute as its implied inverse relationship. The `child` attribute is an array of references to `bUdt`, representing the children of the parent. As in nonrecursive binary associations, in an object-relational implementation the user is responsible for maintaining the integrity of the relationship, although reference checks and delete actions can be specified to support maintenance of the association.

```
create type bUdt as
(...
 parent ref(bUdt) scope b
   references are checked on delete set null,
 child ref(bUdt) scope b array[10]
   references are checked on delete set null, ...)
 instantiable not final ref is system generated;

create table b of bUdt ...
```

N-ary Associations

The mapping of N-ary associations is similar to the mapping of binary associations having descriptive attributes. An association table is defined to represent the N-ary association, and N reference attributes are defined, one for the structured type of each typed table involved in the association. As an example, consider the ternary relationship given in Figure 4.8. In the object-relational mapping that follows, `finance` is the association table having the structured type `financeUdt`, with reference attributes `financedBank`, `financedCar`, and `financedPerson` that respectively refer to the bank, car, and person involved in the transaction. In the inverse direction, the structured types `bankUdt`, `carUdt`, and `personUdt` define reference attributes that point back to the `financeUdt` structured type. The cardinality of each attribute indicates the number of times a row from the typed table can participate in a `finance` association. The attributes in `bankUdt` and `personUdt`, for example, are defined as arrays, indicating that a bank can finance many cars and a person can buy many cars. The attribute in `carUdt` is single valued, indicating that a car can be sold only once.

```
create type financeUdt
(financedBank     ref(bankUdt) scope bank
   references are checked on delete cascade,
 financedCar      ref(carUdt) scope car
   references are checked on delete cascade,
 financedPerson   ref(personUdt) scope person
   references are checked on delete cascade, ...)
instantiable not final ref is system generated;

create type bankUdt /* inverse of financeBank */
(...
 carsFinance ref(financeUdt) scope finance array[10]
   references are checked on delete set null ...)
 instantiable not final ref is system generated;

create type carUdt /* inverse of financedCar */
```

```
(...
 financedBy ref(financeUdt) scope finance
 references are checked on delete set null ...)
 instantiable not final ref is system generated;

create type personUdt /* inverse of financedPerson */
(...
 carsFinanced ref(financeUdt) scope finance array[10]
   references are checked on delete set null ...)
 instantiable not final ref is system generated;

create table finance of financeUdt ...
create table bank of bankUdt ...
create table car of carUdt ...
create table person of personUdt ...
```

Unidirectional Associations

UML conceptual class diagrams have the ability to represent unidirectional associations through navigability. A unidirectional association stores the association in one direction. To define a unidirectional association by using the object-relational features of the SQL standard, define a reference attribute within the structured type of one side of the association. For example, the unidirectional association bc shown in Figure 4.10 is defined as a reference attribute in the structured type bUdt having the type ref(cUdt). The inverse of the unidirectional association is derived by providing a method in cUdt to derive the bUdt reference to which an instance of cUdt is related:

```
create type bUdt
(...
 bTOc  ref(cUdt) scope c
 references are checked on delete no action, ... )
 instantiable not final ref is system generated;

create type cUdt
(... )
 instantiable not final ref is system generated
 method cTOb( ) return bUdt;

create table b of bUdt ... bTOc with options not null ...
create table c of cUdt ...
```

Weak Entities

A weak entity of an EER diagram is typically related to its identifying owner by a 1:N relationship. In Figure 4.11, the Weak class is related to its identifying owner class A by its identifying relationship dependsOn. The candidate key of a weak entity is formed by the combination of the primary key of its identifying owner and its own partial key, which uniquely identifies the weak object in the context of the identifying owner. In the UML diagram of Figure 4.11, dependsOn is represented as a qualified association based on the partialKey.

To map this type of association to an object-relational representation, create a typed table for the weak entity with a composite key that includes the key of the typed table for the owner class. The structured type for the typed table of the weak class can also include a reference attribute to the row of the typed table that represents the owner class:

```
create type aUdt as
(keyOfA           varchar(3),
 linkToWeak       ref(weakUdt) scope weak array[10]
   references are checked on delete set null, ... )
 instantiable not final ref is system generated;

create type weakUdt as
(partialKey       varchar(3),
 keyOfA           varchar(3),
 linkToOwner      ref(aUdt) scope a
          references are checked on delete cascade, ... )
instantiable not final ref is system generated;

create table a of aUdt
(primary key (keyOfA), ... );

create table weak of weakUdt
(linkToOwner with options not null,
 foreign key(keyOfA) references a(keyOfA) on delete cascade,
 primary key(partialKey, keyOfA) ... );
```

For the semantics expressed in Figure 4.11, the reference attribute linkToWeak defined in aUdt represents the array of weakUdt objects associated with an instance of aUdt. The inverse association defined as linkToOwner in weakUdt links an instance of weakUdt to its identifying aUdt owner instance. The a typed table defines the attribute keyOfA as its primary key. In addition, the weak typed table includes the key of the identifying owner (keyOfA) in combination with the partialKey to create a composite key for the weak table.

Constraints on Classes, Attributes, and Associations

In mapping the object-oriented conceptual data models to the relational data model, relevant implementation-level constraints to consider for classes, attributes, and associations include the specification of candidate keys, referential integrity, participation, and multiplicity constraints. Mapping to the object-relational features of the SQL standard can still make use of primary key and uniqueness constraints to specify candidate keys. The referential integrity constraint is also extended to the specification of reference types to make sure that the value of a reference attribute refers to an object identifier in the referenced table. In addition, the scope clause can be used to restrict the reference to be from a specific typed table. The reference type specification in the SQL standard also inherently supports simple cardinality constraints, where arrays can be used with reference types to represent multivalued associations. A total participation constraint is inherently supported by placing a not null constraint on a reference attribute. When a total participation constraint is used together with a multivalued association, the application may need to ensure that an array of references always contains at least one value. Specific upper and lower bounds in multivalued associations must also be enforced by the application. Such constraints can be coded into the behavorial aspects of the structured type definition.

In comparison to their representation in object-oriented databases, the representation of bidirectional associations in an object-relational schema via reference types does not automatically support the specification and maintenance of inverse relationships. The maintenance of inverse relationships must be coded into the behavior of the application.

8.7.2 Checkpoint: Object-Relational Mapping of Classes, Attributes, and Associations

Table 8.2 summarizes the mapping of classes, attributes, and associations to an object-relational representation, using names such as cUdt and sUdt to represent generic type definitions. The first column indicates the component being mapped. The second column indicates the corresponding type to be defined in the schema. The third column, named **Object-Relational Definition**, gives either the type and table definitions associated with the type or the attribute definition that is added to the definition of the type to realize the component in the object model. The mapping summary assumes the use of bidirectional associations. Remember that structured types associated with typed tables must be defined as instantiable and as not final. The specification for generating object references must be consistent between the structured type and the typed table (e.g., system generated in both the structured type and the corresponding typed table). Standard column and table constraints can be defined on the attributes of a structured type in the typed table definition.

Figure 8.5 presents the complete object-relational schema for the unidirectional version of the ABSTRACT ENTERPRISE in Figure 4.13. The specification of the schema is

TABLE 8.2 Summary of Object-Relational Mapping Heuristics for Classes, Attributes, and Associations

Component	Type	Object-Relational Definition
class C	cUdt	create type cUdt as (...);
		create table c of cUdt (...);
single-valued attribute s of C	cUdt	s typeOfS
composite attribute s of C (implemented as a row type)	cUdt	s row(...)
composite attribute s of C (implemented as a structured type)	sUdt	create type sUdt as (...)
	cUdt	s sUdt
multivalued attribute m of C	cUdt	m typeOfM array[n]
binary association: no attributes (1:1 shown)	c1Udt	c1TOc2 ref(c2Udt) scope c2
	c2Udt	c2TOc1 ref(c1Udt) scope c1
binary association ac with attributes (e.g., attrOfAc): Use an association class (M:N shown)	c1Udt	c1TOac ref(acUdt) scope ac array[n]
	c2Udt	c2TOac ref(acUdt) scope ac array[n]
	acUdt	attrOfAC typeOfattrOfAC,
		acTOc1 ref(c1Udt) scope c1,
		acTOc2 ref(c2Udt) scope c2
recursive association c (1:N shown)	cUdt	parent ref(cUdt) scope c,
		child ref(cUdt) scope c array[n]

```
create type aUdt as
(keyOfA          varchar(3),
 attrOfA         varchar(3),
 compositeOfA    row(attrA1 varchar(3), attrA2 varchar(3), attrA3
                     varchar(3)),
 aTOab           ref(abUdt) scope ab array[10]
                     references are checked on delete set null,
 aTOb            ref(bUdt) scope ab
                     references are checked on delete cascade,
 attrOfBA        varchar(3),
 linkToWeak      ref(weakUdt) scope weak array[10]
                     references are checked on delete set null)
 instantiable  not final  ref is system generated
 method derivedAttr() returns varchar(3);

create table a of aUdt
(aTOb with options not null,
 aTOab with options not null,
 primary key(keyOfA),
 ref is aID system generated);

create type weakUdt as
(partialKey      varchar(3),
 keyOfA          varchar(3),
 attrOfWk        varchar(3),
 linkToOwner     ref(aUdt) scope a references are checked on delete
                     cascade)
 instantiable  not final  ref is system generated;

create table weak of weakUdt
(linkToOwner with options not null,
 primary key(partialKey, keyOfA),
 foreign key(partialKey) references a(keyOfA) on delete cascade,
 ref is wID system generated);

create type bUdt as
(keyOfB  varchar(3),
 attrOfB varchar(3),
 parent  ref(bUdt) scope b references are checked on delete set null,
 bTOab   ref(abUdt) scope ab array[10] references are checked
            on delete set null,
 bTOc    ref(cUdt) scope c references are checked on delete cascade)
 instantiable  not final  ref is system generated
 method bTOa() returns aUdt,
 method children() returns bUdt array[10];

create table b of bUdt
(bTOc with options not null,
 primary key(keyOfB),
 ref is bID system generated);

create type abUdt as
(attrOfAB      varchar(3),
 abTOa         ref(aUdt) scope a
                  references are checked on delete cascade,
 abTOb         ref(bUdt) scope b
                  references are checked on delete cascade)
 instantiable not final  ref is system generated;
```

Figure 8.5   The SQL Standard Object-Relational Schema of the Unidirectional ABSTRACT ENTER-
PRISE

```
create table ab of abUdt
(abTOa with options not null,
 abTOb with options not null,
 ref is abID system generated);

create type cUdt as
(keyOfC          varchar(3),
 attrOfC         varchar(3),
 multiValuedAttr varchar(3) array[10])
 instantiable not final  ref is system generated
 method cTOb() returns bUdt;

create table c of cUdt
(primary key(keyOfC),
 ref is cId system generated);
```

Figure 8.5 *(continued)*

more complex than the pure relational version in Figure 4.12. The object-relational version, however, supports the direct representation of multivalued attributes and the use of reference types together with arrays to represent 1:1, 1:N, and M:N associations between classes, where associations are based on object references rather than foreign keys. Arrays of references must be manipulated and queried through the use of SQL routines. Unlike the object-oriented mapping in Chapter 7, the user must maintain inverse relationships. The unidirectional mapping in Figure 4.13, however, illustrates how unidirectional relationships can be used to directly represent the relationship in one direction and to derive the relationship in the opposite direction through the use of a method. (See the method definitions in cUdt and in bUdt that correspond to the inverse of each unidirectional relationship.)

Exercises

1. Map the ECLECTIC ONLINE SHOPPING ENTERPRISE in Figure 1.1 to an object-relational schema. For each constraint associated with the schema, discuss whether the constraint is inherent in the object-relational schema specification or whether it must be captured in the behavior of the objects.

2. Using the dereference operator or the deref() function over the object-relational schema of the ECLECTIC ONLINE SHOPPING ENTERPRISE from Exercise 1, develop solutions for the following queries:

   (a) For each shopping cart, print the order identifier and the first and last name of the customer who owns the shopping cart.

   (b) For each inventory item, print the code, item number, quantity in stock, category identifier, and category description of the item.

   (c) Return the structured type instance for all orders that were placed by customers who live in Arizona.

3. Generate an object-relational schema for the GET FIT HEALTH CLUB ENTERPRISE described in Exercise 2 in Checkpoint 1.1.3. Compare the object-relational schema with the relational and ODL versions of the schema. Identify advantages and

disadvantages of the object-relational schema versus the relational schema. Identify advantages and disadvantages of the object-relational schema versus the ODL schema.

4. Using the dereference operator or the `deref()` function over the object-relational schema of the GET FIT HEALTH CLUB ENTERPRISE from Exercise 3, develop solutions for the following queries:

   (a) For each instance of the class schedule, print the class name, day, time, and first and last name of the instructor.

   (b) Return the structured type instance for all members who have trained with trainer Max Maxwell.

5. Map the MEDICAL PRACTICE ENTERPRISE to an object-relational schema. (See Exercise 3 in Checkpoint 1.1.3 for a description of the enterprise.) Verify that all of the constraints of the enterprise are captured in the resulting object-relational schema, and compare the object-relational schema with the corresponding relational schema and ODL schema.

6. Using the dereference operator or the `deref()` function over the object-relational schema of the MEDICAL PRACTICE ENTERPRISE from Exercise 5, develop solutions for the following queries:

   (a) For each visit, print the month, day, year, and description of the visit, together with the doctor's and patient's names.

   (b) Return the structured type instance for all doctors that have charged more than $50 for a visit.

7. Generate an object-relational schema for the MUSIC AGENCY ENTERPRISE described in Exercise 4 in Checkpoint 1.1.3. Verify that all of the constraints of the enterprise are captured in the resulting object-relational schema, and compare the object-relational schema with the corresponding relational schema and ODL schema.

8. Using the dereference operator or the `deref()` function over the object-relational schema of the MUSIC AGENCY ENTERPRISE from Exercise 7, develop solutions for the following queries:

   (a) For each CD, print the title and the number sold, together with the recording label name and group name of the CD.

   (b) Return the structured type instance for all musical groups that have recorded a CD title with Star Records. (Star is the name of the label.)

8.7.3 Class Hierarchies

The object-relational features of the SQL standard provide inherent support for the specification of class hierarchies. The inheritance of state and behavior is supported by the `under` clause in the structured type and typed table specifications. An example using the `Person` hierarchy from the SCHOOL DATABASE ENTERPRISE was given in Section 8.4.

The EER and UML conceptual data models both provide support for the specification of specialization constraints: disjoint versus overlapping specialization and total or mandatory participation in the class specialization. The object-relational model of the SQL standard does not provide for an overlapping specialization of subclasses. Therefore, by default, a specialization in an object-relational schema is disjoint. As in most object-oriented database implementations, if an overlapping specialization is required for the application, the programmer must simulate the inheritance for all but one of the subtables by using an explicit reference from the overlapping subtables to the supertable and explicitly calling the methods of the supertable to which it is related. The object will, of course, have multiple identifiers, one for each typed table (simulating the overlapping subtables) to which it belongs, and inheritance from the supertable to the overlapping subtables will not be automatically supported. The implementation of the overlapping specialization constraint therefore requires more coding effort on the part of the programmer to correctly represent the semantics of an overlapping specialization. The relational mapping techniques described in Chapter 4 can be used to simulate overlapping specialization.

The total specialization constraint is supported in the SQL standard for hierarchies of structured types, but not for hierarchies of typed tables. In a structured type hierarchy, the supertype can be defined as `not instantiable`, while the subtypes can be defined as `instantiable`. The supertype therefore becomes an abstract type that can be instantiated only at the subtype level. But when structured types are used together with typed table hierarchies, structured types must be defined as `instantiable`. The total specialization constraint must therefore be enforced through the application code by allowing the insertion of objects only at the subtable level.

The object-relational features of the SQL standard do not support the specification of shared subclasses from the EER model or the concept of interface classes from UML class diagrams. Attribute-defined subclasses from the EER model and discriminators from UML are also not inherently supported. If such features are used in a conceptual model that must be mapped to an object-relational implementation, the programmer must find creative solutions to the implementation of such requirements.

8.7.4 Categories

A category in the EER or the xor constraint in UML can be represented by introducing a typed table for the category. Attributes are introduced in the structured type of the category typed table to represent the association to its related superclasses.

The standard example of a category that has been used in previous chapters is the partial `Sponsor` category from the HOLLYWOOD ENTERPRISE, where a `Sponsor` is either a

Person or a Company, but a Person or a Company is not required to be a Sponsor. A uni-directional reference attribute is defined in the structured type sponsorUdt for each class participating in the category: personSponsor with a reference type of personUdt and companySponsor with a reference type of companyUdt. Only one of the unidirectional attributes can have a value at any given time. The other unidirectional attribute must always be null, since an instance of sponsorUdt cannot be related to both a personUdt and a companyUdt. This category constraint must be implemented within the behavior of sponsorUdt.

```
create type personUdt as ( ... )
  instantiable not final ref is system generated;

create type companyUdt as ( ... )
  instantiable not final ref is system generated;

create type sponsorUdt as
(personSponsor ref(personUdt),
 companySponsor ref(companyUdt) ...)
instantiable not final ref is system generated;

create table person of personUdt ...
create table company of companyUdt ...
create table sponsor of sponsorUdt ...
```

When the category is partial, a unidirectional association is preferred. It is still possible to find out whether a person or a company is a sponsor and to find the projects that they sponsor by navigating the unidirectional associations from the Sponsor typed table. If the category is total, requiring that every person and every company must participate in the category, then the category associations can be implemented with bidirectional relationships, where personUdt and companyUdt contain reference attributes that point back to sponsorUdt. The use of bidirectional relationships provides an explicit access path from person and company to the sponsor category table. The total categorization constraint can be enforced in the person and company tables by defining the reference attribute to sponsorUdt to be not null. Again, the person category table must still enforce the exclusive-or constraint of the category.

8.8   Checkpoint

Figure 8.6 presents the complete SQL schema for the SCHOOL DATABASE ENTERPRISE in Figure 2.16. The schema uses the object-relational features of the standard to represent hierarchies and object associations. Whereas the clubs, advises, and chair associations from Figure 2.16 are implemented via bidirectional reference attributes between struc-tured types, the associations for major and worksIn are implemented as unidirectional reference attributes with methods in departmentUdt to derive the inverse values. The mandatory participation constraint on the person hierarchy must be enforced through the application code that controls the insertion of rows into the student and faculty tables (not allowing direct insertion into the person table).

```
create type personUdt as
(pId         varchar(11),
 firstName   varchar(20),
 lastName    varchar(20),
 dob         date)
 instantiable not final ref is system generated;

create type facultyUdt under personUdt as
(rank         varchar(10),
 advisorOf ref(campusClubUdt) scope campusClub array[5]
    references are checked on delete set null,
 worksIn   ref(departmentUdt) scope department
    references are checked on delete no action,
 chairOf   ref(departmentUdt) scope department
    references are checked on delete set null)
 instantiable not final;

create type studentUdt under personUdt as
(status    varchar(10),
 memberOf ref(campusClubUdt) scope campusClub array[5]
    references are checked on delete set null,
 major     ref(departmentUdt) scope department
    references are checked on delete no action)
 instantiable not final;

create table person of personUdt
(primary key (pId),
 ref is personID system generated);

create table faculty of facultyUdt under person;
create table student of studentUdt under person;

create type departmentUdt as
(code         varchar(3),
 name         varchar(40),
 deptChair ref(facultyUdt) scope faculty
    references are checked on delete no action)
 instantiable not final ref is system generated
 method  getStudents() returns studentUdt array[1000],
 method  getFaculty() returns facultyUdt array[50];

create table department of departmentUdt
(primary key (code),
 deptChair with options not null,
 ref is departmentID system generated);

create type locationUdt as
(street varchar(30),
 bldg   varchar(5),
 room   varchar(5)) not final;
```

Figure 8.6 The SQL Standard Object-Relational Schema of the SCHOOL DATABASE ENTERPRISE. © ACM, 2003. This is a minor revision of the work published in "Using UML Class Diagrams for a Comparative Analysis of Relational, Object-Oriented, and Object-Relational Database Mappings," by S. Urban and S. Dietrich in *Proceedings of the 34th ACM SIGCSE Technical Symposium on Computer Science Education* (2003), http://doi.acm.org/10.1145/620000.611923

```
create type campusClubUdt as
(cId      varchar(10),
 name     varchar(50),
 location locationUdt,
 phone    varchar(12),
 advisor  ref(facultyUdt) scope faculty
   references are checked on delete cascade,
 members  ref(studentUdt) scope student array[50]
   references are checked on delete set null)
instantiable not final ref is system generated;

create table campusClub of campusClubUdt
(primary key (cId),
 ref is campusClubID system generated);
```

Figure 8.6   *(continued)*

Exercises

1. Generate an object-relational schema for the ECLECTIC ONLINE SHOPPING ENTER-
   PRISE that was revised in Exercise 1 in Checkpoint 1.2.5 to use class hierarchies.
   Verify that all of the constraints of the enterprise are captured in the resulting object-
   relational schema, and compare the object-relational schema with the corresponding
   relational schema and ODL schema.

2. Map the FICTITIOUS BANK ENTERPRISE described in Exercise 2 in Checkpoint 1.2.5
   to an object-relational schema. Verify that all of the constraints of the enterprise are
   captured in the resulting object-relational schema, and compare the object-relational
   schema with the corresponding relational schema and ODL schema.

3. Generate the complete object-relational schema for the HORSE RACING ENTERPRISE
   described in Exercise 1 in Checkpoint 1.4. Verify that all of the constraints of
   the enterprise are captured in the resulting object-relational schema, and compare
   the object-relational schema with the corresponding relational schema and ODL
   schema.

4. Using the dereference operator or the deref() function over the object-relational
   schema of the HORSE RACING ENTERPRISE from Exercise 3, develop solutions for
   the following queries:

   (a) For each horse, print the horse's name, the name of the horse's trainer, and
       the name of the trainer's stable.

   (b) For each first-place entry (an entry with finalPos of 1) at Evangeline Downs,
       print the race number and date of the race, together with the name of the
       jockey and the name of the horse that won the race.

   (c) Return the structured type instances for all horses owned by Bill Williams.

5. Generate the complete object-relational schema for the HOLLYWOOD ENTERPRISE
   in Figure 7.6. Verify that all of the constraints of the enterprise are captured in the

resulting object-relational schema, and compare the object-relational schema with the corresponding relational schema and ODL schema.

6. Using the dereference operator or the deref() function over the object-relational schema of the HOLLYWOOD ENTERPRISE from Exercise 5, develop solutions for the following queries:

    (a) For each modeling project sponsored by a company, print the project identifier, the project description, and the name of the company sponsor.

    (b) Print the names of celebrities that have been paid more than $1,000,000 for a modeling project.

    (c) Return the structured type instances for agents of female celebrities.

7. Write the code for the getStudents and getFaculty methods of departmentUdt in the object-relational schema of the SCHOOL DATABASE ENTERPRISE in Figure 8.6.

8. Write an SQL procedure for maintaining the inverse relationship between campus clubs and their advisors when a club is assigned a new advisor. Use the object-relational schema of the SCHOOL DATABASE ENTERPRISE in Figure 8.6. The procedure should accept the cId of a club and the pId of a faculty member who will serve as the advisor of the club. The procedure should then assign the faculty member as the advisor of the club and add the club to the faculty member's array of clubs advised. If the club had a previous advisor, what happens to the inverse relationship between the club and the old advisor?

9. Write an SQL procedure for maintaining the inverse relationship between a campus club and its student members when a new member is added to the club. Use the object-relational schema of the SCHOOL DATABASE ENTERPRISE in Figure 8.6. The procedure should accept the cId of a club and the pId of a student who is joining the club. The procedure should assign the student as a member of the club and add the club to the student's list of club membership.

10. Write an SQL procedure for maintaining the inverse relationship between a campus club and its student members when a member resigns from a club. Use the object-relational schema of the SCHOOL DATABASE ENTERPRISE in Figure 8.6. The procedure should accept the cId of a club and the pId of a student who is resigning from the club and take the appropriate action to remove the student from being a member of the club.

11. Modify the mapping for the HOLLYWOOD ENTERPRISE to represent Sponsor as a total category. Compare the mapping for the total category with the mapping for the partial category. How does the mapping ensure the enforcement of the constraints associated with the total category?

8.9   Bibliographic References

In response to the *Object-Oriented Database System Manifesto* prepared by researchers of object-oriented database technology [Atkinson et al., 1990], Michael Stonebraker led a group of researchers in relational database technology in the preparation of the *Third Generation Database System Manifesto*, a document that outlined the manner in which relational technology could be extended to support object-oriented features [Stonebraker et al., 1990]. Rowe and Stonebraker [1987] demonstrated the feasibility of object-relational technology with the development of Postgres, an object-relational version of Ingres [Held et al., 1975] (an early relational database prototype and research tool). Additional sources of information about object-relational technology can be found in Stonebraker [1995], Date and Darwen [1998], and Brown [2001].

The most complete source on the object-relational features of the SQL standard is Melton [2002], with additional information about arrays and row types in Gulutzan and Pelzer [1999] and Melton and Simon [2001]. The complete SQL standards documents can be ordered by contacting the American National Standards Institute or the International Standards Organization.

The use of the SCHOOL DATABASE ENTERPRISE for mapping to object-relational technology was originally presented in Urban et al. [2000], with additional mapping issues addressed in Urban and Dietrich [2003].

Chapter 9

Case Studies: Relational, Object-Relational, and Object-Oriented Database Implementations

Synopsis

This chapter provides relational, object-relational, and object-oriented case studies of database implementations for the SCHOOL DATABASE ENTERPRISE. These case studies reinforce the concepts covered in previous chapters and supplement the material covered in Chapters 3, 4, 7, and 8 with specific examples of database implementations using commercial database products. The relational and object-relational implementations use Oracle, and the object-oriented implementation uses Objectivity/DB. The case studies presented in this chapter provide the opportunity for a comparative analysis of the different database paradigms.

Assumed Knowledge

- Enhanced Entity Relationship (EER) Diagrams (Chapter 1)

- Unified Modeling Language (UML) Conceptual Class Diagrams (Chapter 2)

- The SQL Standard: Advanced Relational Features (Chapter 3)

- Mapping Object-Oriented Conceptual Models to the Relational Data Model (Chapter 4)

- Object-Oriented Databases and the ODMG Standard (Chapter 7)

- The SQL Standard: Object-Relational Features (Chapter 8)

Implementation Examples on Web

- SCHOOL DATABASE ENTERPRISE: Relational Version

- SCHOOL DATABASE ENTERPRISE: Object-Relational Version

- SCHOOL DATABASE ENTERPRISE: Object-Oriented Version

This chapter presents case studies that illustrate the relational, object-relational, and object-oriented database concepts and mapping techniques discussed in the previous chapters. The Oracle database system illustrates relational and object-relational implementations, while Objectivity/DB illustrates an object-oriented database implementation. In all three cases, the SCHOOL DATABASE ENTERPRISE is used to emphasize how the same conceptual model can be implemented in different ways, depending on the underlying database technology. For each mapping, a revised and annotated UML diagram of the enterprise is presented to demonstrate how bidirectional and unidirectional associations provide different mapping directives, depending on the target database. Each case study also exhibits some of the similarities and differences that exist between the relevant standards (SQL and ODMG) and actual database products.

This chapter does not attempt to teach readers how to use each database system. Instead, the sections that follow present representative examples of actual code from each database implementation (available on the Web site for this book) that illustrates the concepts covered in the book.

9.1   Oracle: Relational Database Mappings

Figure 9.1 presents a UML diagram of the SCHOOL DATABASE ENTERPRISE. The diagram has been modified to support the description of a pure relational implementation of the enterprise in Oracle. Besides presenting basic schema definition using the DDL of Oracle, this section illustrates the mapping and constraint enforcement issues addressed in Chapter 4, as well as the PL/SQL language of Oracle for the expression of stored procedures and triggers examined in Chapter 3.

Figure 9.1 has been annotated to summarize the mapping approach taken for generating the Oracle DDL of the schema. The `clubs` association is the only relationship to be implemented as a bidirectional association. Since a M:N association must always be mapped to a separate relationship table in the relational model, illustrating `clubs` as a bidirectional association is the only appropriate modeling choice. The 1:1 and 1:N relationships can be modeled as either bidirectional or unidirectional associations, but a unidirectional representation is used in the figure. As described in Chapter 4, a unidirectional association implies that the association should be mapped with the primary key of one table embedded as a foreign key in the other table. The full Oracle DDL for the relational mapping is presented in Figure 9.2.

9.1.1   Constraints of the Application

The Oracle DDL closely follows the DDL of the SQL standard. The most obvious difference is the `create or replace` syntax in the `create` statement, indicating that

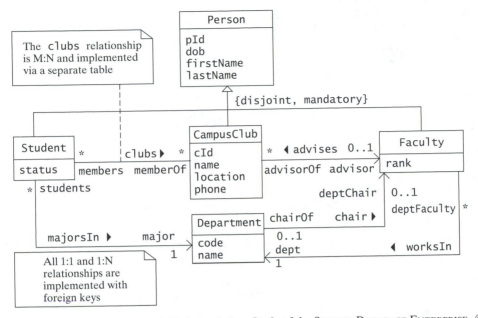

Figure 9.1 UML for the Oracle Relational Case Study of the SCHOOL DATABASE ENTERPRISE. © ACM, 2003. This is a minor revision of the work published in "Using UML Class Diagrams for a Comparative Analysis of Relational, Object-Oriented, and Object-Relational Database Mappings," by S. Urban and S. Dietrich, in *Proceedings of the 34th ACM SIGCSE Technical Symposium on Computer Science Education* (2003), http://doi.acm.org/10.1145/620000.611923.

the statement will either create a new schema object or replace an existing one if a schema object with the same name exists.

The schema in Figure 9.2 illustrates the specification of the `primary key` constraint, the `not null` constraint, and the `check` constraint. The `not null` constraint is used to enforce all cases of total participation (`dept` in the `facultyEDB` table and `major` in the `studentEDB` table), as well as to indicate required attribute values, such as `rank` in `facultyEDB`. The `check` constraint restricts the possible values for the `rank` and `status` attributes of `facultyEDB` and `studentEDB`, respectively. The `foreign key` constraint is expressed for all occurrences of foreign keys, supporting the update and delete options outlined in the SQL standard.

In this mapping, the `Person` hierarchy is represented by creating a table for each class in the hierarchy (`person`, `studentEDB`, and `facultyEDB`). Views are created to present all of the immediate and inherited attributes of the `Student` and `Faculty` subclasses.

Recall the ISA constraint, which states that an instance of a subclass must also exist as an instance of a superclass. Since a pure relational schema does not automatically support the notion of superclass and subclass, the database must be designed to support this feature by providing a way to check the ISA constraint using a view or stored procedure. In this application, the ISA constraint is maintained through a foreign key defined as a primary key in each subclass. For example, `pId` is declared as the foreign key in `facultyEDB`, referencing the `pId` in `person` to support the superclass/subclass relationship. The same

```
create or replace table department
(code      varchar(3)     primary key,
 name      varchar(40)    not null,
 chair     varchar(11));

create or replace table person
(pId                varchar(11)  primary key,
 dob                date         not null,
 firstName          varchar(20)  not null,
 lastName           varchar(20)  not null);

create or replace table facultyEDB
(pId      varchar(11) primary key,
 rank     varchar(10) not null,
 dept     varchar(3)  not null,
 constraint faculty_rank_ck check (rank = 'assistant' or
   rank = 'associate' or rank = 'full' or rank = 'emeritus'),
 constraint faculty_pId_fk foreign key(pId) references person(pId),
 constraint faculty_dept_fk foreign key(dept)
   references department(code));

alter table department add constraint department_chair_fk
    foreign key(chair) references facultyEDB(pId) on delete set null;

create or replace table studentEDB
(pId      varchar(11) primary key,
 status  varchar(10) not null,
 major    varchar(3)  not null,
 constraint student_status_ck check (status = 'freshman' or
    status = 'sophomore' or status = 'junior' or
      status = 'senior' or status = 'graduate'),
 constraint student_pId_fk foreign key(pId) references person(pId),
 constraint student_major_fk foreign key(major)
   references department(code));

create or replace table campusClub
(cId      varchar(10) primary key,
 name     varchar(50) not null,
 phone    varchar(12),
 location varchar(40),
 advisor  varchar(11),
 constraint campusClub_advisor_fk foreign key(advisor)
   references facultyEDB(pId) on delete set null);

create or replace table clubs
(pId      varchar(11),
 cId      varchar(10),
 constraint clubs_pIdcId_pk primary key(pId, cId),
 constraint clubs_pId_fk foreign key(pId) references studentEDB(pId)
   on delete cascade,
 constraint clubs_cId_fk foreign key(cId) references campusClub(cId)
   on delete cascade);
```

Figure 9.2 Oracle DDL for the SCHOOL DATABASE ENTERPRISE Relational Mapping

```
create or replace view faculty as
select p.pId, p.dob, p.firstName, p.lastName, f.rank, f.dept
from    person p, facultyEDB f
where   p.pId = f.pId;

create or replace view student as
select p.pId, p.dob, p.firstName, p.lastName, s.status, s.major
from    person p, studentEDB s
where   p.pId = s.pId;
```

Figure 9.2   (*continued*)

approach is taken to represent the ISA constraint that exists between the Student and Person classes.

Other constraints of the application can be checked by creating views to identify data that violate each constraint. Ideally, the user interface to the application should be designed to prevent constraint violations.

The Disjoint Constraint

The disjoint constraint states that if several subclasses are disjoint, an instance of the superclass can exist in only one of the disjoint subclasses. For example, a Person can be either a Student or a Faculty, but not both. The relational schema in Figure 9.2 cannot enforce this constraint automatically. The following view finds tuples in the person table that violate the disjoint constraint:

```
create view notDisjointPerson as
select *
from person P
where P.pId in
     (select F.pId from faculty F) and
      P.pId in (select S.pId from student S);
```

The Total Specialization Constraint

The total specialization constraint states that an instance in a superclass is required to exist as an instance of at least one subclass. In this application, a Person must exist as either a Faculty or a Student. The notTotalPerson view is used to find the tuples in the person table violating the total specialization constraint:

```
create view notTotalPerson as
select *
from    person P
where   P.pId not in
     (select F.pId from faculty F union select S.pId from student S);
```

Explicit Constraints

In the SCHOOL DATABASE ENTERPRISE, there is an explicit constraint that a faculty member can be the chair only of the department in which the faculty member works. The view deptHasWrongChair finds the department having a chair that does not work in the department, and the view `facultyAsChairOfWrongDept` finds the faculty members that are assigned as chairs to the wrong department:

```
create view deptHasWrongChair as
    select D.*, F.dept
    from   department D, faculty F
    where  D.chair = F.pId and F.dept <> D.code;
```

```
create view facultyAsChairOfWrongDept as
    select F.*, D.Code
    from    faculty F, department D
    where   F.pId = D.chair and F.dept <> D.code;
```

9.1.2 Stored Procedures

Procedural Language/SQL (PL/SQL) is Oracle's version of persistent stored modules, providing a language for creating stored procedure and function definitions that support variable and type declarations, as well as conditional, iterative, and sequential control flow statements. Conditional control statements include the `if-then-else` and `case` statements. The `while loop`, `for loop`, and `exit when` statements are supported as iterative control statements, with the `goto` statement affording sequential control. With PL/SQL, database developers can make use of the data manipulation power of SQL, together with the general-purpose computing capabilities of a procedural language.

For example, the code presented next illustrates the `insertFaculty` procedure, which inserts a faculty member into the `facultyEDB` table and calls another procedure, `insert-Person`, to insert a corresponding tuple into the `person` table.

```
create or replace procedure insertFaculty
    (pId in varchar, dob in date, fName in varchar,
    lName in varchar, rank in varchar, dept in varchar) is
begin
    insertPerson(pId, dob, fName, lName);
    insert into facultyEDB values(pId, rank, dept);
    dbms_output.put_line('Faculty with pId' || pId || ' is inserted.');
end insertFaculty;
```

```
create or replace procedure insertPerson
    (id in varchar, dob in date, fName in varchar, lName in varchar) is
    counter integer;
begin
    select count(*) into counter from person p where p.pId = id;
    if (counter > 0) then
    -- person with the given pId already exists
        dbms_output.put_line('Warning inserting person: person with pId'
        || id || 'already exists!');
    else
        insert into person values (id, dob, fName, lName);
        dbms_output.put_line('Person with pId '|| id || 'is inserted.');
    end if;
end insertPerson;
```

The `insertFaculty` procedure is used to enforce the ISA constraint and the total specialization constraint when faculty data are inserted. The statement `dbms_output.put_line` is a PL/SQL extension to the SQL standard that supports the output of data from a stored procedure, with the symbol ‖ serving as a string concatenation operator.

The procedure `getAdvisedClubs` illustrates the use of cursors to print information about the clubs advised by a faculty member. In this example, a cursor is defined on the basis of the result set retrieved by the `select` statement. The tuples in the result set are then printed with the use of a `for` loop. Oracle fully supports the basic cursor features defined in the SQL standard, such as the `declare`, `open`, `close`, and `fetch` statements (although the Oracle `cursor` statement has a slightly different syntax) as well as extensions that support the definitions of cursor parameters and return types (not shown in this example).

```
create or replace procedure getAdvisedClubs (pId in varchar) is
    cursor c is select * from campusClub cm where cm.advisor = pId;
begin
    dbms_output.put_line('faculty: '‖ pId);
    dbms_output.put_line('cId name');
    dbms_output.put_line('location phone');
    dbms_output.put_line('------------------');
    for rec in c loop
        dbms_output.put_line(rec.cId ‖ ' ' ‖ rec.name);
        dbms_output.put_line(rec.location ‖ ' ' ‖ rec.phone);
    end loop;
end getAdvisedClubs;
```

Other features of PL/SQL are illustrated in the next section through the use of triggers.

9.1.3 Triggers

In Oracle, triggers make use of PL/SQL for the expression of declarative, executable, and exception-handling code. There are three types of triggers in Oracle: DML triggers on tables, `instead-of` triggers on views, and system triggers on a database or a schema. A DML trigger is fired by a DML statement such as an `insert`, `update`, or `delete` statement. An `instead of` trigger is defined on a view to carry out the underlying database operations that cannot be directly executed on the view. A system trigger can be defined to fire in case of a system event, such as a database start-up or shutdown, or a DDL operation, such as table creation.

As in the SQL standard, DML triggers in Oracle are fired either before or after the execution of the specified operation. A DML trigger can make use of implicit parameters that represent the instance of the object type on which the trigger is fired. Parameter `:new` represents new values and `:old` represents existing or old values. Parameter `:new` is applicable to `insert` and `update` triggers, while `:old` is applicable to `update` and `delete` triggers. Row triggers and statement triggers are also supported. DML triggers are typically used to log changes in the database or to enforce complex constraints that cannot be easily enforced through the use of the `check` constraint or the `assertion` statement. In the SCHOOL DATABASE ENTERPRISE, DML triggers are used to maintain inheritance and explicit constraints that are not enforced by declarative constraints in the table definition.

Triggers to Maintain Specialization Constraints

Recall that `Student` and `Faculty` are disjoint and total specializations of `Person`. The code presented next shows an `insert` trigger on the `facultyEDB` table, ensuring that the newly inserted tuple does not violate the disjoint constraint. The trigger is a row trigger that is fired before execution of the `insert` statement on `facultyEDB`. If a violation occurs, an error message will be displayed by means of the exception-handling feature of PL/SQL.

```
create or replace trigger faculty_before_insert_row
     before insert on facultyEDB
     for each row
declare
     counter integer;
     OverLap exception; -- declare exception
begin
     select count(1) into counter
     from student s
     where s.pId = :new.pId;
     if (counter > 0) then
          raise Overlap;
     end if;
exception
     when Overlap then
     raise_application_error(-20001,
     'ERROR: The person already exits as a student');
end;
```

Another trigger on the `facultyEDB` table deletes the corresponding tuple from the `person` table whenever a tuple is deleted from `facultyEDB`. This trigger (together with its counterpart in `studentEDB`) ensures that no person exists without being a faculty member or a student:

```
create or replace trigger faculty_after_delete_row
     after delete on facultyEDB for each row
begin
     delete from person where pId = :old.pId;
end;
```

Triggers to Maintain Explicit Constraints

In the SCHOOL DATABASE ENTERPRISE, a faculty member can be the chair only of the department in which the faculty member works. Three triggers are used over the `department` and `facultyEDB` tables to enforce this constraint automatically.

When a `department` tuple is being inserted, the department cannot have a chair value, since no faculty members have been assigned to the department yet. The `dept_before_insert_row` trigger is used to enforce this constraint:

```
create or replace trigger dept_before_insert_row
     before insert on department for each row
begin
     if (:new.chair is not null ) then
     raise_application_error
     (-20001, 'ERROR: Cannot specify chair on insert.');
     end if;
end;
```

When the chair of a department is updated, the new chair needs to be either null or a faculty member who works in the department being updated. The dept_before_update _row row trigger illustrates the actions to take in this case.

```
create or replace trigger dept_before_update_row
      before update on department
      for each row
declare
      f_obj facultyEDB%rowtype;
      counter integer;
begin
      if updating ('chair') and (:new.chair is not null) then
            select * into f_obj from faculty f where f.pId = :new.chair;
            if (f_obj.dept <> :new.code ) then
            raise_application_error(-20002,
            'ERROR: New chair does not work in this department.');
            end if;
      end if;
exception
      when no_data_found then
            raise_application_error(-20002,
            'ERROR: New chair does not exist.');
end;
```

Note that the type of variable f_obj is declared as faculty%rowtype, specifying that f_obj has the same type and fields as each row of table facultyEDB. In the trigger body, if updating('chair') states that this trigger is fired only when the chair column of the department table is being updated. Notice that two possible error conditions can be raised. The first error condition is explicitly raised as part of the if statement; the second error condition is raised as part of the when no_data_found exception, which is raised when the select statement returns no data as a result.

When a faculty member who is also a department chair transfers to another department, the chair of the original department must be changed accordingly (set to null in this application), as illustrated in the faculty_after_update_row trigger:

```
create or replace trigger faculty_after_update_row
      after update on facultyEDB
      for each row
begin
      if updating ('dept') and :old.dept <> :new.dept then
            update department set chair = null where chair = :old.pId;
      end if;
end;
```

9.2 Oracle: Object-Relational Database Mappings

This section presents an object-relational version of the SCHOOL DATABASE ENTERPRISE implemented with Oracle. The implementation illustrates the use of user-defined types, reference types, and typed tables, as well as Oracle's support for collections in the form of variable-sized arrays (varrays) and nested tables (a feature that is not supported by the SQL standard). As in the relational implementation, stored procedures and triggers are used for constraint enforcement and to maintain inverse relationships between objects. Type and table hierarchies are also supported by Oracle, but these features are not used in the case study due to differences between the use of table hierarchies in the SQL standard and table hierarchies in Oracle.

Figure 9.3 shows a modified UML diagram of the SCHOOL DATABASE ENTERPRISE, with annotations that explain the manner in which the enterprise is mapped to the Oracle object features. Each class in the diagram is translated into a type with an associated typed table. The `clubs` association is implemented as a bidirectional association, with a varray of references on one side of the association and a nested table of references on the other side for an object-oriented approach to the implementation of M:N associations. The `getClubs` method has been added to the `Student` class to provide a way to return the names of the clubs (rather than the references) in which a student participates. The 1:N `advises` association, also bidirectional, is implemented as a varray in `Faculty` to store a collection of references to the campus clubs that a faculty member advises. The `getClubsAdvised` method has been added to `Faculty` to return the names of the advised clubs. In `CampusClub`, an inverse reference attribute is used to point back to the advisor

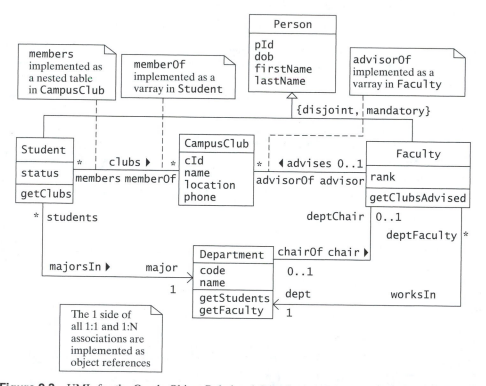

Figure 9.3 UML for the Oracle Object-Relational Case Study of the SCHOOL DATABASE ENTER-PRISE. © ACM, 2003. This is a minor revision of the work published in "Using UML Class Diagrams for a Comparative Analysis of Relational, Object-Oriented, and Object-Relational Database Mappings," by S. Urban and S. Dietrich, in *Proceedings of the 34th ACM SIGCSE Technical Symposium on Computer Science Education* (2003), http://doi.acm.org/10.1145/620000.611923.

of the club. The `chair` association is also bidirectional and is implemented as a reference attribute on each side of the relationship. The `majorsIn` and `worksIn` associations are unidirectional, with a reference attribute in `Student` and `Faculty`, respectively. The `getStudents` and `getFaculty` methods in `Department` are used to derive the inverse of each association. All of the relevant type and table definitions for the Oracle object-relational representation of Figure 9.3 appear in Figure 9.4 and are described in detail throughout the remainder of this section.

9.2.1 Object Types

In conformance with the SQL standard, Oracle supports the basic object-relational feature of object types. An object type is a composite structure that can have a set of attributes and methods. In the following simple example of an object type declaration for the `Person` class without methods, notice that the Oracle definition of an object type does not require the instantiation, finality, and reference generation clauses, as does the SQL standard:

```
create or replace type person_t as object
(pId           varchar2(9),
 firstName     varchar2(20),
 lastName      varchar2(20),
 dob           date);
```

To assign values to an object type, a variable can be created as having the type of the object type. The following example illustrates how to assign values to the attributes of the `person_t` object type in PL/SQL:

```
declare
     p person_t;
begin
     p.pId := 'PR1234567';
     p.firstName := 'Terrence';
     p.lastName := 'Grand';
     p.dob := '10-NOV-1975';
end;
```

Oracle does not support row types from the SQL standard. Instead, *embedded objects* are used to achieve a similar purpose. When an object type is used as the attribute value of another object type, the attribute value is referred to as an embedded object. Embedded objects do not have object identifiers, but provide a way to define an attribute as containing a composite value. In the following example, the `location` attribute of the `campusClub_t` object type is used as an embedded object:

```
create or replace type location_t as object
(street        varchar2(30),
 bldg          varchar2(5),
 room          varchar2(5));

create or replace type campusClub_t as object
(cId           number,
 name          varchar2(50),
 phone         varchar2(25),
 location      location_t, ... );
```

```
create or replace type campusClub_t;
create or replace type campusClub_array as varray(50)
  of ref campusClub_t;
create or replace type student_t;
create or replace type student_array as varray(50)
  of ref student_t;
create or replace type faculty_t;
create or replace type faculty_array as varray(50)
  of ref faculty_t;
create or replace type string_array as varray (50)
  of varchar2(50);


create or replace type location_t as object
(street    varchar2(30),
 bldg      varchar2(5),
 room      varchar2(5));


create or replace type department_t as object
(code           varchar2(3),
 name           varchar2(40),
 deptChair      ref faculty_t,
 member function getStudents return student_array,
 member function getFaculty return faculty_array,
 pragma restrict_references (default, wnds, wnps));


create or replace table department of department_t
(code           primary key,
 name           not null)
 object id primary key;


create or replace type person_t as object
(pId            varchar2(9),
 firstName      varchar2(20),
 lastName       varchar2(20),
 dob            date);


create or replace table person of person_t
(pId            primary key,
 firstName      not null,
 lastName       not null,
 dob            not null)
 object id primary key;


create or replace type faculty_t as object
(super      ref person_t,
 rank       varchar2(25),
 advisorOf  campusClub_array,
 worksIn    ref department_t,
 chairOf    ref department_t,
 member function getClubsAdvised return string_array,
 pragma restrict_references (default, wnds, wnps));
```

Figure 9.4 Oracle DDL for the SCHOOL DATABASE ENTERPRISE Object-Relational Mapping

```
create or replace table faculty of faculty_t
(super    references person not null,
 worksIn references department not null,
 chairOf references department,
 constraint check_chairOf check (chairOf = worksIn),
 constraint faculty_rank_ck
   check (rank='assistant' or rank='associate' or rank='full' or
          rank='emeritus'));

create unique index faculty_idx on faculty(super);

alter table department add (constraint department_chair
   foreign key(deptChair) references faculty on delete set null);

create or replace type student_t as object
(super         ref person_t,
 status        varchar2(10),
 major         ref department_t,
 memberOf      campusClub_array,
 member function getClubs return string_array,
 pragma restrict_references (default, wnds, wnps));

create or replace table student of student_t
(super references person not null,
 major references department not null,
 constraint student_status_ck
   check (status='freshman' or status='sophomore' or status='junior' or
          status='senior' or status='graduate'));

create unique index student_idx on student(super);

create or replace type student_ntable as table of ref student_t;

create or replace type campusClub_t as object
(cId           number,
 name          varchar2(50),
 phone         varchar2(25),
 location      location_t,
 advisor       ref faculty_t,
 members       student_ntable,
 member function isAssociatedMember
 (candidate_member in ref student_t) return boolean,
 member function isAssociatedAdvisor
 (candidate_advisor in ref faculty_t) return boolean,
 pragma restrict_references (default, wnds, wnps));

create or replace table campusClub of campusClub_t
(cId           primary key,
 name          not null)
 object id primary key
 nested table members store as club_members;
```

Figure 9.4 *(continued)*

When an object type is used as the type of a column in a traditional relational table, the value is referred to as a *column object*. Embedded and column objects are accessed and manipulated in the same way that the SQL standard describes for structured types. For example, consider the following table definition with a column object loc:

```
create table courseOffering(code int, loc location_t);
```

Data can be inserted into the table by using the type constructor for location_t:

```
insert into courseOffering
    values (123, location_t ('Orange Mall', 'CPCOM', '207'));
```

Object type definitions may also contain method specifications. The methods of an object type are functions or procedures that model the behavior of objects. Recall that methods in the SQL standard are limited to functions only. As in the SQL standard, the self parameter is an instance of the object type on which a method is invoked. The next example illustrates the PL/SQL code definition of the isAssociatedAdvisor function associated with the campusClub_t object type definition:

```
create or replace type body campusClub_t is
...
member function isAssociatedAdvisor (candidate_advisor in ref faculty_t)
    return boolean is
begin
    return (self.advisor = candidate_advisor);
end isAssociatedAdvisor;
end;
```

The declaration of the function is shown in the campusClub_t type definition in Figure 9.4. The isAssociatedAdvisor function determines whether a faculty member is an advisor of a club. Methods are implemented in the object type body definition for campusClub_t.

The declaration of the isAssociatedAdvisor function, as well as the isAssociated Member function, in campusClub_t of Figure 9.4 is also accompanied by a pragma declaration. Pragmas are compiler directives. Pragmas do not affect the meaning of a program; they simply convey information to the compiler. Pragma restrict_references is used to control side effects in a function, asserting that a function does not read or write any database tables or package variables. The syntax is

```
pragma restrict_references (function_name, option [, option])
```

The function name default can be used to specify that the pragma applies to all functions in the type definition. The pragma options are as follows:

wnds: Writes no database state (does not modify database tables).

rnds: Reads no database state (does not query database tables).

wnps: Writes no package state (does not change the values of package variables).

rnps: Reads no package state (does not reference the values of package variables).

In addition to the methods explicitly defined in an object type definition, every object type has a system-defined constructor method that creates a new instance of an object type and sets up the values of its attributes. The name of the constructor method is the name of the object type. Its parameters have the names and types of the object type's attributes. The constructor method is a function that returns an instance of an object type as its value. For example, the following invocation of the person_t constructor method returns an instance of the person_t object type with the specified attribute values. Unlike the definition of constructor methods in the SQL standard, the built-in constructor for an object type in Oracle accepts parameter values for the attributes of the type.

person_t('PR123456789', 'Terrence', 'Grand', '12-MAY-1975')

9.2.2 Object Tables

An object table is a table in which each row represents an object, each of which has a unique object identifier (oid). Objects that occupy complete rows in object tables are called *row objects*. Oracle allows row objects to be referenced, meaning that other row objects or relational rows may reference a row object by using its oid.

The unique oid value can be specified by means of table constraints as either system generated or based on the row object's primary key. The default oid value is system gener- ated. Figure 9.4 shows how to create an object table based on an object type for each class in the SCHOOL DATABASE ENTERPRISE, where the syntax is similar to that for defining object tables in the SQL standard. For example, object table person is defined on the basis of the object type person_t. The ref is clause of the SQL standard is replaced by the object id clause to specify how object identifiers are generated. In the figure, all of the table defi- nitions indicate that object identifiers are based on primary keys. As in the standard, table and column constraints can be defined in the specification of the object table.

9.2.3 Reference Types

Oracle supports reference types (refs) as defined in the SQL standard, according to which reference types can be used to define object-to-object relationships. In Oracle, a ref is a logical pointer to a row object. For example, in Figure 9.4, the advisor attribute of the campusClub_t object type refers to the object type faculty_t. Also, in the same figure, a ref type is used to model the major relationship between student_t and department_t.

Constraining Reference Types

A ref column or attribute can be constrained by means of a scope clause or a referential constraint clause. When a ref column is unconstrained, it may store object references to row objects contained in any object table of the corresponding object type. Unconstrained references may also lead to dangling references. Currently, Oracle does not permit stor- ing object references that contain a primary-key-based object identifier in unconstrained ref columns.

A ref column may be constrained in Oracle with a referential constraint similar to the specification for foreign keys. The next example, from Figure 9.4, illustrates the use of the references clause to specify a column referential constraint on the deptChair column of the department object table. The clause specifies that a ref stored in a deptChair column must point to a valid row object in the faculty object table. This clause also implicitly restricts the scope of deptChair to the faculty object table.

```
create or replace type department_t as object
(...
 deptChair          ref faculty_t, ... );
```

```
create or replace table department of department_t
( ... ) object id primary key;
```

```
alter table department
     add (constraint department_chair foreign key(deptChair)
     references faculty on delete set null);
```

A ref column may also be constrained by being scoped to a specific object table, using a scope clause as defined in the SQL standard. The scope constraint is different from the referential constraint in that the scope constraint has no implications on the referenced object. That is, deleting a referenced object can still cause a dangling reference. The following alter table statement uses the scope clause to constrain the advisor attribute in the campusClub table to refer to objects in the faculty table:

```
alter table campusClub
    add (scope for (advisor) is faculty);
```

The unique and primary key constraints cannot be specified for ref columns. However, a unique index may be created on a scoped ref column to ensure the uniqueness of the ref values.

Using Reference Types

Queries involving objects make a distinction between row objects, refs, and object types. Oracle provides three functions to support queries involving objects:

- ref() is a function that takes a row object as its argument and returns the ref to that object.

- value() is a function that takes a row object and returns the instance of the object type.

- deref() is a function that takes a ref to an object and returns the instance of the object type.

As an example, consider the campusClub_t object type and its corresponding campusClub object table, together with the following sequence of code:

```
declare
     club_ref   ref campusClub_t;
     club       campusClub_t;
     club_adv   faculty_t;
begin
     select value(c), ref(c), deref(c.advisor)
            into club, club_ref, club_adv
     from    campusClub c
     where   c.name='The Hiking Club';
end;
```

In a select statement such as the one shown in the preceding code sequence, the table alias (c in this case) always contains a row object. To see the values of the attributes of the row object as defined in the object type, use `value(c)`. To get the `ref` to the row object, use `ref(c)`. To get values of the attributes of the object type associated with a `ref`, use the `deref( )` function. The only difference between `value` and `deref` is the input to each function, where `value` takes a row object as input and `deref` takes a `ref` as input. In both cases, the output is the instance of the object type (that is, a tuple of attribute values) associated with the object.

After executing the foregoing query, `club` will contain a `campusClub_t` object type instance, `club_ref` will contain the `ref` of the object, and `club_adv` will contain an instance of the `faculty_t` object type. Recall that `c.advisor` is a `ref` to `faculty_t`. The `deref` function is therefore applied to a `ref` value to return the object type instance of the `ref`.

Reference types can also be used in queries to construct path expressions, as in object-oriented database queries. The following query returns a string value representing the name of the department in which the advisor of Epsilon Sigma works. The expression `c.advisor.worksIn.name` is a path expression, representing implicit joins between the object tables involved:

```
select c.advisor.worksIn.name
from   campusClub c
where  c.name = 'Epsilon Sigma';
```

9.2.4 Inheritance

Oracle enhances object features by supporting type inheritance. The user can create an object type as a supertype and form a type hierarchy by defining one or more subtypes of the supertype. Subtypes inherit the attributes and methods defined in the supertype. Additional attributes and methods can be also defined in subtypes to make them more specialized. Type hierarchies can be of arbitrary depth.

In the following simple example of a type hierarchy for object types `person_t` and `student_t`, note that, unlike the SQL standard, a type at the bottom of the type hierarchy can be specified as `final`:

```
create or replace type person_t as object
(pId            varchar2(10),
 dob            date,
 firstName      varchar2(50),
 lastName       varchar2(50))
 not final;

create or replace type student_t under person_t
(status         varchar2(10))
 final;
```

Object tables can then be defined on the basis of the type hierarchy as in the SQL standard:

```
create table person of person_t
(pId                primary key,
 firstName          not null,
 lastName           not null)
 object id primary key;
```

```
create table student of student_t under person
(pId                     primary key,
 firstName               not null,
 lastName                not null,
 status                  not null)
 object id primary key;
```

Even though type inheritance is supported in Oracle, the instances of object tables in a hierarchy do not behave as described in the final version of that standard, since the Oracle implementation of table hierarchies is based on a preliminary version of that standard. For example, consider inserting an instance of object type student_t into student, using the following insert statement:

```
insert into student values
(student_t ('PR123456789', '01-May-1975','Terrence','Grand','Junior'))
```

In Oracle, the new object is not visible from the person table. As a result, the Oracle object-relational mapping described in this section does not make use of type and table hierarchies for the Person hierarchy. Instead, the person, student, and faculty tables are implemented as independent tables, as shown in Figure 9.4. In addition, the student and faculty tables define a super attribute as a reference type that relates each student and faculty object to its corresponding person object. The super attribute is therefore used to simulate inheritance. Another implementation option is to use table hierarchies and explicitly construct the union of all the data in a supertable and its subtables when there is a need to query the contents of a table hierarchy.

Even though the Person hierarchy is simulated through the use of the super attribute, specialization constraints on the hierarchy can still be enforced. The ISA constraint that an instance of Faculty is also an instance of Person is enforced through the use of the insertFaculty procedure to insert a row object into the faculty table.

```
create or replace procedure insertFaculty
  (id in varchar2, fName in varchar2,lName in varchar2,
  dob in date, rank in varchar2, worksIn in varchar2)
  insert into faculty
  values (newPerson(id, fName, lName, dob), rank,
  campusClub_array(), get_dref(worksIn), null);
  end insertFaculty;

create or replace function newPerson
  (id in  varchar2, fName in varchar2, lName in varchar2, dob in date)
  return  ref person_t is
  p_ref   ref person_t;
  counter integer;
begin
  select count(*) into counter from person p where p.pId = id;
  if (counter = 0) then
      insert into person p values (id, fName, lName, dob)
          returning ref(p) into p_ref;
  else
      raise_application_error
      (-20004, 'Key already exists.');
  end if;
  return p_ref;
end newPerson;
```

The procedure illustrates the fact that when a row object is created in the `faculty` table, the corresponding row object will be created in the `person` table through a call to the `newPerson` function. The `newPerson` function will create the `person` object and return the reference value to be stored in the `super` attribute of the `faculty` row object. An error will be generated if a row object already exists in the `person` table with the same identifier.

Triggers and stored procedures are used to enforce other specialization constraints. The next example illustrates a `faculty_rowdelete` row trigger on the `faculty` object table. The trigger is fired whenever a row is deleted from the faculty object table, preventing a violation of the total subclass participation constraint by deleting the instance in the `person` table that is associated with the deleted `faculty` row object.

```
create or replace trigger faculty_rowdelete
     after delete on faculty
     for each row
begin
     delete person p where ref(p) = :old.super;
end faculty_rowdelete;
```

9.2.5 Varrays and Nested Tables as Collections

In Oracle, variable-sized arrays (varrays) and nested tables can be used to represent the *many* side of 1:N and M:N relationships.

Varrays

Oracle allows arrays to be of a variable size—thus the name varray. A maximum size must be specified when an attribute of type varray is defined. To define an attribute as a varray, a varray type definition must first be created. Creating a varray type does not allocate space, but simply defines a data type that can be used as the data type of a column of a relational table, an object type attribute, or the type of a PL/SQL variable, parameter, or function return value. In Figure 9.4, the varray type definition of `campusClub_array` is used to model the *many* side of the `advisorOf` relationship between `campusClub_t` and `faculty_t`. Since the `advisorOf` relationship is bidirectional, a cyclic reference exists between `campusClub_t` and `faculty_t`.

The code that follows illustrates a forward declaration of `campusClub_t` to support the definition of the `campusClub_array` type. The `campusClub_array` type is then used to define the type of the `advisorOf` attribute in `faculty_t`. The full definition of `campusClub_t` can then appear after the definition of `faculty_t`, as shown in Figure 9.4.

```
create or replace type campusClub_t;
create or replace type campusClub_array as
        varray(50) of ref campusClub_t;
create or replace type faculty_t as object
(...
  advisorOf       campusClub_array,
  worksIn         ref department_t,
  chairOf         ref department_t, ... );
```

Nested Tables

Whereas a varray is an indexed collection of data elements of the same type, a nested table is an unordered set of data elements of the same data type. A nested table has a single column, where the type of the column is a built-in type or an object type. If the column in a nested table is an object type, the table can also be viewed as a multicolumn table, with a column for each attribute of the object type. The use of DML statements on nested tables, such as `select`, `insert`, and `delete`, is the same as that with traditional relational tables.

In a nested table, the order of the elements is not defined. Nested tables are stored in a storage table, with every element mapping to a row in the storage table. Figure 9.4 illustrates a nested table type definition for the `student_ntable` nested table.

```
create or replace type student_ntable as table of ref student_t;
create or replace type campusClub_t as object
(...
  members          student_ntable, ... );

create table campusClub of campusClub_t
(cId              primary key,
 name             not null)
 object id primary key
 nested table members store as club_members;
```

The contents of the nested table are of type `ref student_t`. The type definition is used to define the `members` attribute in `campusClub_t`. The storage table of the `members` nested table, `club_members`, is specified in the `campusClub` table definition. Whereas the programmer accesses the nested table by using the name `members`, the name `club_members` is used internally by Oracle to access and manipulate the nested table.

Although not used in Figure 9.4, a `scope` constraint can be used to constrain the references contained within the storage table `club_members` of the `members` nested table.

```
alter table club_members add (scope for (column_value) is student);
create unique index club_members_idx on
  club_members(nested_table_id, column_value);
```

The constraint indicates that the values stored in the `ref` column must be references to row objects in the `student` table. A unique index is created on the storage table `club_members` by using the `nested_table_id` and `column_value` columns to restrict the uniqueness of the `ref` values. The `nested_table_id` column is a pseudocolumn in nested tables that holds the row identifier of the storage table. The `column_value` column is a pseudocolumn that holds the contents of the nested table (in this case, a `ref` of type `student_t`).

Comparison of Varrays and Nested Tables

Varrays and nested tables are similar in that the data types of all elements in each collection must be the same. But varrays and nested tables differ in the way they are internally managed by Oracle. A varray has the following characteristics:

- A varray cannot be indexed.

- A varray declaration must specify the maximum number of objects to hold.

- A varray is dense, in that all positions, from the first to the last, must be filled. Individual elements cannot be deleted from a varray to leave a `null` value in an array position.

- The elements of a varray are ordered.

- If the size of the varray is smaller than 4000 bytes, Oracle stores the varray in line; if it is greater than 4000 bytes, Oracle stores it in a Binary Large Object (BLOB).

In comparison, nested tables have the following characteristics:

- A nested table is an unordered set of data elements, all of the same data type and having a single column.

- The type of the column in the nested table is either a built-in type or an object type.

- If an object type is used as the type of the column, the table can be viewed as a multicolumn table, with a column for each attribute of the object.

- Nested tables are stored in a separate storage table and can be indexed for efficient access.

- Nested tables are sparse. That is, individual elements can be deleted from a nested table.

The choice between a varray and a nested table depends on the nature of the values or objects stored in the collection. If the number of objects in a multivalued attribute or relationship is large, then a nested table should be used instead of a varray. A varray is normally used when the number of objects contained in a multivalued attribute is small and does not change often.

9.2.6 Accessing Varrays and Nested Tables

Table 9.1 summarizes the functions and procedures that can be used to manipulate collections in Oracle. All functions and procedures in the table apply to nested tables and varrays (indicated by the name `collection` in the table), with the exception of the `delete` procedure. Elements cannot be deleted from a varray.

Varrays

The `listDeptStudents` procedure shows how to retrieve elements from a varray by using the `count` function.

```
create or replace procedure listDeptStudents (dept_code in varchar2) is
     stu_array student_array;
     s_obj student_t;
     p_obj person_t;
begin
     stu_array := student_array();
     select a.getStudents() into stu_array
     from department a
```

TABLE 9.1   Functions and Procedures for Accessing Collections in Oracle

`collection.count`	Function: Returns the number of elements in the collection.
`collection(i)`	Function: Returns the element at location `i` in the collection.
`collection.first`	Function: Returns the lowest-valued index of the collection containing an element (returns `null` if the collection is empty).
`collection.last`	Function: Returns the highest-valued index of the collection containing an element (returns `null` of the collection is empty).
`collection.exists(n)`	Function: Returns true if there is a row in the specified index of the collection.
`collection.next(n)`	Function: Returns the next higher-valued index of the collection where an element exists (otherwise returns `null`).
`collection.prior(n)`	Function: Returns the next lower-valued index of the collection where an element exists (otherwise returns `null`).
`collection.extend`	Procedure: Creates memory for storing an element at the end of the collection.
`collection.trim`	Procedure: Deletes the element at the end of the collection.
`table.delete(n)`	Procedure: Delete row `n` of the nested table (Cannot be used with varrays).

```
      where a.Code = dept_code;
      dbms_output.put_line('Department: ‖ dept_code');
      dbms_output.put_line('pId name');
      for i in 1.. stu_array.count loop
          select deref(stu_array(i)) into s_obj from dual;
          select deref(s_obj.super) into p_obj from dual;
          dbms_output.put_line(p_obj.pId ‖ ' ' ‖ p_obj.firstName
              ‖ ' ' ‖ p_obj.lastName);
      end loop;
      exception
          when no_data_found then
          dbms_output.put_line(dept_code ‖ ' does not exist.');
end listDeptStudents;
```

First, the students of a department are selected into a varray variable called stu_array by calling the getStudents function of department_t (i.e., the function for deriving the inverse of a student's major). Then, a for loop is used to iterate through the elements in stu_array to retrieve and output the pId and name of each student. In this example, the statement select deref(stu_array(i)) into s_obj from dual is Oracle syntax for assigning a value from a table into a PL/SQL variable, where dual is a system table that allows the assignment to occur in the context of a select statement. The deref( ) function has the same meaning as in the SQL standard, returning the object type instance of a reference.

Since a varray is dense, an element can be deleted from a varray only by completely replacing the array with a new array. As an example, consider the case of maintaining the inverse relationship between a campus club and the club's advisor when a club is deleted from the database. Since each `faculty` object maintains a list of clubs advised in the `advisorOf` varray, the club cannot simply be deleted from the array, potentially creating an empty space in the middle of a dense data structure. The `advisorOf` varray must be rebuilt by copying the contents of the old varray into a new varray, omitting the reference to the deleted club.

In the example shown next, a faculty object's `advisorOf` array is selected into `local_array`. The array is copied into `temp_array`, omitting a reference to the deleted student. To perform the copy, the `extend` function is used to add space to the end of `temp_array`, while the `last` function is used to access the index of this last space. The `faculty` object can then be updated with the value of `temp_array`.

```
declare
     deleted_cId number
     c_obj campusClub_t
     f_obj faculty_t
     temp_array campusClub_array
     local_array campusClub_array
begin
     ...
     select f_obj.advisorOf into local_array from dual;
     for i in 1..local_array.count loop
         select deref(local_array(i)) into c_obj from dual;
         if not (c_obj.cId = deleted_cId) then
             temp_array.extend;
             temp_array(temp_array.last):= local_array(i);
         end if;
     end loop;
     ...
end;
```

Nested Tables

Compared with the operations on a varray, a nested table is easier to update and behaves in a manner similar to the way relational tables behave. Values can be directly inserted or deleted from a nested table without moving around other elements.

The next example shows how to insert and delete an element from a nested table:

```
insert into table
     (select c.members from campusClub c where c.name = club_name)
     values (s_ref);
delete from table
     (select c.members from campusClub c where c.name = club_name) t
     where t.column_value = get_sref(member_to_delete);
```

The `table` keyword is used to cast the nested table `c.members` into a relational table for performing `insert` and `delete` operations. The variable `s_ref` contains the reference to be added to the `members` table. The function `get_sref` (not shown) accepts the name of a student and returns the reference to the row object that represents the student.

Whereas a varray must be extracted from a table into a variable for manipulation or querying, a nested table can be queried through the use of a `select` statement. The `isAssociatedMember` function from the `campusClub_t` type body illustrates how to query the members nested table. The nested table is cast into a relational table inside of a select statement, where the count function is applied to the nested table to determine whether the specified student is a member of the club:

```
create or replace type body campusClub_t is
member function isAssociatedMember (candidate_member in ref student_t)
     return boolean is
     cnt integer;
begin
     select count(1) into cnt
     from table(cast(self.members as student_ntable)) t
     where t.column_value = candidate_member;
     return (cnt > 0);
end isAssociatedMember;
...
end;
```

Similar to the insert and delete examples, a nested table can also be queried in an ad hoc manner without embedding the query in a function.

9.2.7 Maintaining Inverse Relationships

There are several options for maintaining inverse relationships. For bidirectional associations, one option is to use triggers on both sides of the association, to take appropriate actions when an update occurs on either side. As an alternative, the application can be constrained so that the update occurs only on one side of the association, using a trigger to update the other side. Stored procedures can also be used instead of triggers to update bidirectional associations. (See the addMembersAssociation procedure in the code for the Oracle case study on the Web site for this book.) For unidirectional associations, the association is stored on one side of the relationship and a function can be used on the other side to derive the inverse relationship (as in the getStudents and getFaculty functions of department_t).

When using triggers to update inverse relationships, it is important to be aware of *mutating tables* in Oracle. A mutating table is a table that is being modified by a DML statement, such as an insert, an update, or a delete statement, or a table that is updated as a result of an on delete cascade referential integrity constraint. SQL statements in a trigger body of a row trigger cannot read from or modify any mutating table of the triggering statement. As a result, it is not possible to get the ref of a new or updated object in a trigger that is fired by the create or update operation on the object. This situation arises in the SCHOOL DATABASE ENTERPRISE when maintaining the relationship between a campus club and its advisor. As a solution, a temporary table is used in combination with a row trigger and a statement trigger.

For example, when a campus club updates the advisor reference attribute, assigning the club a new advisor, two actions must happen with respect to maintaining inverses: The ref to the club must be added to the new faculty member's varray of clubs advised, and the ref to the club must be deleted from the old advisor's varray of clubs advised. But the ref to the club cannot be accessed in a row trigger. Instead, a row trigger is used to record the identifier of the club (cId), together with the refs to the old and new advisors in a temporary table. A statement-level trigger is then used to access the temporary table, get the `ref` to the club, and then update the list of clubs in the old and new advisor objects. Readers are encouraged to examine these triggers in the code for the Oracle case study on the book's Web site. (See the `campusClub_updaterow` trigger and the `campusClub_update` trigger on the `campusClub` object table.)

9.3 Objectivity/DB: Object-Oriented Database Mappings

Objectivity/DB is a distributed client–server object database management system providing an object-oriented approach to managing complex data with scalability and high performance over heterogeneous platforms. In addition to offering a distributed object database server and a set of database administration tools, Objectivity/DB supports application development by providing bindings to object-oriented programming languages such as C++, Java, and Smalltalk. The case study presented in this chapter focuses on the use of the Java language binding, which is referred to as Objectivity for Java.

Figure 9.5 is a UML diagram with annotations that illustrate how the SCHOOL DATABASE ENTERPRISE maps to the object features supported by Objectivity/DB. The Objectivity for Java class definitions that correspond to this figure are presented in Figure 9.6. All classes in Figure 9.5 correspond to *persistence-capable classes* in Objectivity for Java, making use of the built-in support provided for the formation of class hierarchies with inheritance. The `clubs`, `advises`, and `chair` associations illustrate the use of the built-in relationship feature of Objectivity/DB, with automatic support for the maintenance of inverse relationships between objects. In contrast, the `majorsIn` and `worksIn` associations illustrate the use of attributes (or `fields`), together with *persistent collections* for a user-maintained approach to the representation of object associations. The rest of this chapter elaborates on these specific features of Objectivity/DB after first providing the necessary background about the Objectivity/DB architecture and the basic features of persistence-capable classes.

9.3.1 Accessing an Objectivity/DB Database

To understand how to access a database in Objectivity/DB, it is first necessary to understand the four basic types of objects supported by the system: *basic objects*, *containers*, *databases*, and *federated databases*. A basic object is the fundamental unit of storage. All application-defined classes are maintained as basic objects. Basic objects are collected together into containers. A container therefore is a storage unit that allows objects that are frequently accessed together to be physically clustered together on disk for more efficient retrieval. A container also defines the granularity of locking within Objectivity/DB. When a basic object is locked, all of the other objects in the container are also locked. Locking in Objectivity/DB is administered by a lock server, which can run on any machine in the distributed database architecture of the Objectivity/DB environment.

A database in Objectivity/DB is a collection of containers, which can be system generated or application created. Application developers can therefore organize the objects of an application into multiple containers that efficiently support the access patterns of the application. A federated database is a collection of databases. The federated database maintains

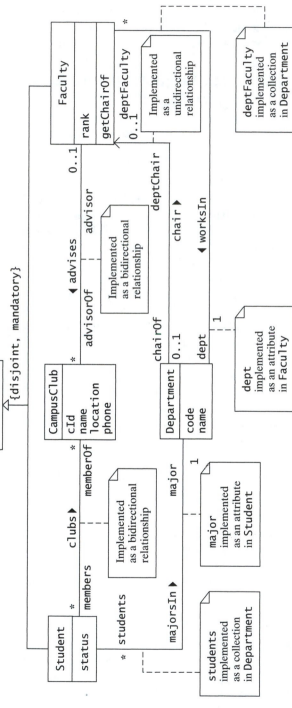

Figure 9.5 UML for the Objectivity/DB Object-Oriented Database Case Study of the School Database Enterprise. © ACM, 2003. This is a minor revision of the work published in "Using UML Class Diagrams for a Comparative Analysis of Relational, Object-Oriented, and Object-Relational Database Mappings," by S. Urban and S. Dietrich, in *Proceedings of the 34th ACM SIGCSE Technical Symposium on Computer Science Education* (2003), http://doi.acm.org/10.1145/620000.611923.

278

```
public class Person extends ooObj
{
  // Persistent fields
  protected String pId;
  protected String dob;
  protected String firstName;
  protected String lastName;

  // Method Definitions
  ...
}

public class Student extends Person
{
  // Persistent field
  protected String status;

  // Persistent field. Inverse of Department::students.
  protected Department major;

  // Bidirectional relationship. Inverse of CampusClub::members.
  private ToManyRelationship memberOf;

  // Method Definitions
  ...
}

public class Faculty extends Person
{
  // Persistent field
  protected String rank;

  // Persistent field. Inverse of Department::deptFaculty.
  protected Department dept;

  //Bidirectional relationship. Inverse of CampusClub::advisor.
  private ToManyRelationship advisorOf;

  // Method Definitions
  ...
}

public class Department extends ooObj
{
  // Persistent fields
  protected String code;
  protected String name;

  // Persistent collection. Inverse of Student::major.
  protected ooMap students = new ooMap();

  // Persistent collection. Inverse of Faculty::dept.
  protected ooMap deptFaculty = new ooMap();

  // Unidirectional relationship with Faculty.
  private ToOneRelationship deptChair;

  // Method Definitions
  ...
}
```

Figure 9.6 Objectivity for Java Class Definitions for the SCHOOL DATABASE ENTERPRISE Object-Oriented Database Mapping

```
public class CampusClub extends ooObj
{
  // Persistent fields.
  protected String cId;
  protected String name;
  protected String location;
  protected String phone;

  // Bidirectional relationship. Inverse of Faculty:advisorOf.
  private ToOneRelationship advisor;
  // Bidirectional relationship. Inverse of Student::memberOf.
  private ToManyRelationship members;

  // Method Definitions
  ...
}
```

Figure 9.6   (*continued*)

the metadata that describe all of the object classes in the federated database. A federated database is also the administrative unit of control for Objectivity/DB, maintaining configuration information. In addition, all recovery and backup operations are performed at this level.

To access an Objectivity/DB database, five steps must be performed: connect to the federated database, create a session, retrieve a federated database from the session, create or get a database, and create or get a container. Furthermore, all access to Objectivity/DB objects, including basic objects, containers, databases, and federated databases, must be performed in the context of a transaction on a session object. The four relevant transaction operations are:

1. `begin`, to acquire access rights (locks) to an object;

2. `commit`, to save all modified data in the database and to release all locks;

3. `abort`, to discard all changes made to objects and to release all locks; and

4. `checkpoint`, to save all modified data, but keep all locks active.

Transactions in Objectivity/DB guarantee the traditional database properties of atomicity, consistency, isolation, and durability (i.e., the ACID properties).

Connecting to a Federated Database

The block of code shown next illustrates how to open a connection to a federated database by utilizing the static `open` method of the `Connection` class.

```
try {
    connection = Connection.open("SchoolDB", oo.openReadWrite);
    } catch (DatabaseNotFoundException exception) {
    System.out.println("Federated database SchoolDB not found");
    return;
    } catch (DatabaseOpenException exception) {
    System.out.println("Connection to SchoolDB already open");
    return;
}
```

The open method receives two parameters: a string of a boot file path and an integer mode. The boot file path is the path name of the boot file of the federated database to which a connection is being opened. The boot file is initially created at the operating system command level (not shown in this example). There are two integer modes to choose from: openReadOnly is used to open the connection for read-only access, and openReadWrite is used to open the connection for read–write access.

Retrieving a Federated Database from a Session

A session is an extended interaction between a user application and the connected federated database. A session can be created and then used to form transactions:

```
Session session = new Session();
...
session.begin()                     //Begin a transaction
ooFDObj sdaFD = session.getFD();    //Get the federated database
...
session.commit()                    //Commit a transaction
```

The session object is used to retrieve the federated database, which is always represented by an instance of the ooFDObj class. After the begin method of the class Session has been called, the user can retrieve the federated database from that particular session. The statement ooFDObj sdaFD = session.getFD() is used to get a federated database.

Creating or Retrieving a Database

Databases are represented by instances of the ooDBObj class. After a federated database has been retrieved, the federated database object can be used to create or get a database. The following code shows how to get an existing database with the if clause and how to create a new database with the else clause:

```
ooFDObj sdaFD;
ooDBobj sdaDB;
Session session = new Session ();
session.begin();
sdaFD = session.getFD();
if (sdaFD.hasDB('SchoolDB'))
      sdaDB = sdaFD.lookupDB("SchoolDB"); //Retrieve existing database
else {
      sdaDB = sdaFD.newDB("SchoolDB");     //Create new database
          }
session.commit();
```

Creating or Retrieving a Container

There are two types of containers in Objectivity/DB: *garbage-collectible* containers and *non-garbage-collectible* containers. A garbage-collectible container is a subclass of ooGC-ContObj. A non-garbage-collectible container is a subclass of ooContObj. Every object in a non-garbage-collectible container is considered a valid object and hence will be stored persistently into the database. A user must explicitly call a delete method to delete an object from a non-garbage-collectible container. By contrast, garbage-collectible containers can contain valid objects *and* invalid objects. Invalid objects are objects that are not connected to valid persistent objects through object relationships. Invalid objects are deleted through garbage collection.

This case study illustrates the use of non-garbage-collectible containers. The following code shows how to get an existing non-garbage-collectible container from the sdaDB database with the if clause and how to create a new non-garbage-collectible container with the else clause:

```
ooContObj Container;
session.begin();
if (sdaDB.hasContainer("Container"))
     Container = sdaDB.lookupContainer("Container");
else {
     Container = new ooContObj();
     sdaDB.addContainer(container, "Container", 0, 5, 10);
     }
session.commit();
```

After a container is retrieved or created, the container can be used to store persistent objects. The next section elaborates on persistent objects in Objectivity/DB as instances of persistence-capable classes.

9.3.2   Persistence-Capable Classes

In Objectivity/DB, Java class definitions must be registered with the schema of a federated database before objects can be stored as part of the database. Java classes can be defined as *persistence-capable classes*. If a class is persistence capable, then objects that are created as instances of the class can be made persistent by storing the objects in a container. An object that is not persistent is a *transient object*, which is not stored as part of the database and is available only within the memory of an actively running process.

A persistence-capable class in Objectivity/DB must be derived from the ooObj class or must implement the interface com.objy.iapp.Persistent. Both basic objects and containers can serve as persistent objects. An object is automatically assigned a unique oid when the object becomes persistent. Persistent objects can also be named to support object retrieval. In addition, indexing capabilities are available for sorting persistent objects according to attribute values.

Defining Persistence-Capable Classes

The code example shown next illustrates how to define the Person class as a persistence-capable class by defining Person as a class that extends ooObj. This declaration of the Person class as a subclass of ooObj allows Person to inherit the necessary methods for creating and manipulating persistent objects.

```
public class Person extends ooObj
{ // Persistent fields
     protected String pId;
     protected String dob;
     protected String firstName;
     protected String lastName;
     // Parameterized Constructor
     public Person(String pId, String dob, String firstName,
```

```
               String lastName)
        {
            this.pId = pId;
            this.dob = dob;
            this.firstName = firstName;
            this.lastName = lastName; }
        ...
}

public class Student extends Person
{
        // Persistent fields
        protected String status;
        protected Department major;
        private ToManyRelationship memberOf;
        // Parameterized Constructor
        public Student(String pId, String dob, String firstName,
          String lastName, String status)
            { super(pId, dob, firstName, lastName);
            this.status = status; }
        ...
}
```

The Student class is defined as a class that extends the Person class. Since Person is a persistence-capable class, the Student class also becomes persistence capable, inheriting persistence capabilities from ooObj and also inheriting attributes and methods from Person. The Student class defines two additional attributes—status and major—and one relationship—memberOf. Relationships are described in more detail in a later section.

The Person and Student classes each have a constructor method with the same name as the class. The parameters of each class correspond to the immediate and inherited attributes of each class. The constructor method for Student calls the super method as a way to invoke the constructor method of the Person superclass.

Creating, Reading, and Writing Persistent Objects

When an instance of a class is initially created, the instance is a transient object. Transient objects become persistent when they are stored or clustered into a persistent container. The following code illustrates how to initially create an object and then make the object persistent by invoking the cluster method on the container of the database:

```
session.begin();
// Create transient student object
Student student =
  new Student("123", "01/15/1984", "JON", "TRUMAN", "freshman");
// Cluster the object in a container to make it persistent
Container.cluster(student);
session.commit();
```

When persistent objects are read, the fetch method is used to obtain a lock on an object and fetch the object from the database. In a similar manner, the markModified method is used to obtain a lock for updating the object. Classes should define access methods for getting and setting every field associated with a class definition. The methods should use fetch and markModified in an appropriate manner to ensure that objects are always left in a correct state. The following code example illustrates access methods for getting and setting the pId of objects in the Person class:

```
public class Person extends ooObj
{
    // Persistent field
    protected String pId;

    // Field access method to get persistent field values
    public String getPId( )
    {
        fetch( );
        return this.pId;
    }

    // Field access method to set persistent field values
    public void setPId(String pId)
    {
        markModified();
        this.pId = pId;
    }
}
```

Objects are retrieved from a class by using the scan method of the Container class. The scan method accepts a persistence-capable class name as a parameter and returns an Iterator object. The iterator object contains the collection of objects that are instances of the persistence-capable class. Methods on the Iterator object can then be used to iterate through the collection of objects returned as a result of the scan method. In the next code sequence, itr is the iterator object.

```
// Print all the Students in the database
public void printAllStudents()
{ ...
    session.begin();
    objCont = sdaDB.lookupContainer("Container");
    Iterator itr = objCont.scan("Student"); // Get all students
    Student s;
    while(itr.hasMoreElements())
    {
        s = (Student)itr.nextElement(); // Get a student
        System.out.println(s.getFirstName() + s.getLastName);
    }
    session.commit();
}
```

The hasMoreElements method is used to determine whether there are more objects to examine in itr. The nextElement method is used to retrieve the next object in the collection of iterator objects.

Selection conditions can also be used in the scan method. A selection is performed by creating a string that contains a predicate. The string is then passed as a parameter to the scan method. In the next example, a predicate is added to the call of the scan function to retrieve students with a status of senior.

```
//Print all senior students
public void printSeniorStudents()
```

```
{
    ...
    String sPredicate = new String("status == "senior"");
    Iterator itr = objCont.scan("Student", sPredicate);
    ...
}
```

In general, the predicate can contain a Boolean combination of conditions over the attributes of a class.

9.3.3 Relationships for Implementing Associations

Associations between object classes can be implemented in Objectivity/DB using *relationships*. Relationships in Objectivity/DB provide a similar functionality as relationships in the ODMG standard, allowing applications to directly model 1:1, 1:N, and M:N associations between objects. Relationships can be either unidirectional or bidirectional. Unidirectional relationships enable an application to locate related objects in one direction only. Bidirectional relationships ensure referential integrity and automatically support the maintenance of inverses. Unlike bidirectional relationships, unidirectional relationships do not guarantee the return of valid objects; thus, dangling references may occur. On the other hand, unidirectional relationships provide less overhead and better performance than bidirectional relationships.

For an association between classes A and B, a relationship definition in A must specify a cardinality to indicate the number of objects in B to which objects in A can be related. The cardinality options in Objectivity/DB nomenclature are follows:

- OneToOne. An object in A can be related to only one object in B (defined on either side of a 1:1 relationship).

- OneToMany. An object in A can be related to many objects in B (defined on the 1 side of a 1:M relationship).

- ManyToOne. Many objects in A can be related to only one object in B (defined on the N side of a 1:N relationship).

- ManyToMany. Many objects in A can be related to many objects in B (defined on either side of an M:N relationship).

The cardinality of ManyToMany can be used only with bidirectional relationships.

Unidirectional Relationships

In the SCHOOL DATABASE ENTERPRISE, a unidirectional relationship is used to model the 1:1 chair association between Department and Faculty by defining the chairOf relationship in Faculty. In this case, the Department object directly accesses a Faculty object via the deptChair relationship. The Faculty object can access the Department object only by writing code to iterate through Department objects.

To define a relationship, the type of the relationship must be defined as either a ToOneRelationship or a ToManyRelationship in the Java class definition for Department. Since the relationship is 1:1, deptChair is defined to be a ToOneRelationship. In addition, a public static relationship definition method deptChair_Relationship must be defined. This method must return an instance of a subclass of the Objectivity for Java Relationship class. The instance must correspond to the cardinality of the association, where the possible subclasses are OneToOne, OneToMany, ManyToOne, and ManyToMany. The relationship definition method is used by Objectivity for Java and is never explicitly called by the application:

```
public class Department {
    private ToOneRelationship deptChair;
    ...
    public static OneToOne deptChair_Relationship() {
    return new OneToOne("deptChair", "Faculty", Relationship.COPY_MOVE,
    Relationship.VERSION_MOVE, false, false, Relationship.INLINE_NONE);
    }
}
```

The deptChair_Relationship method defines deptChair to be a relationship that stores a Faculty object. The following are the meanings of each parameter in the method definition:

1. memberName: Name of the relationship field.

2. otherClassName: Name of the related class.

3. copyMode: Specifies what to do with the relationship when an object is copied. In this case, COPY_MOVE indicates that associations from the original object should be moved to the new object (leaving the original object with no associations). Other options are to copy all association values to the new object (COPY_COPY) and to create a new object with no association values (COPY_DELETE).

4. versionMode: Specifies what to do with the relationship when a new version of an object is created. (The options are the same as in copyMode.) The Java language binding does not support the version capabilities of Objectivity/DB, but the version mode must still be specified.

5. deletePropagate: True if delete operations should be propagated through object associations; false otherwise.

6. lockPropagate: True if lock operations should be propagated through object associations; false otherwise.

7. relationshipStorage: Specifies whether the relationship is stored inline with the object.

After a relationship is defined, accessor methods can be defined to set and get relationships.

```
public Faculty getDeptChair() {
    fetch();
    if (deptChair != null)
        return (Faculty) this.deptChair.get();
```

```
        else
            return null;
}
public void setDeptChair(Faculty chair) {
    markModified();
    this.deptChair.clear();
    this.deptChair.form(chair);
}
```

The getDeptChair method illustrates how to return the Faculty object stored in the deptChair relationship by using the get function. The setDeptChair method illustrates how to set the value of deptChair with the use of the form function. The clear function is used to set a relationship value to null.

Bidirectional Relationships

A bidirectional relationship supports the traversal of an association between two classes in both directions. The advantage of a bidirectional relationship is that inverse relationships are automatically maintained. Furthermore, bidirectional relationships reduce the likelihood of dangling object references. When an object is deleted, all relationships that reference the deleted object are also deleted. Objectivity for Java requires that ManyToMany relationships must be implemented as bidirectional relationships.

In the SCHOOL DATABASE ENTERPRISE, bidirectional relationships are used to implement the 1:N advises association and the M:N clubs association. The following code demonstrates how to declare the bidirectional clubs association in the Student and CampubClub classes so as to indicate that students are members of many clubs and clubs have many students as members:

```
public class Student extends Person {
    private ToManyRelationship memberOf;
    ...
    public static ManyToMany memberOf_Relationship() {
        return new ManyToMany("memberOf", "CampusClub", "members",
        Relationship.COPY_MOVE, Relationship.VERSION_MOVE,
        false, false, Relationship.INLINE_NONE);
    }
}

public class CampusClub extends ooObj {
    private ToManyRelationship members;
    ...
    public static ManyToMany members_Relationship() {
        return new ManyToMany("members", "Student", "memberOf",
        Relationship.COPY_MOVE, Relationship.VERSION_MOVE,
        false, false, Relationship.INLINE_NONE);
    }
}
```

In the Student class, the memberOf relationship is declared as a ToManyRelationship. In the declaration of the static ManyToMany memberOf_Relationship method, there is an additional parameter (the third parameter in the list) to indicate the name of the inverse relationship (members) in the CampubClub class. In the CampusClub class, the `members` relationship is likewise defined as the inverse of the `memberOf` relationship of the `Student` class.

Methods are defined to access the M:N relationship, using special functions for manipulating multivalued relationships. The method `addClub` is defined in the `Student` class to add a club to the list of clubs to which a student belongs. The `includes` function tests for membership in a multivalued association, while the `add` function adds an object to the association.

```java
public void addClub(CampusClub c) {
    if (c != null) {
        markModified();
        if (this.memberOf.includes(c)) {return;}
        this.memberOf.add(c);
    }
}
```

The `removeClub` method illustrates how to remove an object from an association by using the `remove` function:

```java
public void removeClub(CampusClub c) {
    if (c != null) {
        markModified();
        if (this.memberOf.includes(c))
            this.memberOf.remove(c);
    }
    else {
        System.out.println("Cannot delete null CampusClub object!");
        return;
    }
}
```

Iterator objects can also be used with multivalued relationships to iterate through the contents of a relationship. In the `getClubs` procedure, an iterator object `itr` is defined.

```java
public List getClubs() {
    List objects = new ArrayList();
    Iterator itr;
    fetch();
    if(this.memberOf != null)
        itr = this.memberOf.scan();
    else
        return objects;
    if(itr != null) {
        while(itr.hasNext())
            objects.add(itr.next());
    }
    return objects;
}
```

The `scan` function is invoked on the `memberOf` relationship, returning the objects in the association. The `hasNext` and `next` functions are used to iterate through the contents of `itr`, adding each object of the relationship to an array named `objects`.

Since the `clubs` association between `Student` and `CampusClub` is bidirectional, similar methods can be defined in the `CampusClub` class to access the students that belong to a specific club. Furthermore, Objectivity/DB will maintain the inverse relationship when objects are removed from the association. For example, if a club is removed from the memberOf relationship of a student, the corresponding Student object will automatically be removed from the members relationship of the club. Likewise, removing a student from being a member of a club will result in the club being deleted from the student's memberOf relationship.

9.3.4   Additional Features for Implementing Associations

Other features for implementing associations in Objectivity/DB include the use of *fields* and *persistent collections*. A field serves as an attribute of an object, capturing the object's state. When the type of a field is defined to be a persistence-capable class, the field becomes a means for linking one object to another. A field can therefore be used to implement the 1 side of a 1:1 or 1:N association. For 1:N associations, a field can be used in combination with a persistent collection of objects to implement the *many* side of the association. Persistent collections can also be used on both sides of an M:N association. Unlike the relationship feature of Objectivity/DB, the use of fields and collections requires more effort on the part of the programmer to maintain referential integrity and inverse relationships. In the SCHOOL DATABASE ENTERPRISE, fields and persistent collections are used to implement the 1:N worksIn and majorsIn associations.

Fields

The code for the Student class illustrates how to define major as a field that contains a Department object. The class definition includes the getMajor method to return the value of the major field and the setMajor method to assign an instance of Department as the field value:

```
public class Student extends Person {
    protected Department major
    ...
    public Department getMajor() {
        fetch();
        return this.major;
    }
    public void setMajor(Department dept) {
        markModified();
        this.major = dept;
    }
}
```

Collections

A persistent collection is an aggregate object that is used for storing multiple objects. There are several different types of persistent collections in Objectivity/DB. However, the ooMap class is the only collection class that automatically maintains referential integrity, thus making ooMap more appealing for implementing object associations. The SCHOOL DATABASE ENTERPRISE utilizes ooMap to implement the *many* side of the worksIn and majorsIn relationships. The following code illustrates how the Department class defines students as a persistent collection of type ooMap:

```
public class Department extends ooObj {
    protected ooMap students = new ooMap();
    ...
}
```

A persistent collection such as students can contain either objects or key-value pairs. The addStudent method illustrates how to add a new student object into the students collection. The code first determines whether the object already exists in the collection. The student object is then added as a key-value pair, where the object is the value and pId of Student is the key. The use of key-value pairs makes it easier to retrieve objects from the collection or to test for membership in the collection by means of the isMember function.

```
public void addStudent(Student newMajor) {
    markModified();
    String key = newMajor.getPId();
    if (this.students.isMember(key)){
        System.out.println("The student with pId = " + key +
            "already exists in the dept.");
        return;
        }
    this.students.add(newMajor, key);
}
```

The deleteStudent method illustrates how to remove an object from the collection by using the remove function, where the isMember function is used to test for membership before removal:

```
public void deleteStudent(Student major) {
    markModified();
    String key = major.getPId();
    if (this.students.isMember(key))
        this.students.remove(key);
}
```

As illustrated in the findStudent function, the lookup function can be used to find a student object by pId and return the corresponding Student object instance from a key-value pair stored in the collection:

```
public Student findStudent(String pId) {
    fetch();
    if (this.students.isMember(pId)) {
        return (Student)this.students.lookup(pId);
        }
    else {
        System.out.println("The student with pId = " + pId +
            "cannot be found.");
        return null;
        }
}
```

As with classes and relationships, iterators can also be used with collections. The only difference is that the values of the collection are assigned to the iterator by the `elements` function:

```
Iterator itr=null;
...
itr = this.students.elements();
while(itr.hasNext())
{...}
```

Since persistent collections maintain referential integrity, when a `Student` object is deleted, the object will automatically be removed from the `students` collection in `Department`. When a `Department` object is deleted, however, the programmer must write appropriate code to ensure that the `major` field in `Student` is not left with a dangling reference, since fields do not automatically maintain referential integrity.

9.4 Checkpoint

Three case studies of the SCHOOL DATABASE ENTERPRISE demonstrate relational, object-relational, and object-oriented concepts in the context of specific database products. The first case study illustrates the traditional relational mapping, using Oracle, of the SCHOOL DATABASE ENTERPRISE. The relational implementation highlights the fundamental concepts for the enforcement of constraints and the use of stored procedures and triggers. The second case study illustrates the object-relational mapping, using Oracle, of the same application. The object-relational implementation emphasizes the use of object types, object tables, object references, and collections such as varrays and nested tables. The third case study demonstrates a pure object-oriented implementation using the Objectivity/DB object-oriented database system. The UML diagram for each case study makes use of bidirectional relationships and navigation to provide different mapping directives for each implementation.

Exercises

1. Perform a comparative analysis of the three implementations presented in this chapter. In particular, how do these implementations compare with respect to schema design, constraint enforcement, and data retrieval? Comment on any advantages or disadvantages that you find between the relational versus the object-oriented/object-relational implementations or between the object-oriented versus the object-relational implementation. Can you draw any conclusions about how to decide on the use of relational, object-relational, or object-oriented database technology?

2. The SQL files for the Oracle relational case study can be found on the Web site for this book. Modify the files as necessary for implementation on the relational product at your own site. Experiment with writing your own triggers and stored procedures to add functionality to the application.

3. The SQL files for the Oracle object-relational case study can be found on the Web site for this book. If you have an object-relational product other than Oracle, compare the features of Oracle with the object-relational database product at your own site. If necessary, make modifications to get a running version of the application. Experiment with making changes or extensions to the implementation such that you will be able to explore the use of object-relational database technology.

4. The Java classes for the Objectivity/DB case study can be found on this book's Web site. If you have an object-oriented product other than Objectivity/DB, compare the features of Objectivity/DB with the object-oriented database product at your own site. Make modifications as necessary to get a running version of the application. Experiment with making changes or extensions to the implementation such that you will be able to explore the use of object-oriented database technology.

5. Using any of the applications presented in the previous chapters (such as the HOLLYWOOD ENTERPRISE or the HORSE RACING ENTERPRISE), experiment with relational, object-relational, and object-oriented implementations on the database products available at your site. Use these implementations as a way to explore each technology and also as a basis for a comparative analysis of these different database paradigms.

9.5   Bibliographic References

See http://technet.oracle.com for online information about Oracle. Online documentation for Objectivity/DB can be found at http://www.objectivity.com.

The case studies presented in this paper are an elaboration of the comparison originally presented in Urban and Dietrich [2003]. The work in Dietrich et al. [2001] presents an approach to developing a generic graphical user interface (GUI) to object-oriented databases, using XML to communicate schema information between the database and the user interface. Code for the GUI tool, known as the Object Manager, together with an Objectivity/DB implementation of the HOLLYWOOD ENTERPRISE, is available on the Web site for this book (http://www.eas.asu.edu/~advdb).

Bibliography

Abiteboul, S., Buneman, P., and Suciu, D. 2000. *Data on the Web: From Relations to Semistructured Data and XML*. San Francisco: Morgan Kaufmann.

Arnold, K., Gosling, J., and Holmes, D. 2000. *The Java™ Programming Language*, 3d ed. Reading, MA: Addison-Wesley.

Atkinson, M., Bancilhon, F., DeWitt, D., Dittrich, K., Maier, D., and Zdonik, S. 1990. "The Object-Oriented Database System Manifesto." In *Proc. of the 1st Int. Conf. on Deductive and Object-Oriented Databases*, Kyoto, Japan. Elsevier Science Publishers B.V (NorthHolland), pp. 223–240.

Bancilhon, F. 1981. "Update Semantics and Relational Views," *ACM Transactions on Database Systems*, vol. 6, no. 4, pp. 557–575.

Booch, G. 1994. *Object-Oriented Analysis and Design with Applications*, 2d ed. Redwood City, CA: Benjamin/Cummings Publishers.

Brown, P. 2001. *Object-Relational Database Development: A Plumber's Guide*. Upper Saddle River, NJ: Prentice Hall, Inc.

Castro, E. 2001. *XML for the World Wide Web: Visual Quickstart Guide*. Berkley, CA: Peachpit Press.

Cattell, R. G. G., Barry, D. K., Berler, M., Eastman, J., Jordan, D., Russell, C., Schadow, O., Stanienda, T., and Velez, F. (editors). 2000. *The Object Data Standard: ODMG 3.0*. San Francisco: Morgan Kaufmann.

Chaudhri, A., and Zicari, R. (editors). 2000. *Succeeding with Object Databases: A Practical Look at Today's Implementations with Java and XML*. New York: J. Wiley.

Chaudhri, A. B., Rashid, A., and Zicari, R. 2003. *XML Data Management: Native XML and XML-Enabled Database Systems*. Boston; London: Addison-Wesley.

Chen, P. 1976. "The Entity Relationship Model—Toward a Unified View of Data." *Tranactions on Database Systems*, vol. 1, no. 1, March, pp. 9–36.

Codd, E. 1970. "A Relational Model of Data for Large Shared Data Banks." *Communications of the ACM*, vol. 13, no. 6, pp. 377–387.

Cosmadakis, S., and Papadimitriou, C. 1984. "Updates of Relational Views." *Journal of the ACM*, vol. 31, no. 4, pp. 742–760.

Dahl, O.-J., Myhrhaug, B., and Nygaard, K. 1967. "Simula 67 Common Base Language." Oslo: Norwegian Computer Center.

Date, C. J., and Darwen, H. 1998. *Foundations for Object/Relational Databases: The Third Manifesto*. Menlo Park, CA: Addison-Wesley.

Dayal, U., and Bernstein, P. 1978. "The Updatability of Relational Views." *Proceedings of the International Conference on Very Large Databases*, pp. 368–377.

Deitel, H. M., Deitel, P. J., and Nieto, T. 2002. *Internet & World Wide Web: How to Program*, 2d ed. Upper Saddle River, NJ: Prentice Hall.

Dietrich, S. W. 2001. *Understanding Relational Database Query Languages*. Upper Saddle River, NJ: Prentice Hall.

Dietrich, S. W., Suceava, D., Cherukuri, C., and Urban, S. D. 2001. "A Reusable Graphical Interface for Manipulating Object-Oriented Databases Using Java and XML," *ACM SIGCSE International Conference on Computer Science Education*, Charlotte, NC, February, pp. 362–366.

Dietrich, S. W., Urban, S. D., and Kyriakides, I. 2002. "JDBC Demonstration Courseware Using Servlets and Java Server Pages." *Proceedings of the ACM SIGCSE International Conference on Computer Science Education*, Covington, KY, March, pp. 266–270.

Eisenberg, J., and Melton, J. 2002. "SQL/XML Is Making Good Progress." In *ACM SIGMOD Record*, vol. 31, no. 2, June, pp. 101–108.

Eisenberg, J., Kulkarni, K., Michels, J-E., Melton, J., and Zemke, F. 2004. "SQL:2003 Has Been Published," *SIGMOD Record*, vol. 33, no. 1, March, pp. 119–126.

Elmasri, R., and Navathe, R. 2003. *Fundamentals of Database Systems*, 4th ed. Reading, MA: Addison-Wesley.

Elmasri, R., and Wiederhold, G. 1980. "Structural Properties of Relationships and Their Representations", *Proceedings of the National Computer Conference*, AFIPS, volume 49, pp. 319–326.

Elmasri, R., Weeldreyer, J., and Hevner, A. 1985. "The Category Concept: An Extension to the Entity Relationship Model." *International Journal on Data and Knowledge Engineering*, vol. 1, no. 1, May, pp. 75–116.

Fowler, M., and Scott, K. 2000. *UML Distilled: A Brief Guide to the Standard Object Modeling Language*, 2d ed. Reading, MA: Addison-Wesley Publishers.

Garcia-Molina, H., Ullman, J., and Widom, J. 2002. *Database Systems: The Complete Book*. Upper Saddle River, NJ: Prentice Hall, Inc.

Goldberg, A., and Robson, D. *Smalltalk-80: The Language and Its Implementation*. Reading, MA: Addison-Wesley Publishers.

Gulutzan, P., and Pelzer, T. 1999. *SQL-99 Complete Really!* Lawrence, KS: Miller Freeman.

Hamilton, G., Cattell, R., and Fisher, M. 1997. *JDBC Database Access with Java: A Tutorial and Annotated Reference*. Reading, MA: Addison-Wesley.

Held, G., Stonebraker, M., and Wong, E. 1975. "Ingres—a Relational Database System." *Proceedings of the AFIPS National Computer Conference*, pp. 409–416.

Hull, R., and King, R. 1987. "Semantic Data Modeling: Survey, Applications, and Research Issues." *ACM Computing Surveys*, vol. 19, no. 3, September, pp. 201–260.

Jacobson, I., Christerson, M., Jonsson, P., and Overgaard, G. 1992. *Object-Oriented Software Engineering: A Use Case Driven Approach*. Wokingham, U.K.: Addison-Wesley Publishers.

Josuttis, N. 1999. The C++ *Standard Library: A Tutorial and Reference*, Boston: Addison-Wesley Professional.

Kifer, M., Bernstein, A., and Lewis, P. 2005. *Database Systems: An Application-Oriented Approach*, 2d ed. New York: Addison-Wesley.

Koshafian, S., and Copeland, G. 1989. "Object Identity," Chapter 1.1 in *Readings in Object-Oriented Database Systems*, S. Zdonik and D. Maier (editors). San Francisco: Morgan Kaufmann.

Loomis, M. E. S., and Chaudhri, A. (editors). 1997. *Object Databases in Practice*. Upper Saddle River, NJ: Prentice Hall.

Melton, J. 1998. *Understanding SQL's Stored Procedures—a Guide to SQL/PSM*. San Francisco: Morgan Kaufmann Publishers.

Melton, J. 2002. *Advanced SQL:1999: Understanding Object-Relational and Other Advanced Features*. San Francisco: Morgan Kaufmann Publishers.

Melton, J., and Eisenberg, A. 2000. *Understanding SQL and Java Together: A Guide to SQLJ, JDBC, and Related Technologies*. San Francisco: Morgan Kaufmann Publishers.

Melton, J., and Simon, A. 2001. *SQL:1999: Understanding Relational Language Components*. San Francisco: Morgan Kaufmann Publishers.

Meyer, B. 1988. *Object-Oriented Software Construction*. New York: Prentice-Hall Publishers.

Muller, R., 1999. *Database Design for Smarties: Using UML for Data Modeling*. San Francisco: Morgan Kaufmann Publishers.

Object Management Group. 2002. Home Web site, http://www.omg.org.

OMG Unified Modeling Language Specification, Version 1.4. 2001. Object Management Group, Document formal/01-09-67, http://www.omg.org/technology/documents/formal/uml.htm.

Paton, N., and Diaz, O. 1999. "Active Database Systems." *Computing Surveys*, vol. 31, no. 1. March, pp. 63–103.

Peckham, J., and Maryanski, F. 1988. "Semantic Data Models." *ACM Computing Surveys*, vol. 20, no. 3. September, pp. 153–189.

Ramakrishnan, R., and Gehrke, J. 2003. *Database Management Systems*, 3d ed. Boston: McGraw-Hill.

Ramakrishnan, R., and Ullman, J. 1995. "A Survey of Deductive Databases." *Journal of Logic Programming*, vol. 23, no. 2, pp. 125–149.

Reese, G. 2000. *Database Programming with JDBC and Java*, 2d ed. Cambridge, MA: O'Reilly.

Rowe, L., and Stonebraker, M. 1987. "The Postgres Data Model." *Proceedings of the Thirteenth International Conference on Very Large Data Bases*, Brighton, England. September, pp. 83–96.

Rumbaugh, J., Blaha, M., Premerlani, W., Eddy, F., and Lorensen, W. 1991. *Object-Oriented Modeling and Design*. Englewood Cliffs, NJ: Prentice Hall Publishers.

Rumbaugh, J., Jacobson, I., and Booch, G. 1999. *The Unified Modeling Language Reference Manual*. Reading, MA: Addison-Wesley.

Schmuller, J. 1999. *Sams Teach Yourself UML in 24 Hours*, Indianapolis: SAMS Publishing.

Silberschatz, A., Korth, H., and Sudarshan, S. 2002. *Database Systems Concepts*, 4th ed., New York: McGraw-Hill.

Smith, J., and Smith, D. 1977. "Database Abstractions: Aggregation and Generalization." *Transactions on Database Systems*, vol. 2, no. 2, June, pp. 105–133.

Speegle, G. D. 2002. *JDBC: Practical Guide for Java Programmers*. San Francisco: Morgan Kaufmann Publishers.

Stonebraker, M. 1995. *Object-Relational DBMSs: The Next Great Wave*. San Francisco: Morgan Kaufmann.

Stonebraker, M., Rowe, L., Lindsay, B., Gray, J., Carey, M., Brodie, M., Bernstein, P., and Beech, D. 1990. "Third Generation Database System Manifesto." *SIGMOD Record*, vol. 19, no. 3, pp. 31–44.

Stroustrup, B. 1986. *The C++ Programming Language*. Reading, MA: Addison-Wesley.

Taylor, A. 2003. *JDBC: Database Programming with J2EE*. Upper Saddle River, NJ: Prentice Hall PTR.

Ullman, J., and Widom, J. 2002. *A First Course in Database Systems*, 2d ed. Upper Saddle River, NJ: Prentice Hall.

Urban, S. 1999. "Database Models." *Encyclopedia of Electrical and Electronics Engineering*, John G. Webster (editor). New York: John Wiley & Sons, Inc., vol. 4, pp. 604–629.

Urban S. D., and Dietrich, S. W. 2003. "Using UML Class Diagrams for a Comparative Analysis of Relational, Object-Oriented, and Object-Relational Database Mappings." *ACM SIGCSE International Conference on Computer Science Education*, Reno, NV, February, pp. 21–25.

Urban, S. D., Dietrich, S. W., and Tapia, P. 2000. "Mapping UML Diagrams to Object-Relational Schemas in Oracle 8." In Chaudhri and Zicari, 2000, pp. 29–51.

Walmsley, P. 2002. *Definitive XML Schema*. Prentice Hall PTR.

Widom, J., and Ceri, S. 1996. *Active Database Systems*. San Francisco: Morgan Kauffman Publishers.

Wiederhold, G., and Elmasri, R. 1980. "The Structural Model for Database Design." *Proceedings of the 1st International Conference on the Entity-Relationship Approach to Systems Analysis and Design*, pp. 237–258.

Index